ETHNIC CHRONOLOGY SERIES
NUMBER 26

The Chicanos in America 1540-1974

A Chronology & Fact Book

Compiled and edited by

Richard A. Garcia

1977
OCEANA PUBLICATIONS, INC.
DOBBS FERRY, NEW YORK

To my daughter, Misty,
and my son, John

Library of Congress Cataloging in Publication Data

Garcia, Richard A.   1941-
   The Chicanos in America, 1540-1974.

   (Ethnic chronology series ; no. 26)
   Includes bibliographies and index.
   1. Mexican Americans—History—Chronology.
2. Mexican Americans—History—Sources. I. Title. II. Series.
E184.M5G38   973'.04'6872   76-42300
ISBN 0-379-00516-6

Manufactured in the United States of America

TABLE OF CONTENTS

EDITOR'S FOREWORD

Until recently, the Chicanos had been a forgotten ethnic group in American history and society. Although they were in America before the arrival of the Puritans, the majority of them are basically 20th century immigrants to the United States. Chicanos are a product of three cultures -- Spanish, Indian, and Mexican -- and, biologically they are mestizos. They became an ethnic group in America as a result of the United States' war with Mexico in 1848 when, as a result of being defeated, Mexico ceded the Southwestern states of California, Arizona, New Mexico, Texas, and parts of Colorado and Utah. The Mexicans residing in these ceded territories became the "ancestors" of the present day Chicano. Consequently, Chicanos have always been historically, culturally, and geographically within a familiar environment.

Carey McWilliams very aptly stated the neglect of this ethnic group in his book Brothers Under the Skin, when he wrote:

> The Spanish-speaking have spoken out, not once
> but many times, but their voices have been unheard
> and their speeches have gone unheeded. Underlying
> the neglect of the Spanish-speaking is a curious para-
> dox. The Spanish-speaking minority ranks secondly
> only to the American Indians in historical priority,
> yet it happens to be the most recent immigrant group
> in American life. The group is so old that it has been
> forgotten and so new that it has not yet been discovered.

For the most part, Chicano history still lies buried in archives, libraries, newspapers, government documents, census manuscripts, immigration files, and church records. Most of the books available have not been written by Chicanos and have not satisfactorily dealt with the role of this ethnic group and their contributions to American society. Unfortunately, conditions of poverty as well as cultural and racial oppression have not been conducive to the development of a Chicano intelligentsia that could document, interpret, and write the social history of their people. But, since the late 1960s a core of Chicano scholars has emerged, and they have begun to research and write. The rise of these Chicano intellectuals is a direct result of the development of a social and political movement of the Chicano people seeking their identity, striving for better living conditions, better jobs and a better education, and wanting control of their own lives and communities. In essence, Chicanos during this period were demanding their rightful place in American society. As a result of this movement, interest has increased in the study and research of this ethnic group.

This book is intended to provide the student and general reader with a resource tool to begin to research and study the rich and extensive history of the Chicanos. Specifically, the editor hopes that the chronology will provide a brief and useful introduction to this ethnic group, and that the articles and documents enclosed will be the initial starting point of study. In addition, the extensive bibliographical section will provide the student, teacher or general reader with an immediate guide to an in-depth study of the Chicanos in America.

The selections that have been included are important documents to begin a study of this ethnic group. The articles by Jack Forbes, Helen Rowan and Ruben Salazar document the history, problems and plight of the Chicanos in America. While the articles by Mirta Vidal, Philip Ortego, Elma Barrera, Mario Garcia, and the editor highlight the response to these conditions and the important questions Chicanos are dealing with today.

The reading of this resource guide will indicated two basic themes that have always characterized the Chicano population -- oppression and struggle. Thus, it is impossible to produce a chronology or an anthology of articles and documents that do not contain these two themes. But, the reader should also be aware of certain other themes that emerged in the late 1960s and early 1970s. These themes are pride, self-determination, mass political action, and most of all a self-awareness as a community -- as Raza.

Richard A. Garcia
University of California, Irvine

DEFINITIONS

In order to facilitate the study of this ethnic group, the terms Chicano, Anglo, Mexican-American, Raza and Barrio must be defined.

1. The word Chicano has always been used by Mexicans in Mexico. It is not new. But today it is used with different connotations. Although in the past it was applied to lower class Mexicans by the upper class, it now signifies a complete person who has an identity, regardless of class. In the past a Mexican-American was not considered an American; he was hyphenated -- Mexican American. He was looked down upon by Anglos. If the Chicano goes to Mexico he is considered a Pocho, a person who is not quite Mexican. He is too agringado (Anglicized). So, the term Chicano has been chosen by the Mexican-American youth to identify themselves. The Chicano is basically any person of Mexican ancestry who calls himself a Chicano. It provides a sense of identification not given to them by the majority of people in the United States. This word not only furnishes identity; it carries a whole philosophical meaning. A Chicano is a person who is proud of his heritage, a person who is responsible and committed to helping others of his people. The Chicano is a person who may be working class, or middle class; he may aspire to have material things or reject them, but he is a Chicano because he is not ashamed of his heritage nor does he aspire to be what he is not and can never be -- and Anglo. Once the word is accepted, the person who accepts it philosophically accepts his heritage, his brown skin without shame or any reservations. Unfortunately, the young Chicanos have not differentiated between the acceptance of self as a Chicano and the acceptance of different value systems. For example, a Chicano may have middle class economic status and yet still be a Chicano. A Chicano does not necessarily have to be from a barrio.

2. An Anglo is any person who is not Black, Indian, Asian or Latin. In essence an Anglo is any person not in the Third World. The term Anglo is used to identify any person outside the categories named regardless whether they are sympathetic or not. The word Anglo does not carry any negative connotations. When negative connotations are intended, Anglos are referred to as gabachos.

3. Mexican-American. This term carries negative connotations for two reasons. First, most people in the movimiento consider it as a word coined by Anglos to imply that Mexicans in the United States are not equal to Americans -- that is, Anglos. Second, Chicanos consider other Mexicans who identify themselves as Mexican-Americans as people who want to be Anglos and are ashamed of their heritage. The difference between a Mexican-American and a Chicano is a philosophical and ideological one.

4. <u>Raza</u>. <u>Raza</u> is a term literally meaning race, but when most Chicanos refer to themselves as <u>La Raza</u> they do not mean a separate biological race. What is mainly implied is a feeling of <u>carnalismo</u> (fraternity), a feeling of common experience, a feeling of community, of awareness of a certain bond of kinship. <u>Raza</u> as it is used by Chicanos applies not only to a feeling that there is a common bond among themselves, but to all people of Latin America.

5. <u>Barrio</u>. Quite simply, this word refers to the Chicano neighborhood. Any neighborhood where Chicanos live is a <u>barrio</u>. Implied in this term is an area of poverty, but this is not always true.

Due to the colonization of Mexico by Spain (1519-1820), a fusion of Spanish and Indian cultures occurred. In addition, a racial mixture produced the Mestizo, the ancestor of the Mexican and the Chicano.

1540   Explorers from Mexico first entered the Southwest.

1540-1821   Chicano ancestry developed in the diverse aboriginal population of Mexico, especially the Indians of Northern Mexico, such as the Yaquis and the Tarahumaras, and partially American Indian. The key to the Chicanos' ancestry is the Mestizo - Spanish and Indian.

1821   Mexico established its independence and continued to protect its northern frontier -- the present Southwest.

1836   Texas gained its independence. Cultural, racial, economic, and political conflicts continued in Mexico's northern territories between Anglos, Mexicans, and Indians. The Alamo became a historically sensitive question.

1846   The United States engaged in a war with Mexico after a decade of direct hostility.

1848   February 2. The Treaty of Guadalupe-Hidalgo was signed. Articles 5, 8, 9, and 10 of the treaty guaranteed the land, culture, civil rights, and religion of the Mexicans in the area. The treaty specified that Colorado, Arizona, New Mexico, Texas, California, and parts of Utah and Nevada would become American territory. In return, the United States would pay Mexico 15 million dollars.

The New Mexican population was divided into two classes Los Ricos and Los Pobres. The Ricos (rich) were lighter color but fewer in number. The Pobres (poor) increased their number by intermarrying with the Indians. Illiteracy characterized both classes. The Ricos constituted one-fifth of the population, but by the 1860s, the Ricos largely ceased to exist as a "governing class." The remaining population was of soldier-settler-mestizo origin rather than Spanish.

The Texas population totaled 14,500 - 15,000. Most Mexicans lived in the border areas. The class structure consisted of the lower class of peons which were Mexican-Indian, but often more Indian than Mexican; the landowners and vaqueros (cowboys) were more mestizos. The small upper class also consisted of Anglo landowners. The social and political structure was similar to California; the majority of Chicanos were in the lower class.

Mexican population outnumbered the Anglo population in California.

1849
September. California's first constitutional convention was held. Eight Mexican representatives (Californios) out of a total of forty-eight attended. Jose A. Carrillo was the only one who voted for free blacks to be admitted to California.

After the discovery of gold at Sutter's Mill, Anglos outnumbered Mexicans in California. Out of one hundred thousand people only thirteen thousand were Mexicans.

1850-1870
Mexican (Chicano) upper classes in Arizona, New Mexico, Texas, and California lost most of their lands.

1850
The California Foreign Miners Tax Law was passed. It deprived almost all Latins of their mining occupations. This began a decade characterized by violence against Mexicans. This period has been referred to by Chicanos as the period of Linchocracia (lynch-democracy).

1851
All native Mexicans were excluded from the California State Senate. Also the California Land Law was passed which deprived Mexicans of their lands. At this time, 200 Mexicans owned fourteen million acres of land, including all land valued at over $10,000. The Mexican community was divided between the rich Chicanos called Californios and the poor, which were the majority, called Cholos.

Downieville, California, was the only place in mining history that hanged a woman - a Chicana named Juanita.

1852-1874
"El Bandido" Tiburcio Vasquez captured the imagination of Mexicans in California and the wrath of the Anglos. He was labeled a nationalist by the Mexican community and a bandit by the white community. He is reputed to have said, "Given $60,000, I would be able to recruit enough arms and men to revolutionize Southern California."

1853
The Gadsen Purchase completed the transfer of the Southwest from Mexico to the United States. The purchase caused

great concern between Arizona and Sonora, Mexico, over the question of mineral wealth.

1854-55   Mexicans already represented 16 to 20 percent of the inmates at San Quentin prison.

1855   The Bureau of Public Instruction in California ordered that all schools teach exclusively in English.

California passed a law prohibiting vagrancy. It was called the Greaser Law.

Jesus Islas established the Pan-Mexican Movement. He founded the emigration society called Junta Colonizadora de Sonora. Its purpose was to have Mexicans in the United States settle in Sonora, Mexico.

1855-1859   Francisco P. Ramirez published El Clamor Publico, a Chicano paper, in Los Angeles, California. The paper defended Chicano rights, was anti-establishment and was committed to the advancement of the Chicano people. In 1872, Ramirez published another paper in Los Angeles, the Cronica.

1856   Juan Flores and Poncho Daniel, two bandidos, rallied fifty Mexicans to a nationalist cause and attacked Anglos around the San Juan Capistrano, California area.

Los Angeles, California, split along racial lines, because the Anglos felt that Mexicans were on the verge of revolting.

Anglo-Americans in Los Angeles, California, split the county into two parts in order to increase their influence. Thus began the problems Chicanos have experienced with gerrymandering.

1859   The Juan Cortinas revolt against the Anglos began in Texas.

1860s   The period of the bandido ensued.

1870   The Mission Camp Affair in Arizona began a decade of heightening antagonism between Anglos and Chicanos.

Mexican land holdings were reduced by three-fourths in California.

1872   The Mexican Border Commission reported continued border hostility between Texans and Mexicans.

Juan Patron, a school teacher and later a speaker of the house in New Mexico, emerged as a leader in New Mexico's Lincoln County War, 1876-1878.

1878   The El Paso Salt War began. Texas Chicanos revolted against the prohibition of the use of certain salt fields.

1880s   The United States Immigration Acts prohibited contract labor, but Mexican contract labor began to be widespread. El Paso, Texas, during this period became the clearinghouse for Mexican labor into the United States.

1880   The Mexican population in Arizona numbered 9,330; in California 8,648; in New Mexico 5,173; and Texas 43,161.

             No persons with Spanish surnames held any California public office by this date.

1883   Juan Gomez, signed a first attempt to organize an agricultural union in Texas.

1889-1891   Chicano resistance in New Mexico to the appropriation of land began. Chicano groups, the Gorras Blancas and Mano Negras, led the resistance.

1890-1900   Unionization began in the Southwest, but it was anti-Mexican in practice. This caused friction within the labor movement.

1890   The Mexican population decreased in California to 7,164 and to 4,504 in New Mexico.

             The United People's Party, the political arm of the Gorros Blancos, ran candidates for local elections in New Mexico. The party existed for only a year.

1891   A court of private land claims was established in California to examine the confusing land grant claims. In the course of this, control of most of the California resources shifted to the Anglos.

1894   The Alianza Hispano Americano formed in Tucson, Arizona. A mutalista organization, it provided funeral and insurance benefits. It later engaged in political activities and published its own magazine.

1897   Wealthy Mexicans in Texas established El Colegio Altamiro to preserve the Mexican culture for their children.

1900   Growth of the Mexican population throughout the Southwest
            occurred because of increased migration.

1901   The Arizona Rangers were formed. They closely resembled
            the Texas Rangers. Their role was to break strikes and
            stop cattle rustling. As in Texas, Mexicans considered them
            primary enemies.

1903   Chicanos were in the leadership of the Clifton-Morenci Mine
            Strike. The strike came to be known as the Mexican Affair.
            Two thousand Chicanos marched through Morenci, Arizona,
            during the strike.

1904   Ricardo Flores Magon and his brother Enrique, two Mexican
            revolutionaries, published their newspaper Regeneracion in
            San Antonio, Texas, and later in St. Louis, Missouri. By 1906,
            the newspaper had a circulation of 6,000.

            The St. Louis-Brownsville-Mexican railroad line was com-
            pleted. This helped to bring American culture and education
            to the isolated Mexicans on the Texas border.

            A small middle class of Chicanos in South Texas developed.

1906   January 14. Thirty Mexican workers formed the Union Li-
            beral Humanidad in Cananea, Mexico. This liberal club af-
            filiated with the Magonist party (PLM) and proved instrumen-
            tal in the Cananea mine strike.

            Some Chicanos began to join the International Workers of the
            World (IWW) and began to unionize in Arizona and New Mex-
            ico.

1907   The Magon brothers founded El Partido Liberal Mexicano
            (PLM), a militant political party that functioned in Southern
            California and Baja, California. Many of the Magons' follow-
            ers organized Mexican workers in the United States.

1910   By this year immigration swelled the Mexican population to
            29,987 in Arizona, 32,694 in California, 11,018 in New Mex-
            ico and 125,016 in Texas. Prior to 1908 only about 60,000
            Mexican immigrants entered annually.

1910-1914   Eighty-two thousand, five hundred eighty-eight Mexicans im-
            migrated to the United States.

1911   Migration of Mexicans to the United States shifted from
            northern Mexico to the Mexican states of Guanajuato, Jalisco,
            and Mexico D. F. Eventually this shifted one-eighth of Mex-
            ico's population to the United States. The Report of the Im-
            migration Commission stated that the Mexicans came as
            transient and migratory unskilled labor rather than settlers.

1912   Arizona and New Mexico attained statehood. Unlike Chicanos
            in New Mexico, Arizona Chicanos held few political offices.
            In both states, Anglos controlled the main industries.

1914-1919   Over 91,000 Mexicans immigrated during this period. The
            total for the decade exceeded 173,000.

1915   Chicanos predominated in the leadership of the Arizona
            Western Federation of Miners, an affiliate of the IWW. Be-
            cause of its strike activities, the state forced it to abandon
            its IWW affiliation and join the Arizona State Federation of
            Labor, an affiliate of the AF of L.

1917   The Immigration Act of 1917 placed a head tax on Mexicans
            and applied the literacy provision of the act to them. The
            act was ignored by industrialists and agricultural growers
            who pressured the government to finally waive sections of
            the law.

1918   A small middle class arose in New Mexico. It sought to dis-
            tinguish itself from the Mexican lower class by calling it-
            self Spanish or Hispano.

1919   Chicano and Mexican workers organized the Sociedad Muta-
            lista Benito Juarez of El Centro, California.

1920s   Educational systems introduced Americanization programs
            to make the Mexican immigrant an American and to accul-
            turate them.

            American labor unions lobbied for quotas on Mexican immi-
            gration. They claimed Mexican labor depressed domestic
            wages and served as strikebreaker.

1920   Sixty to seventy per cent of the Chicano population was on
            relief because of their poor economic status.

            Over twelve thousand Chicanos from New Mexico were leav-
            ing the state every year for seasonal work in other states.
            The migrant stream thus began.

1920-1930 Labor was needed in the Southwest, and Mexico was in a
state of revolution. This push-pull effect brought in the following number of immigrants per year: 1920 -- 52,361;
1921 -- 30,758; 1922 -- 19,551; 1923 -- 63,768; 1924 --
89,336; 1925 -- 32,964; 1926 -- 43,316; 1927 -- 67,721; 1928
-- 59,016; 1929 -- 40,154; 1930 -- 12,703. The legal migration was increased by the undocumented workers who
crossed the border undiscovered.

1921 La Sociedad Mutualista Hidalgo was formed by Chicano and
Mexican workers in Brawley, California.

La Liga Protectiva Mexicana was organized in Kansas City.
It was an anti-deportation organization.

La Orden de Hijos de America was established in San Antonio, Texas. It was limited to native-born or naturalized
Chicanos. An integrationist and assimilationist organization,
it fought for basic civil and constitutional rights for the
Chicanos.

1924-1930 Congress debated extensively the 1924 Immigration Act and
the Box Bill in addition to holding hearings in 1928 and 1930
on the problems of immigration. Nativism versus immigrants was the central question. Quotas imposed on European and Asian immigrants were not extended to Mexicans.
The Department of State and southwestern industrialists
joined hands to keep open immigration from Mexico.

1925 The Border Patrol of the United States Immigration and Naturalization Service was given absolute search and seizure
authority over Mexicans. Their job was to search out and
deport undocumented workers. Many Chicanos suffered illegal searches and abuse of their constitutional rights.

1925-1927 American labor unions and Mexican labor unions held talks.
Mexican labor officials wanted to force Mexican workers
entering the United States to join unions and have the American labor unions issue them international union cards.
American labor refused.

1927 La Confederacion de Uniones Obreras Mexicanos (CUOM)
was formed by Mexican and Chicano workers and held its
first convention on May 5,1968 in Los Angeles, California.
CUOM organized twenty locals and had a membership of approximately 3,000 within a few years. It combined both urban and rural workers.

1928   La Union de Trabajodores de Valle Imperial, a predominantly Chicano agricultural workers' union, called the cantaloupe workers strike in the Imperial Valley of California.

The League of United Latin American Citizens (LULAC) was formed in Texas. It purported to help Mexicans become acculturated and assimilated into American society by emphasizing the learning of English.

1929   The Trade Union Unity League, formed by the Communist Party, organized Mexican workers when the AFL failed to do so.

1930s   Chicano deportations continued in this decade.

1930   January. The Mexican Mutual Aid Society, formerly the Union de Trabajadores de Valle Imperial, led another strike there. The demands centered on wages, end of discrimination, and better working conditions.

The census showed the following in Southwest states: 5,400 Chicanos in clerical jobs, 1,092 in teaching jobs, 93 lawyers and judges, and 165 physicians and surgeons. The total population of Chicanos numbered an estimated three million.

1930-1931   The Communist Party and Mexican workers established the Agricultural Workers Industrial League which led several strikes. It later reorganized under the name of the Cannery and Agricultural Workers Industrial Union (CAWIU). This union stood in the forefront of Chicano strike activities during the early 1930s.

1931-1934   United States' records indicate that some 300,000 Mexican citizens were deported.

1933-1937   Chicanos in California's colleges and universities organized the Mexican Youth Conference or the Mexican American Movement (MAM). It emphasized education and published a monthly newspaper, La Voz Mexicana.

1933   June. Over 500 workers, including Chicanos, Japanese, and Filipinos, led the Berry Strike in El Monte, California. Union recognition was the main demand.

June-July. Five thousand workers, predominantly Mexican, walked of the celery fields of Santa Monica and Culver City, California, and began a large scale strike.

June 15. The Mexican union locals of Los Angeles held a convention and formed La Confederacion de Uniones de Campesinos y Obreros Mexicanos del Estado de California (CUCOM). By 1934, this union of peasants and workers of California had a membership of around 10,000. Its purpose was to culturally educate the Mexicans and help them by striking to end exploitation.

1934   Chicano workers appealed to Mexico for help. The national labor union in Mexico, La Confederacion Regional Obrera Mexicano, told its members to respect the wave of Chicano strikes in the United States. In addition, Plutarco Elios Calles, a former president of Mexico, sent financial contributions to the striking Chicano workers. Strikes continued in California for the next few years, although they were branded as Red Strikes.

La Liga Obrera de Habla Espanola, which concerned itself with the problems of poor Chicanos, was formed in New Mexico. By 1935, its membership had grown to 8,000.

1937   Many Chicano workers joined the United Cannery, Agricultural, Packing and Allied Workers of America (UCAPAWA) which was chartered by the newly formed CIO and led by John Lewis.

1938   February 1. The San Antonio Pecan Sheller's Strike was called. The pecan industry employed basically unskilled Mexican workers. The average salary for the five to ten thousand sorkers two dollars a week. This proved to be the largest strike of the 1930s led by Chicanos.

El Congreso de Pueblos de Habla Espanola held a national conference of all Spanish-speaking peoples. Luisa Moreno from the UCAPAWA was the main organizer.

1940s   Chicanos formed Unity Leagues in California which fought against discrimination and segregation. The Unity Leagues oriented towards trade unionists and desired to stimulate political activity.

The Chicano youth protests against American culture emerged in the form of the Pachuco or the Zootsuiter.

1942-1944   The Sleepy Lagoon Defense Committee gained national prominence. It was involved in the case of a young Mexican

killed by an alleged Mexican gang. Elements of sensational-
ism and police brutality highlighted the case. Chicanos won
a victory in the courts.

1941-1945 The Chicanos serving in World War II were the most deco-
rated ethnic group in the United States. They won more Me-
dals of Honor than any other group.

1941 Carey McWilliams, commissioner of immigration and housing in California, Dr. George Sanchez of the Univeristy of
Texas, C.J. Correan, a Chicano legislator in Arizona, and
others submitted a plan for the improvement of Anglo-His-
pano relations to the federal government. As a result of this
action and a further survey of the conditions of the Southwest,
the Spanish-Speaking Peoples Division was established as
part of the office of Inter-American Affairs.

1942-1943 Sponsored by the federal government, a series of conferences were held throughout the Southwest on the problems
of Spanish-speaking people. Grants in aid and scholarship
monies resulted.

1942 May 22. As a result of the labor shortage created by World
War II, agricultural growers and the federal government established the Bracero Program, Public Law 45. Mexico
agreed to send an undetermined number of workers to the
United States, and in return, certain wages would be paid
the Mexican workers. The resulting stream of workers fur-
thered the growth of the Chicano culture and slowed the process of acculturation of Mexicans already in the United States.

The Los Angeles County Sheriff's Department attempted to
explain the delinquency problems among Chicano youth by
stating, "his [the Mexicans] desire to kill or at least to
draw blood . . . This is an inborn characteristic that has
come down through the ages."

1943-1944 Zoot-suit riots occurred in response to anti-Mexican propa-
ganda, racial prejudice, and wartime tension. Sailors in San
Diego, Los Angeles, and Oakland attacked Chicano youths.
Racial riots occurred in Philadelphia, Chicago, Detroit, New
York, and Texas, as well.

1943-1947 Labor organizations and Chicano leaders opposed the open
border and the Bracero program, although Chicano leaders
did want immigrant status for Mexicans.

The federal government appropriated some one hundred and twenty million dollars for the labor importation program. This subsidized the agri-business. Braceros numbered over four thousand in 1942, and their total subsequently rose to 55,000 by 1947.

1944   The Comite Mexicano Contra el Racismo was formed in Mexico to attempt to lend assistance to Chicanos in the United States in the fight against racism. It published Fraternidad.

1945   March 21. Judge Paul J. McCormick ruled that the segregation of Mexican youngsters found no sanction under California law, and that it violated the equal protection clause of the fourteenth amendment of the United States Constitution. The United States Supreme Court upheld the decision.

1946-1947   The American Council on Race Relations sent an organizer into the Southern California communities to expand the Unity League programs.

1947   October 1. A major strike was called against the Di Giorgio Corporation at Arvin, California. It was led by Local 218 of the AFL and involved 860 Mexican workers. National industrial and governmental support helped break the strike.

Mexico's ambassador to the United States, Antonio Espinosa de los Monteros, called upon the people of the United States to make an effort to do away with racism and offer the Mexican in the United States equal opportunities.

The Community Service Organization (CSO) was established in 1947 using the model of the Unity Leagues. Its work in registering Chicano voters proved instrumental in electing Edward Roybal to the Los Angeles City Council in 1949. Roybal was the first Chicano to be elected to the council since 1881.

1948   The Mexican Civic Committee was organized to stimulate grass roots democracy in Los Angeles.

Chicano veterans of World War II founded the American G.I. Forum in Corpus Christi, Texas. Essentially a non-partisan organization, its purpose was to promote political and social reform for Chicanos. The organization grew to include ladies auxiliaries and junior organizations.

1950   Strong nativist pressure forced many of the Chicano organi-
               zations to prove their Americanism or be subjected to
               fierce red-baiting and viewed as having Communist leanings.

               With the war over, the United States needed less labor and
               Operation Wetback was undertaken. Mexicans were indis-
               criminately rounded up and returned to Mexico.

1951-1953   Chicano activists were deported as a result of the McCarthy
               era. Luisa Moreno, Frank Corona of the shoeworkers, An-
               tonio Salgado, a trade union organizer, and others were
               sent to Mexico.

1951   Public Law 78 renewed the Bracero program, since domes-
               tic workers were refusing to work in the fields. The Bra-
               cero Program presented the major obstacle to the unioniza-
               tion of farmworkers.

1952   July. The melon pickers of the Imperial Valley organized
               and struck. Braceros were used to break the strike.

               The Walter-McCarran Act was passed. It was responsible
               for setting the tone and practice of the Operation Wetback
               period. Mexican and Chicano residents of the United States
               suffered harassment and intimidation.

1953-1956   A third decade of deportations commenced. During these
               years more than two million Mexicans and Chicanos were
               deported to Mexico. Homes were illegally searched and
               civil rights abused.

1954   The Los Angeles Committee for the Protection of the Foreign
               Born reported that many of the Chicanos it was defending
               against deportation charges had been long time residents of
               the United States.

               Seven hundred and fifty immigration agents descended on
               East Los Angeles barrios and arrested thousands of Mexi-
               cans and Chicanos. Elysian Park was converted into a reten-
               tion center. Deportations took place without due process.
               During this year over a million Mexicans were deported
               from the Southwest back to Mexico.

               Edward Roybal made an unsuccessful bid for state office in
               California.

1957   The Hernandez v. Driscoll court case in the southern dis-
              trict of Texas challenged the Texas practice of requiring
              all Mexican children to spend two years in the first grade.

1960   The national census documented the Chicanos' impoverished
              conditions. Their per capita income was $968 as compared
              to $2,047 for Anglos and $1,044 for blacks. Chicanos ob-
              tained an average of four years less education than Anglos,
              they had higher unemployment, and sixty percent of Chicanos
              held unskilled jobs.

              Viva Kennedy clubs were established throughout the South-
              west and helped increase Chicano voter registration. The
              Chicano vote played a significant role in the Kennedy-John-
              son victories in Texas and California. This stimulated fur-
              ther Chicano political activity, including the formation of the
              Mexican American Political Association (MAPA) in Califor-
              nia.

              Official figures placed the Chicano population at four million,
              and unofficial estimates placed it at as high as ten million.
              Over 80 percent were urbanized.

1962   Cesar Chavez left the Community Services Organization and
              began to organize farm workers, forming the National Farm-
              workers Association. By 1965, the union claimed 1,700 mem-
              bers.

1963   Reies Lopez Tijerina, a national figure in the Chicano move-
              ment, organized La Alianza Federal de Mercedes. Its pur-
              pose was to gain the lands back for Chicanos that rightfully
              belonged to them under the Treaty of Guadalupe Hidalgo.

1964   The Bracero Program terminated.

              The War on Poverty brought new programs into the barrios
              which stimulated and increased political awareness in the
              Chicano communities. Moreover, the Civil Rights movement,
              the Black Power struggle, and campus activities increased
              the impetus for the Chicano movement.

1965   September 16. The National Farmworkers Association
              (NFWA) voted to support the Filipinos of the Agricultural
              Workers Organizing Committee (AWOC) in their strike
              against the Delano, California, grape growers. Chavez
              emerged as the central figure of the strike and as a national
              leader of the rising Chicano movement.

A new immigration and naturalization bill, which sought to correct injustices against the Mexican and Chicano peoples, was introduced by liberal congressmen.

The Chicano youth who participated in the South's civil rights movement returned to organize, in their own communities.

1966   Rudolfo "Corky" Gonzales organized the Crusade for Justice, a community-based, independent organizing unit, in Denver, Colorado. Using a philosophy of nationalism, it sought self-determination for Chicanos. Tactically it used mass demonstrations, electoral activity through the La Raza Unida party, and educated its members through its school, Tlatelolco.

Fifty Chicano delegates, administrators and professionals walked out of an Equal Opportunity Commission meeting in Albuquerque, New Mexico. They protested the lack of Chicano staff members on the commission's board.

September 4. Farmworkers and supporters, totaling 8,000, marched in Austin, Texas, protesting poor farm worker conditions and in support of Cesar Chavez's Union.

October 15. Tijerina and the Alianza occupied the national forest area known as the Echo Ampitheater, declaring it their land and establishing a governing body. Within a week, police officials arrested Tijerina; he was convicted in 1967 but appealed. Two years later he lost the appeal and was sentenced to serve time in prison.

El Teatro Campesino, a Chicano theater group, formed by Luis Valdez, emerged from the Delano Huelga. Its actors were often workers, and they traveled throughout the United States dramatizing the plight of the farm workers, the story of the migrant and the Chicano struggle.

The Schenley Corporation became the first signer of a contract with Cesar Chavez's union. Soon afterwards, Gallo, Christian Brothers, Masson, Almaden, Franzia Brothers, and Noviatiate signed contracts.

The Di Giorgio Corporation, one of the largest grape growers announced it would allow Chavez to hold elections; the Teamsters and the NFWA unions clashed. The United States Senate investigated the Chavez union for Communist inflitration. Also, the United Farmworkers Organizing Committee was formed.

1966-1967   Texas Rangers in Starr County, Texas were used as strike breakers when Cesar Chavez tried to organize farm workers in South Texas.

1967   June. As a result of the growing ferment among Chicanos, the federal government appointed Vicente Ximenes to the Equal Employment Opportunity Commission. Shortly afterwards he was appointed to head the newly created Interagency Committee on Mexican American Affairs. In addition, President Johnson promised to have a White House conference for Chicano leaders. This was never held.

October. President Johnson held cabinet committee hearings at El Paso, Texas, to examine the problems of the Chicanos. None of the nationally recognized leaders of the Chicano movement were invited. Consequently, activist Chicano groups boycotted and picketed the conference. They held a rump conference in the barrio of El Paso. A manifesto proclaimed the formation of the Raza Unida which became the precursor to the Raza Unida Party.

Cesar Chavez's union, which was not under the National Labor Relations Act (NLRA), used the secondary boycott to continue to pursue contracts from intransigent growers. Boycott activities spread across the United States and to Canada and Europe. The U.S. Department of Defense increased its grape purchases from 468,000 pounds in 1965 to over 4,000,000 pounds in 1969.

"Corky" Gonzales wrote the epic poem "I Am Joaquin," which became one of the most influential pieces of literature for the Chicano movement. The poem put the Chicano within a historical perspective and gave a nationalist direction to the movement. It concluded with a resounding "I will endure."

Reies Lopez Tijerina gained national fame by leading a raid on the Tierra Amarilla Courthouse in northern New Mexico. He touched off the largest manhunt in New Mexico's history. Tijerina had been harassed by police and not allowed to have a planned conference at Tierra Amarilla. He entered the courthouse to make a citizen's arrest of the District Attorney. Shooting broke out and the manhunt began. Tijinera was arrested but pleading his own case, the jury found him not guilty of any charge.

Brown Berets were established in East Los Angeles under

the leadership of David Sanchez. They were a paramilitary group and by self-definition purported to defend the Chicano community. They proved instrumental in fostering nationalist consciousness in Chicano youth, especially in the high schools. In addition, they spearheaded the organizing of the Chicano Moratorium in August, 1970. Brown Beret chapters organized throughout the Southwest, but the organization officially disbanded in 1973.

The Federal Bilingual Act was passed by the government. It made available funds for bilingual education pilot projects.

The Mexican-American Youth Organization (MAYO) was organized by Jose Angel Gutierrez, Carlos Guerra and Mario Compean at St. Mary's College in San Antonio, Texas. Within two years, MAYO, principally under the leadership of Gutierrez, organized chapters throughout Texas, organized marches, and boldly threatened the control of Mexican Democrats in the Texas political arena. Using MAYO as the skeleton, Gutierrez and Compean turned the Mayo organization into the Raza Unida Party in 1970. A third force in Texas politics was created.

La Raza magazine was established by Elizar Rico, Joe Raza, Raul Ruiz, and others. The magazine has served as a chronicle of major events of the Chicano movement.

El Grito: A Journal of Contemporary Mexican-American Thought first appeared. Published by the Quinto Sol Publications, it is a scholarly journal dedicated to creating awareness in the Chicano community and serving as an outlet for the Chicano intellectuals.

1967-1968   Chicano studies departments were first established throughout the Southwest, especially in California. Massive protests by Chicano students usually occurred before permission was granted to set the new programs into motion.

1968   March. Chicano students walked out of five Los Angeles high schools. This set in motion the Chicano student movement. The students demanded courses in Chicano history and culture, Chicano teachers and administrators, and an end to discrimination against Chicanos. The walk-outs, referred to as blow-outs, gained massive sympathy and support from the Chicano community. The Los Angeles Grand Jury indicted several participants, but all charges were found to be unconstitutional by the courts.

El Plan de Santa Barbara, defining what a Chicano Studies
Department should be, was written by students, professors,
and community members at a conference in Santa Barbara,
California. The plan served as the model for the construction of Chicano studies departments throughout the Southwest.

Trade unionists from the barrio formed the East Los Angeles
Community Union. They sought assistance from major unions
like the United Auto Workers to help create a new organization of barrio workers regardless of union affiliation. It
planned to establish a strong membership of dues-paying
and share-holding members and gradually create community
control of local barrio businesses.

1969   June 5. "El Tigre" Tijerina again attempted to occupy Kit
                Carson National Forest. He and his wife were arrested.

September 2. Santa Clara Judge Gerald S. Chargin aroused
Chicanos' anger when he remarked at a Chicano's incest trial,
"You are lower than animals and haven't the right to live in
organized society. . . Maybe Hitler was right. The animals in our society probably ought to be destroyed because
they have no right to live among human beings." Two congressmen called for a federal investigation and Chargin's
dismissal.

Chicano university and college students formed El Movimiento Estudiantil Chicano de Aztlan (Mecha). The name grew
out of the Santa Barbara conference. Mecha is the acronym
for flame. Mecha was to serve as the catalyst for the Chicano movement throughtout the Southwest.

The Mexican American Education Commission (MAEC) was
formed by the Los Angeles school system. This was in response to the Chicano community's demand for greater Chicano involvement in the running ot the barrio schools. The
Los Angeles School District also established an in-service
teacher training program to sensitize Anglo teachers regarding Chicanos.

The Crusade for Justice held the first annual Chicano Youth
Conference in Denver. Youth groups and individuals from
throughout the United States, but in particular the Southwest,
attended. The conference called for the coordination of national activities, national student walk-outs on the 16th of

September to register protest against discrimination in the educational system, building of Raza Unida parties, and anti-war moratoriums. Most important of all, the conference adopted the Plan de Aztlan, which provided an ideological framework for the nationalist movement and outlined a program of action.

The organization Catolicos Por La Raza was formed to protest the lack of support by the Catholic Church to the Chicano struggle.

The Ford Foundation funded the Mexican American Legal Defense Fund (MALDF), which was established to furnish legal services to Chicanos.

The U.S. Conference of Catholic Bishops became more involved with the farm worker boycott. It played a large part in engineering negotiations between the growers and the farm workers.

1970-1972   La Raza Unida Party (LRUP) chapters were organized throughout the Southwest. LRUP fielded complete slates of candidates or partial slates in Colorado, Texas, California, Arizona, and New Mexico.

1970-1973   Raza Contra La Guerra groups were organized throughout the Southwest to coordinate Chicano anti-war participation in national, state, and local anti-war demonstrations.

1970   June. Coachella and San Joaquin Valley growers signed contracts with Chavez's union. By the end of the year, the majority of the table grape industry had signed contracts with Chavez. Chavez then moved to organize the lettuce workers.

August 29. The Chicano Moratorium was organized in Los Angeles. Thirty thousand Chicanos of all ages protested the war in Vietnam. This was the largest protest of its kind by any minority group. Violence ensued from a police attack, and several Chicanos lost their lives, including Ruben Salazar, a popular writer and journalist.

September 16. Chicanos in California celebrated Mexico's Independence Day by organizing two to three hundred thousand to protest against the violence and police brutality following the Chicano Moratorium. Cries of "Chicano Power," "Viva La Raza," "Who Killed Ruben Salazar," predominated.

The Catholic church established the Fund for Human Development, a nationwide collection taken up on a yearly basis in Catholic churches throughout the United States. The money was to be distributed to Chicano grassroots organizations.

Lawyer Oscar Zeta Acosta challenged the systematic exclusion of Chicanos from grand jury duty in Los Angeles County. He contended that in the previous ten years only three Chicanos served from a total of two hundred and ten grand juries. In March of 1971, the Los Angeles Superior Court ruled against the challenge. It said Chicanos had not been systematically excluded "because in each of the last ten years at least one Mexican American was nominated for grand jury duty."

Ricardo Romo, a Chicano, ran for governor of California on the Peace and Freedom Party ticket.

J. Edgar Hoover, head of the F.B.I., stated, "You never have to bother about a president being shot by a Puerto Rican or Mexican. They don't shoot very straight. But, if they come at you with a knife, beware."

Patrick Fernandes Flores became the first Chicano priest to be elevated to a major church post. He was appointed to the post of auxiliary bishop and subsequently invited Chicano activists to the ceremony.

1971

April 3. La Raza Unida candidates ran in Crystal City, Texas. LRUP swept the board of education and city council elections, gaining a majority on both boards. Crystal City was over 80 percent Chicano.

June. The First Chicana's Conference was held in Houston, Texas. Chicana women from throughout the United States gathered in Texas to analyze their role in the Chicano movement.

Spring. The National Committee to Defend Los Tres was established. It sought to defend three Chicano activists accused of killing a police officer who was posing as a drug pusher.

The United Farmworkers Organizing Committee signed a pact with the Teamsters that gave the Teamsters jurisdiction over the food-processing workers and gave the UFWOC jurisdiction over the field workers.

Abogados (lawyers) de Aztlan were funded by the Catholic
church's fund for Human Development. It was to be a firm
of Chicano lawyers whose express purpose was to help the
people of the barrio.

The Mid-West Conference of La Raza met in Muskegan,
Michigan, to organize Raza United Party chapters in the
Midwest.

1972   April 13. Ricardo Chavez Ortiz hijacked a Frontier Airlines
jet to highlight the plight of his family.

August. Members of the Brown Berets occupied Catalina
Island off the coast of California. The protest, according to
the Brown Berets, symbolized the takeover of Mexican lands
by the United States during the past century.

September. La Raza Unida Party held its first national convention in El Paso, Texas. The third party conference dealt
with two major issues: first, should there be a national
LRUP ticket and second, what position the LRUP should take
toward the Democrats and Republicans. The convention
voted no to the first question and decided against giving support to either of the two major political parties. A National
Committee was also established.

October. Reies Lopez Tijerina called a National Land and
Culture Conference to be held in Albuquerque, New Mexico.

El Centro de Accion Social Autonoma (CASA) was organized
under the leadership of Bert Corona, long time Chicano activist. It was established as an organization for Chicano and
Mexican workers which would fight deportations.

The California state legislature passed the Dixon-Arnett
Law which stipulated that employers who knowingly hired
undocumented Mexican workers would be fined. The state
supreme court ruled the law unconstitutional.

Ramsey Muniz, a Chicano lawyer, ran for governor of Texas
on the Raza Unida Party ticket.

Some 4,000 Chicano workers, predominantly women, struck
the Farah pants factories in El Paso, San Antonio, and Vic-
toria, Texas. The workers demanded unionization, and after
a two year struggle, which gained national attention, the
strikers won.

Ramona Acosta Banuelos, a prominent Mexican-American businesswoman from Los Angeles, was appointed and confirmed as the treasurer of the United States.

1973   The Chicano Social Scientists' Association was formed at a conference held at the University of California, Irvine.

1974   August 31. Over 2,500 Chicanos marched in East Los Angeles protesting deportation of undocumented workers. Similar marches were held throughout the United States.

November. Raul Castro became the first Chicano to win election as governor of Arizona. The Raza Unida Party ran partial or complete electoral slates in California, Texas, and Colorado in state and local elections. Olga Rodriguez, a Chicana activist and feminist, ran unsuccessfully for governor of California on the Socialist Workers Party ticket.

Attorney General William B. Saxbe called for deporting one million "illegal aliens, mostly Mexicans, because they constituted a severe national crisis." Angry Chicanos throughout the United States quickly responded that the government was to blame for the economic ills of the country not the undocumented workers.

DOCUMENTS

THE SIGNIFICANCE OF THE MEXICAN-AMERICAN PEOPLE

Dr. Jack D. Forbes in this article emphasizes three main points. First, the Chicano people in the United States have a definite cultural history; second, the Southwest of the United States would not exist as it is without the Mexican-Spanish heritage and third, the proximity of the Mexican border guarantees the continuance of the Chicano as a distinct bicultural and bilingual ethnic group in the United States.

Source: A report prepared for the U.S. Department of Health, Education and Welfare by the Far West Laboratory for Educational Research and Development, 1970, entitled Mexican-Americans: A Handbook for Educators.

Approximately five million persons of Mexican ancestry reside in the United States. Most live in the states of California, Arizona, New Mexico, Texas, and Colorado, but a large number have made homes in the greater Chicago area and in other industrial centers. In many sections of the Southwest, particularly along the border from San Diego, California to Brownsville, Texas Mexican-Americans are the majority population, and their language and culture serve to provide the entire region with much of its charm and distinctiveness.

Modern-day Mexican-Americans play a vital role in the industrial, agricultural, artistic, intellectual, and political life of the Southwest but the significance of this group cannot be measured solely in terms of present-day accomplishments. It is certain that the Southwest as we know it would not exist without the Mexican-Spanish heritage. That which sets New Mexico off from Oklahoma and California off from Oregon is in large measure the result of the activities of the ancestors of our fellow citizens of Mexican descent. Our way of life has been and is being immeasurably enriched by their presence north of the present-day international boundary.

THE MEXICAN HERITAGE OF THE UNITED STATES:
AN HISTORICAL SUMMARY

What is a Mexican?

Prior to 1821 (when the modern Mexican nation won its independence from Spain), a Mexican was usually a person who spoke the Mexican or Aztec language (Nahuatl). In fact, the early Spaniards almost always referred to the Aztec people as Mexicans. This practice has continued in modern Mexico where the Nahuatl language is called

"Mexicano" by the common people and where writers usually speak of the Mexican Empire rather than the Aztec Empire. The modern people of Mexico, who are said by scholars to be about 80% native Indian in their ancestry, are proud of their descent from the ancient Mexicans and trace the history of their people back to the builders of the magnificent cities of Teotihuacan, Monte Alban, and Chichen Itza.

Our Ancient Mexican Heritage

The Mexican heritage of the United States commences long before the time of Christ. About the year 4000 B.C. Indians living in southern New Mexico learned how to raise corn (maize) as a result of contacts with Mexico (where that remarkable plant was first domesticated after what must have been a long and tedious process). Other crops, including squash and beans, were subsequently borrowed and still later (about 500 A.D.) Southwestern Indians began to develop the Pueblo Indian Civilization. This advanced way of life, which still flourishes in Arizona and New Mexico, was largely based upon Mexican influences in architecture, pottery-making, clothing, religion and government.

In about 1000 A.D., according to some scholars, a people known as the Hohokam moved from northern Mexico into what is now southern Arizona. They brought many advanced traits with them, including the construction of monumental irrigation systems, stone etching techniques, and, very possibly, new political concepts. The Hohokams constructed a large center at Snaketown, Arizona and spread their influence widely, apparently establishing a colony at Flagstaff and trading their pottery as far as the San Fernando Valley in California. During the same general period Mexican influences seem to have reached the Mississippi Valley and advanced cultures developed there. The Indians of the southern United States developed a Mexican-style religious and political orientation and constructed small pyramid-temples while the Ohio River Indians built fanciful effigy mounds, sometimes in the shape of serpents.

The Vitality of Mexican Civilization

It is not at all surprising that ancient Mexico had a great impact upon the area of the United States. The Mexican people were extremely creative, industrious, and numerous (perhaps numbering 20,000,000 in central Mexico alone in the 1520's). Great cities such as Teotihuacan were developed very early and at the time of the Spanish conquest Tenochtitlan (Mexico City) was perhaps the largest and certainly the most modern city in the world. In fact, our cities of today are not as well planned and are probably not as well cared for as was Tenochtitlan.

The ancient Mexicans excelled as artists, craftsmen, architects, city planners, engineers, astronomers, statesmen, and warriors. They also developed centers of higher education (called calmecac by the Aztecs), wrote excellent poetry, produced many historical and religious works, and were very interested in philosophical questions. One philosopher-king, Nezahualcoyotl, put forth the view that there was only one Creator-God, while Maya scientists developed a calendar which is more accurate than the one we use today.

Mexican traders (pochteca) traveled great distances, going as far south as Panama. They helped to spread Mexican culture and also prepared the way for colonists to settle in places such as El Salvador and Nicaragua and for the last Mexican empire (that of the Aztecs) to expand. By the 1520's the Mexican language was the common tongue of the region from north central Mexico to Central America.

The Spanish Invasion

In the 1520's the Spaniards commenced their conquest of Mexico. Although the Aztecs were conquered quickly, in spite of a noble defense of Tenochtitlan led by Cuauhtemoc (the present-day national hero of Mexico), the rest of what is now Mexico was subdued only very gradually. In fact, many Indian groups in northern Mexico and in the jungles of Yucatan-Guatemala were never conquered. Also, many of the Mexicans who were subdued never lost their identity and this explains why at least one-tenth of the people of modern Mexico speak native languages, often in addition to Mexican Spanish.

The Spanish invasion did not bring an end to the vitality of the Mexican people. Most Spaniards came to rule, not to work, and the magnificent churches, aqueducts, and palaces of the colonial period are essentially the result of native labor and craftsmanship. Educated Mexicans helped to record the history of ancient Mexico and for a brief period a Mexican university, Santa Cruz del Tlaltelolco, flourished, training many persons of native ancestry. The conquering Spaniards, if of high rank, often married native noblewomen and the common Spaniards married ordinary Indian women, in both cases contributing to the mixture of the Spanish and native Mexican races.

The Hispano-Mexican Northward Movement

The number of Spaniards who came to Mexico was always very slight and the growth and expansion of the Spanish Empire depended upon the use of native and mixed-blood (mestizo) servants, settlers, craftsmen, miners, and soldiers (the Tlaxcaltecos, Mexicans of Tlaxcala, were particularly relied upon as colonists and soldiers). The conquest of the north would have been impossible without Mexicans and every major settlement, from Santa Fe, New Mexico, to Saltillo, Coahuila, had its Mexican district (barrio or colonia). Many of the settlers taken by Diego de Vargas to northern New Mexico in the 1690's were called "Espanoles Mexicanos," that is, "Aztec-Spaniards;" and Juan de Onate, the first Spanish governor of New Mexico, was married to a woman of Aztec royal ancestry and their son, Cristobal de Onate, was the second governor of that province. Every major expedition, including those of Coronado and De Soto, utilized Mexicans, and eight Mexican soldiers were stationed at San Diego, California in 1769 by Gaspar de Portola. The northward movement of Spain into the southwestern United States was, therefore, a Spanish-Mexican affair. It was Spanish-led but depended for its success upon Mexicans and mixed-bloods. In California, for example, well over half of the Spanish-speaking settlers were of Indian or mixed ancestry and the forty-six founders of Los Angeles in 1781 included only two persons called Spaniards, and their wives were Indian.

The Creation of Modern Mexican Culture

Gradually the way of life brought to America by the Europeans became mixed with native Mexican influences, until the life of the common people became a blend of Spanish-Arabic and Indian traits, much as the culture of England after 1066 became a blend of French-Latin and Anglo-Celtic traditions. The Spaniards used the Mexican language for governmental, scholarly, and religious purposes for several generations and many Mexican words, such as coyote, elote, jicara, tamal, chile, chocolate, jacal, ocelote, and hundreds of others, became part of Spanish as spoken in Mexico. Roman Catholic religious practice was modified by many Indian customs and devotion to the Virgin of Guadalupe has had a lasting impact upon the Catholic faith.

Meanwhile, the Mexican people intermixed with diverse tribes and eventually began to absorb both the non-Mexican Indian and the Spaniard himself. This process of migration and mixture made possible the creation of the independent Mexican republic in 1821, after a ten-year struggle for freedom.

The Mexican Republic in the North

Independent Mexico was to have a lasting impact upon the southwestern United States. Many Mexican leaders were imbued with new republican and equalitarian ideals and they sought to implement these reforms. Legislatures and elected local councils were established in California and elsewhere, the Indians and mixed-bloods were granted complete legal equality and full citizenship, and foreigners were encouraged to take up a new life as Mexicans. On the other hand, many persons found it hard to break with the authoritarian legacy of Spain, and republican reforms were often subverted. Foreign settlers did not always choose to become good Mexican citizens, as for example the Anglo-Texans who refused to set their slaves free or to obey Mexican land-title and tariff regulations.

The early Mexican governments were often beset by financial difficulties and progress was difficult in the face of widespread illiteracy and an unequal distribution of wealth and power. Gradually, however, these negative conditions were overcome and the Mexican people advanced along the road of democracy, albeit with backward steps from time to time.

In what is now the United States Mexicans were active in the development of new mining regions (gold was discovered in California in 1842, for example), opening up new routes for travelers (as from Santa Fe to Los Angeles via Las Vegas, Nevada), founding schools (some twenty-two teachers were brought to California in the 1830's and a seminary was established at Santa Ynez), establishing new towns (Sonoma, California is an example), and setting up printing presses (as in

California in 1835). The north was a frontier region and was, therefore, not in the forefront of Mexican cultural progress, but it did benefit from developments originating further south.

Mexican Miners and Colonists in the North

Commencing in the 1830's Mexican settlers began moving north once again. Some 200 craftsmen, artisans, and skilled laborers sailed to California in that decade, and soon overland immigrants from Sonora were joining them. Thereafter a steady stream of Sonorans reached California, only to be turned into a flood by the discovery of gold in the Sierra Nevada foothills in 1848. The Sonorans were often experienced miners and their techniques dominated the California Gold Rush until steam-powered machinery took over at a later date. Chihuahuans and other Mexicans also "rushed" to California by sea and by land and they too exercised an impact upon mining as well as upon commerce.

The United States-Mexican War of 1846-1848 did not immediately alter the character of the Southwest greatly, except in eastern Texas and northern California. The Gold Rush changed the language of central California after 1852 (when Mexican miners were largely expelled from the Sierra Nevada mines), but Mexicans continued to dominate the life of the region from San Luis Obispo, California, to San Antonio, Texas. Southern California, for example, remained a Spanish-speaking region until the 1870's with Spanish-language and bi-lingual public schools, Spanish-language newspapers, and Spanish-speaking judges, elected officials, and community leaders. The first Constitution of the State of California, created in part by persons of Mexican background, established California as a bi-lingual state and it remained as such until 1878. Similar conditions prevailed in other southwestern regions.

Anglo-Americans Become Dominant

Gradually, however, Anglo-Americans from the east who were unsympathetic toward Mexican culture came to dominate the Southwest. Having no roots in the native soil and being unwilling to become assimilated to the region, these newcomers gradually transformed the schools into English-language institutions were no Spanish was taught, constructed buildings with an "eastern" character, pushed Mexican leaders into the background, and generally caused the Mexican-American, as he has come to be termed, to become a forgotten citizen.

By the 1890's on the other hand, tourists and writers began to rediscover the "Spanish" heritage and "landmark" clubs commenced the process of restoring the decaying missions of the Southwest. A "Spanish" cultural revival was thus initiated, and soon it began to influence architectural styles as well as the kind of pageantry which has typified much of the Southwest ever since. Unfortunately, the Mexican-Indian aspect of the region's heritage was at first overlooked and the Mexican-American people benefited but little from the emphasis upon things Spanish.

Twentieth-Century Mexican "Pioneers"

In the early 1900's a new group of Mexican immigrants began to enter the United States, attracted by job offers from agricultural developers who wished to open up virgin lands in southern California, Colorado, Arizona, and south Texas. During World War I and the 1920's this movement became a flood, a flood which largely overwhelmed the older group of Mexican-Americans (except in northern New Mexico and southern Colorado) and became ancestral to much of the contemporary Spanish-speaking population in the Southwest.

These hundreds of thousands of new Mexican-Americans had to overcome many obstacles as they attempted to improve their life patterns. Anglo-Americans were prejudiced against people who were largely of native American, brown-skinned origin, who were poor, who of necessity lived in substandard or self-constructed homes, who could not speak English, and who were not familiar with the workings of a highly competitive and acquisitive society. Gradually, and in spite of the trauma of the Great Depression (when all sorts of pressures were used to deport Mexican-Americans to Mexico), los de la raza, as Mexicans in the United States frequently refer to themselves, climbed the economic ladder and established stable, secure communities in the Southwest.

The Internal Development of the Mexican-American Community

The Mexican-American community was not simply a passive force during this long period of transition. Everywhere mutual benefit societies, patriotic Mexicanist organizations, newspapers, social clubs, small stores and restaurants were founded, and artisans began to supply Anglo-American homes with pottery and other art objects (the first gift I ever gave to my mother was a pottery bowl made by a Mexican-American craftsman who fashioned ceramics in a shop behind his home on our street in El Monte, California).

Mexican-American mutual benefit organizations soon commenced the task of helping to upgrade the status of agricultural and industrial workers by seeking better wages and conditions of employment. During the 1920's and 1930's Mexican-American labor organizers, with little formal education and less money, traveled from region to region, helping in the unionization process. Ever since, labor leaders have played an important role in Mexican-American affairs and Spanish speaking union officers are a significant element in the structure of organized labor in the Southwest. Current efforts directed toward the unionization of agricultural workers and obtaining a minimum wage for agricultural laborers, from California to south Texas, are being led by organizers of Mexican ancestry.

During the past twenty years the cultural and political life of Mexican-Americans has advanced remarkably. Today, fine Spanish-language newspapers blanket the Southwest and Far West, some of which are daily periodicals with the latest dispatches from Europe and Mexico. Magazines, including bi-lingual ones, issue forth with slick paper and exciting photographs. Spanish-language radio and television stations reach much of the Southwest, and theatrical-musical productions of a folk or modern nature are frequently staged for the benefit of both los de la raza and Anglos.

Mexican-American civic, business and political leaders are now prominent in many regions, and they include within their ranks members of Congress, mayors, and all types of professional people. The image of the Mexican heritage has vastly improved due not only to the activities of individual Mexican-Americans, but also due to the cultural renaissance occurring in Mexico itself concurrent with the incredible richness of the Mexican past revealed by contemporary archaeological discoveries. Anglo-Americans have ceased emphasizing the Spanish legacy at the expense of the Mexican, and a more healthy climate of mutual understanding has evolved.

Educational Progress

Educationally, Mexican-American progress has been striking in individual cases but has been slow over-all. Generally speaking, whenever Anglo-Americans gained control over a particular state or region in the Southwest they chose to import the kinds of public schools developed in the Middle West or East. Hispano-Mexican and bi-lingual schools were replaced by English-language, Anglo-oriented schools from which Mexican-American children were sometimes excluded. After the turn of the century greater numbers of Spanish-speaking youth began to attend schools, but the latter were either irrelevant to the background, language, and interests of the pupils (as in New Mexico) or were segregated, marginal elementary schools (as in much of California and Texas). Normally, secondary-level education was not available to Mexican-American pupils except in an alien Anglo-dominated school (and even that opportunity was often not present in many rural counties in Texas and elsewhere).

During the post-World War II period segregated schools for Mexican-Americans largely disappeared, except where residential segregation operated to preserve the ethnic school. Greater numbers of Mexican-Americans entered high school and enrollment in college also increased, although slowly. Nevertheless, drop-out rates remain high, even today; and it is also true that the typical school serving Mexican-Americans makes little, if any, concession to the Mexican heritage, the Spanish language, or to the desires of the Mexican-American community.

A Six Thousand Year Old Heritage

In summary, the Mexican heritage of the United States is very great indeed. For at least 6,000 years Mexico has been a center for the dissemination of cultural influences in all directions, and this process continues today. Although the modern United States has outstripped Mexico in technological innovation, the Mexican people's marked ability in the visual arts, music, architecture, and political affairs makes them a constant contributor to the heritage of all of North America. The Mexican-American people of the United States serve as a bridge for the diffusion northward of valuable Mexican traits, serve as a reservoir for the preservation of the ancient Hispano-Mexican heritage of the Southwest, and participate directly in the daily life of the modern culture of the United States.

THE MEXICAN-AMERICAN WAY OF LIFE

The United States' five million citizens of Mexican origin do not form a homogeneous group with identical values, customs, and aspirations. One can divide the Mexican-American community along class (economic) lines, from the affluent rancher, businessman, or public official to the migrant farm worker or isolated self-sufficient farmer in the mountains of New Mexico. One can also divide the Mexican-American community on the basis of the degree to which the individual has become Anglicized and integrated into the larger society. One can further classify Mexican-Americans according to the degree of Caucasian ancestry which they possess, or according to whether or not they object to being called "Mexicans" and prefer to be called "Spanish-American." But whichever type of classification system one uses, it is clear that there is no single way of life possessed by our Mexican-American people.

Nonetheless, it is possible for purposes of generalization to ignore those individuals who are non-typical and to concentrate upon the large majority of Mexican-Americans who have many things in common.

First, the Mexican-American community is basically proud of being of Mexican background and sees much of value in the Mexican heritage. By means of folk-level educational agencies, such as benevolent societies, patriotic organizations, and the extended family, many Mexican traits are kept alive, either as functioning parts of the individual's personal life or at least as items with which he feels some degree of familiarity. Mexican arts and crafts, music, dances, cooking, family structure, concepts of the community, the Spanish language, and other characteristics, are maintained in this manner. Spanish-language radio and television stations, newspapers, and magazines, and Mexican-American political organizations, help to carry on this process as well as to bring in new cultural influences from Mexico. In short, the Mexican-American community possesses many internal agencies which serve to maintain a sense of belonging to "la raza" and which also serve to carry forward worthy aspects of the Mexican heritage.

In many rural areas of the Southwest, as well as in some wholly Mexican urban districts, most adults can be described as belonging primarily to the culture of northern Mexico. The Spanish language is universally favored over English and the bilateral extended family provides a satisfying and strong social background for the individual. In other urban districts, as well as in suburban regions and on the fringes of Mexican neighborhoods in rural areas, one finds numerous Mexican-Americans who are completely bi-lingual, or who in some cases favor English over Spanish. These people have not become "Anglos", but their Mexican cultural heritage has become blended with Anglo-American traits.

Unfortunately, many younger Mexican-Americans, educated in Anglo-oriented schools, have not been able to relate in a positive manner toward either the north Mexican or Mexican-Anglo mixed cultures, primarily because their parents have been unable to effectively transmit the Spanish language and Mexican heritage to them. At the same time the public schools have either attacked or completely ignored that heritage and have attempted to substitute an often watered-down Anglo heritage. The youth subjected to this pressure have not ordinarily become Anglos, though, because of a feeling of being rejected by the dominant society (because of frequently experienced prejudice and discrimination) and by the schools (because the curriculum is so totally negative as regards their own personal and cultural background). These young people have frequently developed a mixed Anglo-Mexican subculture of their own, based upon a dialect of Spanish heavily modified by an ingenious incorporation of English words and new expressions and upon a "gang" style of social organization.

Another important factor which retards the complete absorption of partially Anglicized Mexican-Americans into the larger society is the fact that more than 95% of Mexicans are part-Indian, 40% are full-blood Indians, and most of the mixed-bloods have more Indian than non-Indian ancestry. Mexican-Americans are, therefore, a racial as well as a cultural minority and the racial differences which set them apart from Anglos cannot be made to "disappear" by any "Americanization" process carried on in the schools.

The larger Mexican-American community is in a process of rapid cultural transition, wherein most individuals are acquiring a mixed Anglo-Mexican culture, while smaller numbers are marrying into or otherwise being absorbed into the dominant Anglo society. An unfortunate aspect of this process is that extremely valuable Mexican traits, such as the strong extended family, the tendency toward mutual aid, the Spanish language, artistic and musical traditions, folk dances, fine cooking, and such personality characteristics as placing more emphasis upon warm interpersonal relationships than upon wealth acquisition tend to be replaced by what many critics might suggest are the lowest common denominator of materialistic, acquisitive, conformist traits typical of some elements within the Anglo-American population. That this is occurring is largely a result of the fact that many Mexican-American graduates of the public schools feel ambivalent about their own self-identity and about cultural values. They have been deprived of a chance to learn about the best of the Mexican heritage and, at the same time, have been, in effect, told to become Anglicized. They tend, therefore, to drift into the dominant society without being able to make sound value judgements based upon cross-cultural sophistication.

On the other hand, the Mexican-American community considered in its entirety is a vital, functioning societal unit with considerable ability to determine its own future course of development. It may well succeed in developing a reasonably stable bicultural and bilingual tradition which will provide a healthy atmosphere for future generations and which may prove attractive to many Anglos. In any case it is clear that the proximity of Mexico will insure a continual flow of Mexican cultural influences across the border and the Mexican-American community, as a bicultural population, will not soon disappear.

MEXICAN AMERICANS IN THE SOUTHWEST

Using extensive empirical data and concrete examples, Helen Rowan proves her thesis that there has been a consistent and systematic oppression of Chicanos in every sector of American life since 1848. Rowan clearly establishes that racism, injustice, discrimination and overall oppression permeate Chicanos' lives and are rooted within American society.

Source: Mexican Americans in the Southwest. A report prepared for the U.S. Commission on Civil Rights by Helen Rowan, 1968.

Spanish-speaking persons have been in what is now New Mexico since 1590, and had settled communities over much of what is now the American Southwest by the middle of the nineteenth century. The land was ruled by Spain until Mexico achieved independence in 1821. But by 1853, the United States had acquired, by purchases and by force-- primarily the latter--nearly one million square miles of Mexican territory, of half of all Mexico.

The Treaty of Guadalupe Hidalgo in 1848 ended the Mexican-American War. In establishing the rights of Mexicans in territories ceded to the United States, the Treaty stipulated that ". . . property of every kind, now belonging to Mexicans not established there, shall be inviolably respected. The present owners, the heirs of these, and all Mexicans who may hereafter acquire said property by contract, shall enjoy with respect to it guarantees equally ample as if the same belonged to citizens of the United States." The treaty contained no language that guaranteed language and cultural rights. Mexican Americans assert that since then the land grants made by and protected in the Treaty have been largely usurped from the families and pueblos which held them, and that the rights guaranteed by the Treaty have been consistently violated.

In 1967, the Mexican American associate director of a State migrant council described the status and experience of the resident Mexicans who in 1853 became American at the stroke of a pen:

They had all the disadvantages of a vanquished nation, but none of the advantages of a Marshall Plan, or even the understanding that there are differences in cultural groups. They were now subject to impositions of a new and powerful nation whose cultural orientation and social and legal systems were diametrically opposed to theirs. The new government proceeded to exploit what was beneficial to it, and ignore what was not. A new language was introduced, but little effort was made to provide instruction in it. Then the new economy which was superimposed was different, but no effort was made to educate people to relate to it. Taxes were imposed on the land; it became a commodity rather than a meaningful possession. Gradually it was lost.

By the turn of the century, most of the States had already enacted language laws which inhibited Mexican American participation in voting and judicial processes and in the schools. Segregation, either by school or classroom, was widespread. Some parts of Texas even maintained three separate systems: for Anglos, Mexican Americans, and Negroes. There were many incidents of violence against Mexican Americans and Mexican citizens in the United States. By 1922, they had become so severe that the Secretary of State warned the Governor of Texas that action would have to be taken to protect Mexicans.

However bad conditions and wages may have been on this side of the border, they obviously appeared better than those in Mexico to the millions of Mexicans who entered the United States over the years, some temporarily, many to stay. The succeeding and fluctuating waves of immigration have reflected economic and political conditions in Mexico as well as opportunities for work in the United States: first in the mines and on the railroads, then in agriculture, more lately industry. And over recent years, first because of displacement caused by the bracero program and more recently as machines have increasingly taken over the cultivating and harvesting of the fields and vineyards, Mexican Americans, along with many other Americans, engaged in the great internal migration to the towns and cities.

"If we speak of the East Los Angeles area as being a port of entry, people immediately associate it with the port of entry for people from a foreign country," a Mexican American said recently. "I speak of a port of entry to the thousands of our people that are moving to the area from the Valley, where 135,000 farms ten years ago have been reduced to approximately 80,000, highly mechanized. And here are the people who lack the basic language skills and trade skills that are moving into the urban areas, looking for an opportunity. It is the poverty of opportunity that we must overcome."

The Mexican American barrios and colonias tabulate the familiar statistics of the urban poor: relatively high delinquency and social dependence, educational deprivation, disintegrating family life, and, of course, unemployment. But the urban barrio--indeed, the entire Mexican American community in the Southwest--is subject to an additional set of economic and social pressures. Immigrants from Mexico-- about 40,000 a year--bring with them the same kinds of social handicaps as do the new arrivals from the American rural areas. They represent direct competition for the few available jobs (and are particularly susceptible to exploitation in sweatshops), they place added pressure on schools and health and welfare agencies, and they add to the burden of the existing Mexican American community which must both absorb them and act as interpreters and mediators between them and the unfamiliar, complex, and impersonal Anglo world. Between 1960 and 1964, nearly 218,000 Mexican immigrants arrived, of whom more than 78 percent were either unskilled or of low skills; only 30 percent of all immigrants of the United States during that period fell into that category.

The Mexican American birth rate is extraordinarily high, considerably greater than that of any other single group in the country, about 50 percent greater than that of the population as a whole. The population is unusually young, with a median age 11 years below Anglo. Almost 42 percent of Mexican Americans are under the age of 15, compared with 29.7 of Anglos and 36.6 of nonwhites. Families tend to be large; the proportion of families of six persons or more is about three times that of Anglos.

The large-family, low-income pattern makes housing a particular problem for the Mexican Americans, with familes often forced to choose between adequate space in dilapidated housing or very crowded space in more desirable dwellings. Frequently, housing is both crowded and dilapidated.

Residential segregation is widespread, although there are large variations in its extent from place to place. The barrios tend not to be "central city" concentrations, however, as are the newer Negro ghettos. Rather, the old colonias which often ringed the Southwestern towns and cities were engulfed as the towns grew. The result is that in many places there are several concentrations of Mexican Americans rather than just one, which means, of course, that Mexican American "target areas" for social agencies are dispersed.

Health statistics for Mexican Americans across the Southwest are not available because the government agencies which collect them break them down into white and nonwhite categories only; hence Mexican Americans cannot be distinguished from the rest of the white population. What little information is available, however, notably for the State of Colorado and the city of San Antonio, indicate that, as would be expected, a larger proportion of Mexican Americans than of the general population, die from causes which are usually associated with low socioeconomic conditions. And in Colorado, at least, there is a marked difference in longevity, with the mean age at death of Spanish-surnamed persons being 56.7 years in contrast to 67.5 years for others.

A recent report by two members of the School of Public Health at the University of California at Los Angeles noted that there is "a complete lack of data on the health services available to Mexican Americans and the degree to which these services are utilized by members of the group."

Although more than 85 percent of the Mexican American population is native born, political participation is relatively low, and Mexican Americans have few elected representatives in Congress and, except for New Mexico, only a handful in the State legislatures, with none at all in California. Mexican American organizations totally lack the funds and resources necessary to mount effective voter registration drives, and neither political party has shown much inclination to provide them.

Mexican American political strength is potentially large, but it is still largely potential. The numerous Mexican American organizations therefore carry most of the burden of pressing community interests, but these organizations have very little money, usually no paid staff, few research facilities, and limited opportunities for the leaders even to meet together. There is no Mexican American organization equivalent of the National Association for the Advancement of Colored People (NAACP) of the National Urban League; no Mexican American colleges; and virtually no financial or other help from outside the community itself. It has thus been extremely difficult for the leadership to develop and pursue strategies which would force public agencies and institutions to pay greater and more intelligent attention to Mexican American needs and to make changes, where necessary, to meet them.

CIVIL RIGHTS AND THE ADMINISTRATION OF JUSTICE

Many Mexican Americans have suffered violations of their constitutional rights, and they have not had full or ready access to all of the processes involved in the administration of justice. Often they are denied such access; often it appears that they fail to seek it.

Preliminary investigations by staff members of this Commission, and a survey conducted independently by a team from the NAACP Legal Defense and Educational Fund Inc., lead to the belief that denials of civil rights which have been documented are repeated elsewhere, undocumented; many violations have doubtless been suffered in silence, or where they have been protested have not been proved. The Commission on Civil Rights has begun an investigation into the administration of justice throughout the Southwest.

Three recurring complaints are made with special frequency by Mexican Americans: of police brutality, illegal arrest, and exclusion from juries.

Allegations of the use of unnecessary force on the part of law enforcement officers have been made in many towns in all the Southwestern States, and every Mexican American attorney interviewed by the NAACP team cited police brutality as a major issue in his area. Mexican American youths have died while in police custody in California, Colorado, and Texas. In 1966, the Council on Mexican American Affairs took testimony in nearly 30 cases of alleged brutality in the Los Angeles area alone and demanded Federal investigation of the findings.

In 1967, the Texas Advisory Committee to the Commission on Civil Rights, having heard testimony concerning a farm labor dispute in Starr County, Texas, concluded that excessive force was used by local police and Texas Rangers against striking Mexican American workers, and that there were other infringements of their civil rights. The Advisory Committee asked that the Department of Justice investigate the case. A Senate investigating subcommittee also concluded that excessive force had been used. The National Council of Churches and the AFL-CIO have supported lawsuits to enjoin the Rangers from interfering with the strikers. The Rangers are regarded with great resentment and distrust by many Mexican Americans. One said to the Committee: "There's a lot to the saying that you hear in South Texas that all of the Rangers have Mexican blood. They have it on their boots."

Mexican Americans in Los Angeles complain that the police use "dragnet" arrest techniques, taking into custody everyone at or near the scene of a crime. Allegations of other forms of illegal arrest-- such as entering houses late at night and making arrests, without warrants, for petty offenses--are made in other parts of the Southwest. Recent cases in Northern New Mexico have aroused particularly widespread resentment among Mexican Americans throughout the Southwest. In June of 1967, an organization formed to press Mexican American claims to ancestral and land grants had scheduled a rally to be held in the countryside. The district attorney of Rio Arriba County warned leaders that the meeting would not be tolerated; as Mexican Americans arrived he arrested them on a variety of minor charges, including mistreatment of animals, and held them incommunicado for several days before dismissing the charges. In reprisal, a group of Mexican Americans attempted a citizen's arrest of the district attorney at the Rio Arriba County Courthouse in Tierra Amarilla. In the ensuing melee the attackers wounded two officers. Following this episode, 50 Mexican Americans, including women and children, were held in an open sheep pen for 36 hours, with no charges brought against them then or later.

More subtle, but undoubtedly much more widespread, than physical brutality is what Mexican Americans regard as psychological brutality on the part of many police officers. As the background report of the President's Crime Commission noted, there is the feeling that police are discriminatory, condescending, and paternalistic; that there is excessive patroling in Mexican American districts, frisking of adults and youths; and the use of degrading or condescending terms such as "pancho," "muchacho," and "amigo" in addressing Mexican Americans.

It appears that a major element in the friction between police and the Mexican American community is the relative dearth of policemen of Mexican descent. A Mexican American alleged in 1966 that the Oakland, California, police force of 617 included only five of Spanish surname, two of whom spoke Spanish. There are cities in Colorado with Mexican American populations exceeding 20 percent in which there are no Spanish-speaking policemen.

Mexican Americans and the Border Patrol

Many Mexican Americans have a sense of special grievance against the Border Patrol of the Immigration and Naturalization Service, a unit of the U.S. Department of Justice. Officers of the Border Patrol are authorized to interrogate, without a warrant, any person believed to be an alien on his right to be or to remain in the United States, and to search conveyances, such as buses or railway cars, within 100 miles of the border. The result is that many U.S. citizens of Mexican descent are accosted and questioned in what they often term as harassment. They point out that no other American citizens, as a group, are subject to such trouble and humiliation.

It appears that an important cause of intense Mexican American resentment against the Border Patrol is the widespread belief that its fluctuating activities reflect the wishes of powerful agricultural interests in the Southwest. They cite the fact that before the mid-1950's, millions of Mexican "wetbacks" managed to enter the U.S. illegally to provide a supply of cheap agricultural labor despite the Patrol. Yet after the initiation of the bracero program in 1951, which provided for Mexican nationals to work on contract under government supervision, the Border Patrol suddenly and unaccountably became more efficient. Within five years, it rounded up and deported nearly four million wetbacks, more than a million in 1954 alone. In 1967, a Mexican American economist told the Commission on Civil Rights: "American immigration policy is a function of American economic policy. . . . Whether or not the border is open or closed . . . whether or not the Border Patrol is very stringent in picking up wetbacks or whether it is very liberal in picking them up depends upon the condition of production in the United States."

The Judicial Process

It is charged that Mexican Americans are totally excluded or are represented in only token numbers on juries throughout the Southwest. In 1954, the Supreme Court ruled in the Hernandez case that the equal protection clause of the 14th amendment extends to "any identifiable group in the community which may be the subject of prejudice," and that the Mexican Americans constitute such a group. In the case in point, no Mexican American had been summoned for jury duty in 25 years although the area had a substantial Spanish-speaking population.

In Texas, it is the practice for jury commissioners to ask persons prominent in the community to suggest names for the jury panels. Under this "key man" system, it is alleged, very few Mexican Americans are suggested. In Nueces County, Texas, a Mexican American told the Texas Advisory Committee: "They had 288 grand jurors selected and only 16 Latin Americans over a period of nine years. . . . Our people had rather plead guilty than go to a jury system like that."

Atascosa County, Texas, is 45 percent Mexican American. For the week beginning August 11, 1966, the names of 48 persons were on the petit jury panel; two were Mexican American, of whom one was alive.

All of the Southwestern States except New Mexico require that a juror be able to speak and understand English (except that in Texas a court may waive the requirement if English-speaking jurors cannot be found). The requirement has not been tested in the courts.

Arizona, California, and Colorado require that court proceedings be carried on in English; New Mexico and Texas have no such requirement. All States allow for the use of interpreters, but it appears that the language barrier that colors many Mexican Americans' attitudes toward the courts may affect not only their ability to defend themselves but also their motivation to do so. One Mexican American, describing a friend who pleaded guilty to a charge "just to avoid the fuss" said,

"I wonder how many thousands of Mexicans this has happened to in the State of California that want to get it over with and be guilty because of the language problem."

Many Mexican Americans believe that if they are brought into court and found guilty of a crime or misdemeanor they are likely to receive a more severe sentence than an Anglo. There has been testimony that much harsher sentences have been meted out to Mexican Americans in towns where Anglos who committed similar crimes were treated lightly. And an Anglo scholar who studied the court records of a small town in California said that they "reveal that the punishments meted out to Anglos were significantly less severe than that given to Mexican Americans convicted on the same charges. Anglos, for example, are fined for drunkenness and sometimes kept in jail overnight. Mexicans have been fined and jailed for up to 60 days, though their conduct while drunk was essentially the same as that of the Anglos." Similar complaints are voiced concerning the handling of juveniles.

Voting

In some areas Mexican Americans have testified that their right to vote has been compromised by means ranging from outright intimidation to restrictive laws which make registration difficult.

Only Arizona and California require that a voter be literate in English. In Texas, however, a new registration law enacted in 1966 has been described by some Mexican Americans as actually constituting a substitute for the poll tax, which was repealed at the same time. After studying the registration act, the Texas State Advisory Committee to this Commission requested that the Commission in consultation with the Department of Justice review the law to determine if it "violates the civil rights of citizens or if it presents a serious obstacle to increased registration."

Mexican Americans have described other kinds of registration difficulties. It was claimed in 1967 that local officials in two Northern California counties refused to give registration books to Mexican American volunteer deputy registrars.

In a Texas town, Mexican Americans described a variety of attempts to lower the Mexican American turnout. They alleged that welfare recipients were intimidated, that police ticketed cars for minor defects on election day, and that election officials attempted to confuse Mexican American voters by asking "Where is your property?" instead of "Where do you live?" thus making some eligible voters believe they must own property in order to vote.

Access to Justice

There has been no concerted legal attack on the civil rights problems of Mexican Americans. Very few suits have been brought against the police in cases of alleged brutality. While more than a dozen cases involving exclusion of Negroes from juries have reached the Supreme Court, only one such involving Mexican Americans has gone to the Court.

Only a handful of cases have been brought under Federal and State law prohibiting discrimination in employment, only a handful in cases of school or classroom segregation.

Until very recently, there has been no Mexican American organization with the funds or legal expertise necessary to mount a systematic legal attack on various civil rights disabilities. Individual Mexican Americans who have been, or think they have been, discriminated against (and often they are ignorant of their rights) usually lack the money necessary to hire a lawyer and prosecute a case. Often they appear to lack the will as well. A Mexican American member of the Texas Advisory Committee explained why some are reluctant to use administrative and legal processes:

> In general the low income people, the low education people, are afraid of anybody coming at them with a piece of paper. Either it's a bill collector or the law. And it's not that they know the law that well--it's the lack of knowledge that the law is there to protect them. They have been abused so long that they just are afraid of everybody.

As of 1960, only 2 percent of lawyers in the Southwest had Spanish surnames. Most of them have a large volume of cases and low incomes which make it impossible for them to donate the time necessary for difficult civil rights cases. Very few have experience in civil rights litigation, which is so complex that it is now recognized as a specialty within the law.

In May 1968, the Ford Foundation announced the establishment of the Mexican American Legal Defense and Education Fund. A small legal staff based in San Antonio will work with local lawyers throughout the Southwest in identifying and preparing civil rights cases for litigation. The Fund will also carry on an educational program designed to inform Mexican Americans of their civil rights.

EDUCATION

Taking the Southwest as a whole, Mexican Americans on the average have about eight years of schooling, or four years less than Anglos, two years less than nonwhites. Educational statistics must be scrutinized closely, however, by State and county and city. In Texas, for example, 40 percent of all Mexican Americans are functionally illiterate.

Obviously the dropout rate among Mexican Americans is very high, with most of the dropouts occurring by eighth or ninth grade. High dropout rates at the high school level then come as no particular surprise, and they appear more ominous when they occur in urban settings where occupations require relatively high levels of skill and education. In 1966, two predominantly Mexican American high schools in Los Angeles had dropout rates of 53.8 percent and 47.5 percent.

Nor is it surprising that Mexican American enrollments in college are low. About two percent of California's college population, for example, is of Spanish surname.

Apart from statistics about educational level and dropouts, far too little sound information is available about the education of Mexican American children in the Southwest. Except for California, statewide figures showing the amount of school segregation are not available. Too little is known about the sporadic educational experiences of the 40,000 to 50,000 migrant children. The degree to which the facilities, teachers, and educational programs of predominantly Mexican American schools are not equal to those of Anglo schools has not been established.

Although there is little of what academicians would regard as "hard" evidence, there is a wealth of impressionistic, anecdotal, and eyewitness accounts of what goes on in the schools. And the mere statistics themselves, of course, suggest a few reasonable inferences.

Mexican Americans make many specific complaints: crowded and run-down facilities, large class size, poor counseling and guidance, poor vocational education, testing and tracking practices that isolate Mexican Americans within schools if they are not in segregated schools, inappropriate textbooks and other teaching materials. It is clear, however, that there is also a more general and overriding concern: that the schools function as mirrors of some of the more destructive attitudes of the dominant society.

"It's the way the schools feel, the attitudes of the schools toward the Mexican American," a parent said in Los Angeles in 1967. In fact, grievances about education have provided the impetus for community and parental action and organization. The groups thus formed, however, greatly need technical advice and educational programs of their own.

Mexican American parents are, of course, not alone in challenging some of the prevailing attitudes. In 1967, a Colorado State Government report on Spanish-surnamed citizens found that it is the prevailing opinion among many school administrators that Mexican American youth "because of their cultural value system . . . do not aspire to educational success." But, the report asserted:

> The lack of aspiration in any Spanish-surnamed student is probably not his failure to accept prevailing cultural goals, but his awareness that he cannot make it. Assuming he has the ability, as do many Spanish-surnamed students who drop out of school, it is the educational system and the majority society which kill his aspiration, not an inner deficiency.

English must be used as the language of classroom instruction except in New Mexico and California, and California repealed its "English only" law just last year. Until recently, the practice has been widespread (and some assert that it still is today) to prohibit resolutely the speaking of Spanish even on the playground. A Mexican American leader in Phoenix deplored the "bigoted approach on the part of the schools which immediately puts in the child's mind that the Spanish language is inferior--not socially acceptable--since you cannot use it in public.''

In 1964, a group of seventh grade students in Texas was asked to write essays about their experience in elementary school. They described some of the methods used to punish them for speaking Spanish: having to stand on the "black square" for an hour or so; being charged a penny for each Spanish word uttered; and having to write three pages of "I must not speak Spanish in school."

Educators' reasons for prohibiting the use of Spanish are, of course, that the children must learn English. But some of the essays showed that suppression of Spanish did not necessarily insure success in the teaching of English.

One girl wrote:

I have fell in the for grade. Some of the rules were. No talking in class. No getting up from there chairs. And no speaking spanish. If any baby that speaking spanish would get a leeking, are would be speted from school. P.S. They would get 3
leeking a day.

In integrated schools, it is reported that Mexican American children are sometimes separated from their Anglo classmates in the classroom, on the playground, and in extracurricular affairs. In a rural California district, Mexican American students are always seated behind Anglos at graduation ceremonies. "It makes for a better looking stage," the school principal explained.

Numerous academic and social practices are such as to impress Mexican American students with the idea that they are not only different but inferior. One teacher explained why she always calls on Anglo children to "help" Mexican American children when they hesitate for an answer: "I think it is better if the Mexican pupils get 'help' from an American pupil who knows what he is talking about than from another Mexican who doesn't. Besides, it is good educational practice to have the American children help the Mexicans. It draws them out and gives them a feeling of importance."

The curriculum in general and textbooks in particular neglect to inform both Anglo and Mexican American pupils of the substantial contributions to the Southwest made by Mexicans and Mexican Americans, and of the rich history and culture of Spanish-speaking people. Denied full status as Americans ("They're told they're Americans and yet they're treated as Mexicans," a school counselor in Los Angeles said), the Mexican American students are also deprived of the chance to gain understanding and pride in their heritage. A Los Angeles high school student said recently:

The teachers' negative opinion of Mexico would not bother me
so much, except that this is the only image portrayed to us here
in America of what we are. We look around for something to
be proud of, we question our parents, but all they tell us, 'just
be proud you are a Mexican,' because they are too busy working or taking care of the little kids or too uneducated to tell

us all we have to be proud of . . . all the thousand things we
have to be proud of. And since they cannot tell us these things,
and the schools will not, we begin to think that maybe we are
inferior, that we do not belong in his world, that, as some
teachers actually tell students to their faces, we should go back
to Mexico and quit causing problems for America.

The crisis in identity is obviously acute for many Mexican American youngsters. A Mexican American teacher in a Los Angeles school
noted differences in behavior between native-born Mexican Americans
and Mexican-born students at a Cinco de Mayo assembly: "The Mexican youngster knew who he was and had no difficulty, while the Mexican
American youngster was very much ashamed, very insecure."
In some cases, school personnel display an insensitivity which
borders on brutality. In 1967, a Los Angeles mother testified before
the State Advisory Committee to the Commission:

We have another mother in the school in the San Fernando Valley, which is having nine children, and which, with the wages
the husband make, was not enough to put an adequate lunch for
the children when they went to school. Yet the school kept constantly calling her back telling her that the beans--a sandwich
of beans--was not enough. I think she knew that. She knew that
very well. The point was, she didn't have enough money to put
anything better.
        And that is not the problem I'm referring about. The prob-
lem is that this was told to the children in front of the rest of
the class. What kind of teacher would make the children feel
bad because of that--not once, three, four, five times. When
a teacher is doing this, this is making damage on the child itself. He can no longer concentrate on trying to improve, trying to do his best. He's already been branded.

Mexican American educators, parents, and students, and also
many Anglos, are demanding that textbooks and other teaching materials
be revised so as to give a proper representation of Mexican history
and culture, and that teachers, administrators, and guidance and counseling personnel be properly trained in the same subjects as well as
in appropriate ways to deal with Mexican American students. Little
has been done so far, however. At El Paso, a Mexican American educator referred to an NDEA Institute he directed for teachers on the
role of Negroes and Mexican Americans in American history. "It was
unique for two years in a row," he said, "while scores of others dealt
with such vital questions as new insights on the French and Indian
wars or the adjustment to industrialism in the Western world."

Isolation by School or by Class

Although adequate statistics are not available about the extent of
school segregation as a whole, a look at the schools suggests that it is

widespread. On the west side of San Antonio there are three elementary schools within walking distance of each other. Their names--Sojourner Truth, Hidalgo, and Will Rogers--accurately reflect the ethnic compositions of their student bodies.

California has released an ethnic breakdown of its schools, which shows that 57 percent of Mexican American students in the eight largest school districts attend schools that are segregated according to California's definition: the ethnic composition of the student body is not within 15 percent of the composition of the school district. Only 2.25 percent of California's teachers have Spanish surnames.

Testing, "ability" grouping, and counseling practices often result in Mexican American segregation within "integrated" schools. There is serious question in many educators' minds about the reliability of "intelligence" tests, yet in California, Mexican Americans comprise more than a quarter of the children assigned to classes for the mentally retarded.

"Why is it that in our Head Start program we found out that when you gave tests in Spanish the children's I.Q. increased, and yet when the school tested them, their mental capacities were much lower?," a Mexican American community leader demanded.

The charge is frequently made that counselors guide Mexican American students into "realistic" vocational and business programs rather than a curriculum that might prepare them for more education. A recent study in Los Angeles showed that only a fifth of Mexican American students are in an academic program while half the Anglo children are.

Language

The schools' attitudes toward the Spanish language obviously play a role in strengthening or shaking a child's self-esteem. In addition, there are, of course, serious educational problems involved in teaching children whose first language is not English. The traditional approach of the schools has not solved these problems.

"As the Spanish-speaking child has seldom mastered the basic grammatical concepts of the Spanish language before he is forced to deal with English, he seldom learns either Spanish or English well," a Mexican American educator said recently. "The school districts of the Southwest have the unique honor of graduating students who are functionally illiterate in two languages." State and national educational organizations have recently been taking a much greater interest in the problems of Mexican American education, and some Anglo teachers have made special efforts to learn Spanish and to understand the cultural background of their pupils.

There is now great pressure from the Mexican American community for bilingual teaching programs which would enable children to learn English as a second language while taking basic subjects in Spanish. Some promisive experimentation with bilingual programs is now going on, and more will be supported if funding is provided. The fact that much research must still be done, and teaching materials

developed, is an indication of the lack of interest the region's universities have shown in the educational needs of the area's largest minority
group. This lack of attention also has been reflected at the national
level. A Mexican American educator recently pointed out: "Odd as it
may seem, the United States Government has done more to help citizens of other countries learn English in their own lands than it has
done for non-English-speaking American citizens in this country. We
know that there are texts and tapes and teacher training programs
available through the State Department for overseas use. Why can't
these materials be made available to our teachers and students of
English?"

Migrant Education

Children whose parents are migratory workers suffer more
severe educational deprivation than any others. They are moved from
school to school, few of which welcome them, and it is alleged that
some schools will not admit migrant children or, if they do, put them
in segregated classes under the instruction of substitute or non-cre-
dentialed teachers. It is reported that school attendance laws are seldom
enforced in the case of the migrant children.

Some Federal and State funds have been provided for special
assistance in migrant education; in California, such funds provide
services, directly or indirectly, to only about one of every eight migrant
children in the State.

Since 1963, Texas has tried to improve the education of migrants
by establishing an intensive six-month program for children who leave
the area early in the spring and return late in the fall. The program
emphasizes intensive training in language development. Critics, however, have attacked it as being naive as well as segregationist.

Pressures for Change

Mexican American groups, with support from an increasing number
of Anglo educators, are pressing for a great variety of changes in the
schools. They ask for more research on bilingual, bicultural education,
improved and more relevant training for the teachers who will instruct
Mexican American students, and the development of new teaching materials. They urge the recruitment of more Spanish-speaking teachers,
and suggest that certification requirements should be revised. They
ask that existing ability tests be reviewed for cultural bias, and that
vocational education programs be evaluated and brought up to date.
And they insist that the Mexican American parents and community
must be more closely involved in the education of the youth. They
allege that the "Upward Bound" program for recruiting and helping
minority or poor youngsters into college has not been effective in
reaching many Mexican Americans and urge much greater scholarship assistance from private foundations.

EMPLOYMENT

As a group, Mexican Americans have been unable to move into the mainstream of American economic life. Taking the Southwest as a whole, their unemployment rate is about double that of Anglos. As is so often the case, overall statistics tell less than the whole story. They understate the case for Mexican Americans because, among other things, unemployed farm workers are not included in unemployment statistics. Furthermore, regional figures hide the severity of the situation as it exists in many barrios where Mexican Americans are concentrated. The unemployment level hovers at about 20 percent in one Denver ward, 12 percent in a Los Angeles census tract.

More important, perhaps, than the gross unemployment picture are other characteristic patterns:

There is widespread underemployment. Many Mexican Americans do not have full-time, year-round jobs. A 1966 survey by the Department of Labor showed that 47 percent of the men in a Mexican American district of San Antonio were either unemployed, underemployed, or earning less than $60 per week.

Mexican Americans are heavily concentrated in the lowest paying jobs. This condition holds for public employment-- Federal, State, county, and city--as well as private. In 1960, 79 percent of all Mexican American workers labored in unskilled and semi-skilled jobs. This statistic makes it evident that Mexican Americans have difficulty gaining promotion once they are employed, probably due in part to the generally low level of education and skills, and probably in part to discrimination.

There are certain important kinds of business and industry in which Mexican Americans appear not to have made significant inroads at any level. In Los Angeles County, they have been well represented, since World War II, in the food, steel, automobile assembly, and diecast aluminum industries. But it is alleged that in others which include some of the most important growth industries and companies--aircraft, telephone, space, and electronic and allied industries--Mexican American employees total 5 percent or less, though they constitute from 12 to 14 percent of the County population as a whole.

Public Employment

The single largest, and the best-paying, employer in the Southwest is the United States Government. As of mid-1966, having made dramatic increases in a short time, it employed Mexican Americans in almost direct proportion to their percentage of the total labor force-- about 10 percent--taking the Southwest as a whole.

Again, however, overall statistics do not present a complete picture, for in California, which has the largest concentration of Mexican Americans of all the Southwestern states, Mexican American

Federal employees were only 4.9 percent. And in Los Angeles County, which has the largest concentration of Mexican Americans in the country, they were only about 4 percent. In that county, the Post Office employs 43 percent of all Federal employees, but only 4.1 percent of those employees are Mexican American.

Resentment against Post Office hiring and promotion policies runs high among Mexican Americans in California, both because the Post Office is such a large employer and because it has made special efforts to help another minority group.

"It is a fact that last year in San Francisco," a Mexican American testified before the California State Advisory Committee to this Commission, "after the Negro uprising, 700 positions were created to pacify and alleviate the problems of unemployment in the Negro community. The Civil Service exams were waived in the mentioned case. Yet, when the Mexican American organizations requested that the same be done for the Mexican American, the Administration refused to acknowledge that the Mexican American community was faced with the same problem in employment. Will we have to burn some buildings to obtain justice from our Government?"

As is true in the private sector of the economy, Mexican Americans in Federal service are clustered in the lowest pay scales. In the postal service, 91 percent are in the lowest paying positions, grades one through four. Overall, nearly 70 percent are at entry level.

Employment of Mexican Americans by State, county, and city governments varies but in general is less than Federal. In California, only about 4 percent of the State employees are Mexican American, and that percentage represents a sharp increase over what it was just a few years ago.

A study recently conducted by the Commission showed that in Houston and the San Francisco Bay area, persons of Spanish surname held 7.7 percent and 2.4 percent of municipal jobs, respectively. They constitute 6.4 percent of the total population in both places.

In some important cases, it is difficult to obtain figures. The city of Los Angeles, for example, home for 260,389 Mexican Americans at the time of the 1960 census, insists that it makes no ethnic head count and that it cannot even estimate the number of city employees who are of Mexican descent. The city does, however, now keep an ethnic count of appointments made in any given year; in 1965-66, they were running about 6 percent Mexican American.

Private Employment

It is difficult to obtain precise ethnic breakdowns for private businesses and industries. Those available, however, suggest that there are wide variations in the employment pattern, but that Mexican Americans are greatly underrepresented in certain kinds of employment in many Southwestern towns. In Mathis, Texas, where 65 percent of the population is of Spanish surname, the only bank had no Spanish-speaking employee in 1966, nor did the power and light company. There were no Mexican American journeymen or masters in skilled trades. In Roswell,

New Mexico, which is 14.2 percent Mexican American, neither the telephone company nor the public utility company had any Mexican American employees at any level in 1964.

Mexican American spokesmen claim that many large employers have poor records in hiring and promoting Mexican Americans. In 1966, an official of a large oil company testified before the Texas Advisory Committee of the Commission on Civil Rights:

> In the counties of Kleberg, Nueces, and San Patricio we have 883 employees. Of Latin American and Negroes there are 8, which is a percentage of 1. . . . I might say that we are an equal rights company, the Humble Oil and Refining Company.

Mexican Americans constitute 40 percent of the population of the three counties.

Discrimination and Other Causes

Discrimination against Mexican Americans is often difficult to prove because employers may cite lack of skill or facility in the English language as grounds for refusing employment or promotion. And it is unquestionably true that much of the Mexican American employment situation in general must be laid to the low educational level and lack of occupational skills on the part of many members of the community. Nonetheless, the Anglo and Mexican American observers are convinced that overt discrimination is widespread.

In 1967, the director of the Los Angeles office of the Equal Employment Opportunity Commission testified before the State Advisory Committee of the Commission on Civil Rights that "our experience has been, and certainly is still, there is much too much discrimination against Mexican Americans."

He went on to say: "I am reminded of an employer in Arizona who said to us, 'Yes, we discriminate against Mexican Americans. We always have. We have never permitted Mexican Americans to get higher than a certain level in this company.'

"I am also reminded of the union representative who said he believes the best way to integrate his union is to hire a Negro to work with his own people.

"We have had at least one employer who has used the techniques of not hiring anyone on any given day when Negroes and Mexican Americans are the best qualified, but hiring on days when these people did not appear as applicants."

Charges of discrimination, particularly in promotion, have been brought by Mexican American organizations against Federal installations as well as private companies, many of which hold Government contracts which prohibit discrimination. The Kelly Air Force Base in San Antonio has been a frequent target; so have other military installations. Charges of differential pay and treatment have been made against the Kingsville Naval Air Station. It was alleged that Mexican American Navy Exchange employees are paid 80 cents an hour and Anglos $1.25, and that the Navy has contracts with a cleaner who hires Spanish-speaking employees at 50 cents an hour. A Mexican American supervisor charged that he was ordered to sweep and clean his area while no Anglos of the same (or even lower) rank have been asked to perform such duties.

Mexican Americans complain that, although they must be paid good wages (though often they are not), they cannot rise into higher positions. One in Los Angeles testified that when he was the logical choice to become foreman, his employer (who acknowledged the man's ability) told him:

"John, the men won't take orders from you."
"I said, 'What men?' "
"He said, 'The American men.' "
"So, being from Afghanistan, I figured that's right. So I was given a raise of 25 cents an hour and I was happy with that."

Many observers believe that private firms, and Civil Service itself, often establish totally irrelevant requirements which have the effect, intended or not, of screening out Mexican American applicants. A high school diploma is often necessary to gain very simple sorts of jobs.

"This high school fetish that is still adhered to by some employers is harmful to the dropout and is also harmful to the industry itself," the Anglo manager of training for an aircraft company in Los Angeles told the California State Advisory Committee of the Commission on Civil Rights in 1967. "A few years ago Douglas and Lockheed collaborated in a study of minimum requirements for factory occupations. We found that 18 jobs could be performed by people with less than eighth grade education, 11 jobs with eighth grade ability level, and 27 jobs with tenth grade ability level."

Tests of various kinds often present unnecessary obstacles to employment for Mexican Americans. It is acknowledged that tests seldom accurately measure the ability of different language or cultural groups. And in some cases, it is difficult to see what relationship a given test has to a given job. In 1967, the San Francisco Chronicle reported that several of the best gardeners in the city's Recreations and Parks Department had lost their jobs because, having been hired on a temporary basis until they could meet Civil Service requirements, they could not pass a written test which a reporter described as a "watered-down version of a college entrance exam." It included such questions as "He treated me as though I _____ a stranger."

The dismissed gardeners were described by a superior as men who "can spot plant diseases and know just what to do, but put it down in writing--never!"

Employment of Non-resident "Residents"

There is an additional factor--a crucial one--which affects the employment and wage possibilities of the many Mexican Americans living along the great border which stretches from Brownsville, Texas to San Diego, California. Each day, at least 44,000 Mexican citizens and about 18,000 American citizens commute to jobs in the American border towns from their homes in Mexico.

These commuters, whose wages are high by Mexican standards but would not provide a bare subsistence in the United States, are admitted each day under what Judge Luther Youngdahl of the Federal District Court in Washington has termed "an amiable fiction": that they are bona fide immigrants to the United States. The American Government grants them the immigration documents from which they derive the designation "Green Carders" despite the fact that there is no proof that they intend ever to establish residence in this country and, in fact, every evidence that they do not.

There have been many allegations that commuters have been used as strikebreakers in labor disputes in the United States. And there is substantial evidence that their daily migration depresses wages and creates unemployment for Mexican Americans who live along the border.

In 1966, unemployment in Texas border towns was almost 95 percent higher than in the interior. Wages in the same towns were 31 percent below the State average. On one day in 1966, 2,581 Green Carders crossed into Laredo where 3,365 American citizens were unemployed and where the local unemployment rate was 12.6 percent. In El Paso, 11,772 crossed on a day when 5,050 were unemployed. In California's Imperial Valley, where some 7,500 commuters work, the unemployment rate in 1966 was twice the State average.

It appears unlikely that many of the commuters possess skills which are not available on the American side of the border. When a spot survey was made in 1961, for example, two garment manufacturing firms in Laredo were employing 88 Green Carders as sewing machine operators at the same time that applications from 156 out-of-work American sewing machine operators were on file at the Texas Employment Commission office in Laredo.

The U.S. Attorney General is required by law to refuse entry to commuters if domestic workers are available. The evidence suggests that this law is not enforced.

Under immigration law, the commuter is officially a "resident alien". There is no authority in the law for a resident to be non-resident.

Despite the damaging effect of the commuters on the domestic job situation and wage structure, Mexican American spokesmen and organizations appear to have ambivalent feelings about how or whether to attack the problem. Although all deplore the use of Green Carders as strikebreakers, there have been few concerted efforts to get the border closed. Reluctance to press for this solution may spring from the fear that the already increasing tendency for the border to develop as a "Hong Kong economy" will be spurred. Already "runaway industries" are establishing plants just inside the Mexican border, with the encouragement of the Mexican government which allows the plants to import machinery, raw goods, and semi-finished goods duty-free, and to export the finished products freely. Moreover, a Mexican American

labor official pointed out, "when these products are shipped into the
U.S., Section 807 of the Tariff Code provides a special, very low tariff--
not on the value of the products, but on the cost of the value added in
the Mexican plant, which is essentially the low wages of the Mexican
workers."

Agricultural Labor

While it cannot be stressed too strongly that the Mexican American problems of today are primarily urban problems, the condition of
the dwindling number of Mexican American workers in agriculture
deserves special mention.

As of 1960, 16 percent of all Mexican American employment
was in agriculture. Today, perhaps 250,000 Mexican Americans subsist entirely or primarily by farm labor. Mexican Americans from
Texas dominate the migrant labor force which fans out across the
Midwest, the Rocky Mountain States, and up the Pacific Coast. Resident Mexican Americans, many of them former migrants who settled
down, comprise most of the farm labor force of California, Arizona,
and Colorado.

Wages for farm labor are low, employment is seasonal and often
irregular even during the season, the work is backbreaking without
offering the opportunity for advancement, and living and working conditions are often indescribably bad.

In January of 1967, farm labor wages ranged from $1.09 an hour
in New Mexico to $1.62 in California. The annual income for farm
workers in 1964 averaged $1,213, with migrants earning less than
$1,000 on the average.

Women and children form an important portion of the farm labor
force. "A mother cannot work, yet she must work," a woman in California said, and the low prevailing wage makes clear why. For the
families who follow the crops, education is interrupted, health and
welfare programs are often inaccessible owing to residence requirements and for other reasons, and the miserable housing is notorious.
A health official in Indiana testified before the Indiana State Advisory
Committee to this Commission that inspections of 329 labor camps in
the State found only four which were certifiable by State standards.
(None of them was closed, however, and the Department of Labor
continued interstate recruitment of migrant workers although it is
required not to do so when housing does not meet State requirements.)
New Mexico and Texas have no provisions or requirements covering
migrant housing. A Mexican American in Colorado described migrant
housing this way: "On various places, they just run out the chickens
and the migratory worker moves in. When he moves out the chickens
move back in." An Anglo professor doesn't think the chickens are so
well-off either; he says he saw labor camps in 1967 "that aren't fit
for animals."

Threatened by competition from Mexican immigrants even more
desperate than they, the Mexican American farm workers find little
protection from American law. Farm labor is specifically excluded

from the right to bargain under the National Labor Relations Act, and it is limited in its coverage under Social Security and minimum wage laws. State laws vary but none provides unemployment insurance, and even so basic a protection as workmen's compensation for injury suffered on the job is limited.

Enforcement of such regulations as do exist to protect the farm worker is spotty.

PUBLIC POLICIES AND PUBLIC AGENCIES

In testimony before the Commission and various of its State Advisory Committees, at a Cabinet-level hearing in El Paso in October of 1967, and in numerous speeches and protests, Mexican Americans have made clear their community's growing frustration and anger. The condition of the large proportion of the community, they say, signifies the failure of public policies and public agencies to provide equal access to the institutions, services, and programs of American society.

The failures they cite are of several different, though often overlapping, kinds. The first is one common to all societies: priorities and the allocation of resources tend to favor the haves rather than, and sometimes at the direct expense of, the have-nots. Second, even where legislated or administrative policies or standards might protect the poor, it is charged that public agencies sometimes, because of the influence of powerful private interests, sometimes withhold services, apply the policies wrongly or differentially, and enforce the standards sporadically or not at all. In many cases it is acknowledged that agencies lack the funds and personnel necessary for implementation, but this, again, it is said, represents a system of priorities. Finally, even when programs are specifically designed and sincerely meant to benefit poor people, they are often ineffective either for reasons which are generic to bureaucracies or because of the inability of bureaucrats to make the programs accessible or useful to the Mexican American community.

Many Mexican Americans are extremely distrustful of the intentions as well as the practices of Federal as well as State and local agencies. At El Paso, one said:

We who have for thirty years seen the Department of Labor stand by, and at times connive, while farm labor unions were destroyed by agri-business; we who have seen the Immigration and Naturalization Service see-saw with the seasonal tides of wetbacks; we who are now seeing the Department of Housing and Urban Development assist in the demolishment of the urban barrios where ex-farm laborers have sought a final refuge; we who have waited for a Secretary of Education who would bristle with indignation, back it with action, at a system that continues to produce that shameful anacronism--the migrant child; we who have seen the Office of Economic Opportunity retreat with its shield, not on it, after calling the Mexican poor to do battle

for maximum feasible participation in their own destinies. . . .
We, may I say, are profoundly skeptical.

Mexican Americans are well aware of the public subsidies that
increase the advantages of those who are already well off. The President's Commission on Rural Poverty reported that Federal programs
to help rural Americans are "woefully out of date" and charged that
some of them "have helped to create wealthy landowners while largely
bypassing the rural poor."

Mexican Americans are also keenly aware of the fact that the
mechanization of agriculture, which has driven many from farm to
barrio without skill or training, has been accomplished through gen-
erous public subsidy. An economist declared at El Paso:

"The research that has made possible the chemical, physical,
and genetic progress that underlies mechanization is subsidized research. The University of California campus at Davis has been for
decades the public supported Academy of Science of agri-business."
He went on to refer to another kind of subsidy:

> The gigantic irrigation projects by which corporate farming
> takes water at bargain rates, [are] capitalizing this unearned
> dividend into rapidly rising land values that place it out of the
> reach of the small grower. The corporate farms can tap this
> no-cost benediction by laying a siphon onto the nearest con-
> crete ditch or sinking a $75,000 well. Their promised land is
> not over Jordan; it is just over the Central Valley Canal. Ver-
> ily, the Federal Government has laid a water-table for them
> in the presence of their critics.

A Mexican American union official said at El Paso: "The loud
hue and cry being raised today about the curtailment of bracero importation is coming from those who seek to perpetuate this rotten system. The agricultural industry, already heavily subsidized with taxpayer money, wants the additional advantage of having its dirty labor
performed at starvation wages and at conditions that no decent person
should be forced to endure."

At a San Francisco hearing in 1967, a Mexican American said
that the Department of Labor tells "statistical lies" in order to accommodate growers wishing a supply of braceros from Mexico. Still
on the subject of labor, it was said at El Paso:

> The employment of Mexican citizens who have entered this
> country illegally has become a regular feature of the agri-
> cultural labor market. This illegal supply of labor rests on
> the willingness of corporate farmers to hire, of intermediaries
> to transport, of Congress to tolerate, and of the Department
> of Justice to accommodate to this vicious black market in hu-
> man toil.

An Anglo scholar charged at El Paso that "the Departments of
Interior and of Agriculture have a direct responsibility for heavy land

loss among the subsistence Spanish American farmers located along
the major river systems of New Mexico. The development of almost
every major irrigation and flood control district in the State . . . drove
thousands of Spanish Americans from their lands through their inability to pay the financial charges imposed upon their small farms.
The policies of both departments are such that the majority of their
programs benefit the larger commercial heavily subsidized Anglo
American farmer. . . . ''

He added:

> The harsh refusal of the dominant Anglo American population
> and Anglo dominated state legislatures to permit the expendi-
> tures of state funds for programs to assist Spanish Americans
> is quite ironic in view of the fact that the Anglo American pop-
> ulation is far more subsidized by state and Federal Govern-
> ments than the Spanish Americans. This statement is supported
> by an examination of the evidence. The network of superhigh-
> ways constructed by state and Federal funds somehow always
> bypass the Spanish American areas suffocated by an inadequate
> transportation system. Lavish airports seldom utilized by the
> Spanish Americans mark the Anglo American cities . . . con-
> siderable funds are spent on the natural forests for the Anglo
> American hunter, fisher, and camper to the neglect of the gra-
> zing facilities needed by the small Spanish American village
> livestock owner.

Testifying before a Congressional subcommittee in 1967, a Mexican American said: "This year in Fresno County, one cotton grower
received $2 1/2 million in government subsidies for his cotton crop
allotment, while the antipoverty funds for the entire county totaled
only $1 1/2 million. This is another contrast in terms of how govern-
ment welfare is expended in the State of California. . . . ''

Policies of the Department of Housing and Urban Development,
as well as those of State and local agencies, have come under sharp
attack because they have destroyed Mexican American communities
in the name of urban renewal. Barrios in San Antonio, Los Angeles,
and San Jose, as well as many smaller communities, have been de-
molished, and in San Francisco efforts were made to blueprint 2,700
families and nearly 2,000 single individuals out of the heavily Spanish-
speaking Mission District.

"It's easier to attract money for tourist attractions than for
housing the poor," a Mexican American community organizer said
bitterly, apparently referring to the fact that Mexican Americans in
San Antonio were displaced for construction of the Hemisfair and in
Los Angeles for the construction of a baseball stadium.

States, counties, and local communities can, and often do, thwart
Federal efforts to help the Mexican American poor. Thirty-two of the
44 Texas counties with Mexican American populations of 25 percent
or more participate in Federal food (either surplus commodities or
food stamps) programs. It is charged that some schools do not take

advantage of the program providing free lunches to eligible children even though funds are available to do so. It is charged that some school districts divert into their general fund Federal money earmarked for the education of poor children. And some school districts will not accept such help for their disadvantaged children. A suit has recently been brought against a district in Orange County, California, which has failed to accept more than $1 million to which it is entitled, although it scores lowest of all California county districts on a statewide reading test. Mexican American enrollment in the schools is 29 percent. The superintendent of a district in Texas which is about 70 percent Mexican American explained that the schools had not accepted Federal funds because, "We feel like we are doing a pretty good job." Median school years completed by Mexican Americans in the county are 2.1.

As for the application or enforcement of existing policies Mexican Americans claim that local sheriffs and police often allow migrant workers to sleep in ditchbanks or cars during the harvest, then roust them as soon as the season ends. They charge that the Farm Placement Service of the Department of Labor recruits workers without assuring itself that wages and working conditions are as advertised and that they meet minimal Federal and State standards (where they exist). And the condition of much farm labor housing is proof that authorities cannot or will not, in any event do not, effectively enforce those State requirements which do exist.

An Anglo professor said at El Paso that wages for labor in sugar beet production are determined on the basis of annual regional hearings which "are dominated by sugar processors and producers." As of 1967, the wage was set at $1.40 per hour, but the Department of Agriculture gives producers the option of paying at that rate or on a piecework basis. "As a practical matter," the professor said, "the rate paid is the latter" because in most cases it averages out at less than $1.40, in some cases as low as 75 cents an hour. Producers are required to comply with the wage standard in order to receive their annual subsidy from the government.

Spokesmen claim that Federal agencies have not been energetic in promoting equal job opportunities for Mexican Americans, and that some State and local agencies are at best indifferent in doing so. In some cases it appears that lack of staffing and resources inhibits the making of positive efforts to increase Mexican American employment. In some cases it appears also that there is a reluctance to apply available sanctions. As of June 1967, for example, the Office of Federal Contract Compliance of the Defense Contract Administration Services Region, Department of Defense, in Los Angeles had not cancelled a single Federal contract on the grounds of noncompliance with nondiscriminatory requirements. The director of the office acknowledged that he did not know, even roughly, the employment rate of Mexican Americans in the large aircraft industry in the area, and when pressed as to whether the aircraft companies are in compliance with the law said, "Some may be and some may not be."

The Los Angeles staff had only 10 employees, who were responsible for ensuring that 2,000 prime contractors and an unknown number of primary and secondary subcontractors do not discriminate. Small wonder that the staff has not been able to engage in much positive work with contractors. In cases where it has been able to, however, good results are apparent. Fifty contractors with which the Office had made special efforts now have an average of 13.9 percent Mexican Americans employed; 50 similar companies with which the Office had not worked have only 9.3 percent. Furthermore, the firms which receive special attention had 6.7 percent more skilled Mexican Americans craftsmen than the others. Such results lend credence to the argument of many Mexican Americans that equality of job opportunity must be pursued through affirmative efforts rather than merely adjudicating specific complaints of discrimination.

The Equal Employment Opportunity Commission (EEOC) has been a special target of Mexican American organizations, both because they believed it was not active in attempting to solve Mexican American employment problems and because there was no Mexican American member of the Commission. In 1967, a Mexican American was appointed to the five-member EEOC. The EEOC has put primary emphasis on responding to specific complaints of discrimination, lacking sufficient staff and resources to pursue a substantial program of affirmative action with employers.

. "The Spanish American is not prone to complain about discrimination," a Mexican American said, and the experience of the EEOC bears him out. During the first eight months its Los Angeles office was open, for example, it received complaints from 130 Negroes and only 36 Mexican Americans. The Director of the Office said to the State Advisory Committee to the Commission on Civil Rights that "we need to take a look at how to develop new ways of meeting Mexican American needs."

Bureaucratic Failures

In El Paso, the Mexican American director of a Los Angeles service center said:

> The fact that traditional agencies cannot relate directly with
> people in poverty pockets, who have withdrawn behind barriers
> of distrust and suspicion, has been in evidence for a long time.

Even when these agencies make special efforts they often fail, as do some of the programs of the newer agencies specifically created to help the poor. Some examples may suggest some of the reasons why:

> In some areas, many Mexican American children do not take
> advantage of federally funded free lunch programs to which
> they are entitled. The children are given different colored tick-
> ets to obtain the food, or they must eat it at a different time
> or in a different place from their classmates. "Many children
> will go without lunch rather than be embarrassed in this way,"
> a Mexican American mother says simply. "This is a nutri-
> tional problem and an educational problem." It is also an

example of institutionalized insensitivity to cultural values.

A psychiatric social worker in California testifies that the Mexican American community cannot take full advantage of the new Community Mental Health Program for two basic reasons: the paucity of bilingual specialists in the field of mental health, and the inability of the community, owing to its generally impoverished status, to subsidize the staffing of such centers even if staff could be found. This is a problem in the field of mental health. It is also an example of how well-intentioned government programs sometimes fail to help the very people they were created for.

A probation official points out that few institutionalized programs for rehabilitating alcoholics or narcotic addicts are effective with Mexican Americans, who would be much more likely to respond to treatment in small centers in their own neighborhoods. This is a health problem, and also an example of planners' ignorance of cultural patterns.

The Department of Agriculture administers a loan program for the rural poor. In Texas, which has 140,000 Mexican American families officially classified as poor, only 242 out of 1,928 loans active as of mid-1967 were held by Mexican Americans. This is an economic problem. It is also another example of a governmental program aimed at serving the poor, which, for whatever reasons, is not serving many Mexican American poor.

A University of Colorado professor who spent last summer among sugar beet workers reports that of all the families he met, many of them without food or money, not one had ever heard of the Food Stamp Program. This is a problem of hunger; it is also a communications and information breakdown.

Officials operating a Head Start program for the children of migrant workers in California were surprised when few appeared for class at 9:00 in the morning. Since 5:00, the children had been in the field with their parents, who had no place to leave them. This is an educational problem, and also an example of bureaucratic ignorance or indifference to the facts of migrant life.

Housing officials in Tulare County, California, agreed to build new public housing for Mexican American farm workers. The planned housing will be too small for their large families and too expensive for their low incomes.

There is a California elementary school with a large Mexican American enrollment which is named Sal Si Puedes. Those who gave the school a Spanish name doubtless meant to acknowledge in a positive way the background of most pupils. But Sal Si Puedes means, "Get out if you can." This represents either ignorance of the Spanish language or a perverse sense of humor.

There are similarities and differences among these examples. Some represent bureaucratic failures, some show insensitivity, some appear to be the result of ignorance. All of them represent institutional failures to deal effectively with individuals or groups of Mexican Americans.

"The problem of our Mexican Americans are unique and plead for a clearer understanding by government agencies," a Mexican American social agency head recently declared.

Manpower training programs, for example, have in general not been effective in reaching and helping Mexican Americans. Until recently, most Federal training programs were not linked to English language problems. Potential trainees with language problems were passed over for people who could be trained faster and at lower cost.

The Department of Labor, however, has recognized the failure of most training programs to reach the Mexican American unemployed, and has contracted directly with Mexican American organizations for special recruiting, counseling, placement, and information services. Some spokesmen express the wish that other agencies would follow such a policy.

A major reason for institutional ineptness in relation to Mexican Americans is simply that very few Mexican Americans are in positions of influence in government agencies, in private enterprise, and in schools and universities.

"You have a lot of problems and they always go back to a problem being solved for the Mexican by another group, by Anglos, by another minority. That is the main problem I think we have," a Mexican American said recently.

Mexican Americans claim that they are greatly underrepresented even in agencies, including the Commission on Civil Rights established specifically to deal with minority problems.

"You find these commissions discussing us but never appointing us," one points out.

While government agencies (as well as private businesses) often say that they have difficulty recruiting Mexican Americans, community spokesmen claim that efforts to do so are haphazard and sporadic. They add that Mexican Americans frequently must measure up to standards that would never be applied to Anglos or Negroes.

Selective Service boards across the Southwest have slightly less than 6 percent Mexican American membership. Mexican Americans account for nearly 20 percent of the Southwesterners killed in Vietnam.

At El Paso, a Mexican American attorney remarked: "Those agencies that have exercised diligence and sincerity have been rewarded for their work. Our draft boards have not had the same difficulty finding qualified people as have our jury commissioners. In Nueces County over 75 percent of the men killed in Vietnam bear Mexican American names. ... I simply use this illustration to point out that where an agency wants minority group participation, this is accomplished quickly and in full measure--protests, language handicap, lack of training and all else notwithstanding."

GROWING SENSE OF IDENTITY

The most pervasive force among Mexican Americans today is a growing sense of identity and a quest for unity to achieve equality of opportunity in every phase of life. In cities and towns throughout the Southwest, Mexican Americans are coming together in issue-oriented and action-committed organizations. The effects of these efforts for unity have not been lost on Federal agencies and private organizations.

In May 1967, the President announced the establishment of the Interagency Committee on Mexican American Affairs, consisting of the Secretaries of Agriculture; Labor; Health, Education, and Welfare; and Housing and Urban Development; and the Director of the Office of Economic Opportunity. Vincente T. Ximenes, a member of the Equal Employment Opportunity Commission, was named to head the Interagency Committee. The Committee's first major activity was to hold two days of hearings in El Paso in October 1967, at which four Cabinet officers and several agency heads listened as Mexican American spokesmen defined in their own terms the character of major problems facing the community in agriculture, employment, health, education, welfare, housing, anti-poverty programs, and economic security.

At the same time that the hearings were underway, Mexican Americans who sought an entirely different kind of confrontation with the same problems convened in the heart of El Segundo, an El Paso slum district, to hold the Conference of La Raza Unida. La Raza, literally translated "the race", actually connotes the historical and cultural ties uniting all Spanish-speaking peoples. There was one common theme stressed at the conference: the urgent need for unity, greater communication, greater group awareness, the development of political strength, the development of clear definitions of purpose and methods of operation, and the need for coalitions with other minority groups to achieve common goals.

A direct outgrowth of La Raza Unida Conference was the formation of the Southwest Council of La Raza, funded in June 1968 by the Ford Foundation. The Southwest Council will encourage and help finance the formation of community organizations in the barrios of the Southwest to achieve civil rights and equal opportunity. Units have been established in San Antonio, Texas, and Oakland, California.

The Mexican American Legal Defense and Educational Fund, patterned after the NAACP Legal Defense and Educational Fund Inc., is headquartered in San Antonio and provides legal and financial assistance for civil rights cases involving Mexican Americans. The Fund received a 7-year Ford Foundation grant this year.

The unionizing movement of farm workers which began more than three years ago in a small area of the San Joaquin Valley in California by the United Farm Workers Organizing Committee, has expanded into a national effort to boycott California fresh table grapes in order to arouse national interest and concern for the plight of the agricultural worker.

In an effort to eradicate the stereotype of a sombrero-wearing, siesta-loving, and shiftless creature into which the Mexican American has been cast by the advertising industry, the Washington, D.C.-based Mexican American Anti-Defamation Committee has been formed to pressure advertising agencies and their clients into rejecting the stereotype and projecting a positive, or at least neutral, image of the chicano on television, billboards, and in the news media.

Recently, Dr. Hector P. Garcia, a physician from Corpus Christi, Texas, and founder of the American GI Forum, was appointed by the President as a member of the U.S. Commission on Civil Rights. He is the first person of Spanish surname to serve as a member of the Commission. Several Federal agencies have recently established task forces on Mexican American affairs and assigned liaison officers with major responsibility for Mexican American matters.

The essential force of the Mexican American movement is hardly told by the listing of names of new organizations or new appointees. It really lies in the mounting interest and activism of young Chicanos who may be credited with pushing their elders into more active roles in the drive for human dignity. At the El Paso La Raza Unida Conference, for example, a youth remarked: "If nothing happens from this [conference], you'll have to step aside or we'll walk over you."

In East Los Angeles last spring, Mexican American students staged walkouts in five high schools in protest of conditions there. Protest walkouts also have occurred in Texas; chicano students have demonstrated against college programs in California, and conducted a separate commencement for chicano youth at a California college last June. The trend is toward more active and aggressive assertion of rights.

The level of organization, of awareness, and of identity is constantly rising. The impact of improved communications through an increase in the chicano press, a struggling network of barrio newspapers and magazines, is a significant addition to the effort to develop philosophy and ideology among chicano groups. In fact, every aspect necessary to the development and sustaining of a movement is being activated and, most importantly, obtaining financial stability.

La Raza has become more than a slogan; it has become a way of life for a people who seek to fully realize their personal and group identity and obtain equality of rights and treatment as citizens of the United States.

STRANGER IN ONE'S LAND

Ruben Salazar, using the records of the 1969
San Antonio Hearings of the United States Civil
Rights Commission, presents an "oral history"
of the Chicanos' personal and psychological
dilemmas as they confront poverty, injustices,
educational and labor problems. This article
conveys the personal reality of a people who find
themselves "Strangers in One's Land."

Source: Clearinghouse Publication No. 19,
U.S. Government Printing Office, May 1970.

INTRODUCTION

The San Antonio hearing of the U.S. Commission on Civil Rights
which probed into the social anguish of Mexican Americans was
born in protest and began in controversy.

As the country's second largest minority, Mexican Americans had
been virtually ignored by public and private reformers. There was vague
realization that they had educational, employment, and cultural problems. But it was felt that language was the basic reason for these
problems. And, it was concluded, once this accident of birth was re-
paired, Mexican Americans would melt into the Caucasian pot, just
as Italians, Germans, and Poles had.

Then came the black revolution.

It exploded partly from a condition which had been known all along but was now the basis for a black-white confrontation: the color of one's skin was all too important in America. White was good. Black was bad.

Faced with an identity crisis, many young Mexican Americans—excited by black militancy—decided that they had been misled by their elders into apathetic confusion. It came as a shock at first: Mexican Americans felt caught between the white and the black. Though counted as "white" by the Bureau of the Census, Mexican Americans were never really thought of as such. Though the speaking of foreign languages was considered highly sophisticated, Mexican Americans were condemned for speaking Spanish.

The ambivalence felt vaguely and in silence for so long seemed to crystalize in the light of the black revolution. A Mexican American was neither Mexican nor American. He was neither white nor black. What was he then and where was he going? The young, the militant, and the angry wanted to know.

When the Commission met in San Francisco in May 1967, Mexican Americans walked out protesting there was not a Mexican American Commissioner to represent them or enough attention accorded their problems.

In October of that year, the U.S. Inter-Agency Committee on Mexican American Affairs held a hearing in El Paso on the problems of the Spanish-speaking. The hearing, conducted at the same time President Johnson officially returned to Mexico a disputed piece of border land [El Chamizal], ended on a sour note.

Governor John Connally of Texas, accused of allowing the use of Texas Rangers to break strikes by Mexican American farm workers in the Rio Grande Valley, was roundly booed and hooted by Mexican Americans in the presence of President Johnson. Because the President was there, the incident was given wide publicity and it marked a rare national exposure of rising Mexican American militancy.

In other areas of the Southwest, the strike-boycott of California table grapes led by Cesar Chavez was becoming a national and international cause. Reies Lopez Tijerina's land grants struggle in New Mexico and its adversaries introduced violence to the movement. There were the high school walkouts in East Los Angeles by Mexican American students, and Rodolfo (Corky) Gonzales, head of the Denver-based Crusade for Justice, was preaching ethnic nationalism. Many Mexican Americans joined the Poor People's Campaign in Washington, D.C. in the summer of 1968.

For the first time, many Americans became aware of Mexican American discontent. There was talk now of brown power.

In November 1968, President Johnson named the first Mexican American to the Commission, Dr. Hector P. Garcia, a physician from

Corpus Christi, Texas, and founder of the American G.I. Forum. A Commission hearing which would center on Mexican American problems was scheduled for December 9–14, in San Antonio.

Protests helped bring it about. Now the controversy would begin.

Some Mexican American leaders charged that Washington was meddling in something it knew nothing about and so would make things worse instead of better. They felt any problems Mexican Americans might have should be solved locally, by local leadership. The younger and the more militant Chicano leadership retorted that the problems had intentionally been ignored and that national exposure would bring new, more imaginative solutions. Traditional leadership, they claimed, had failed.

These strong points of view, aired publicly before the Commission met, hint at the diversity of thought and feeling found among the some six to seven million Mexican Americans, most of whom live in California, Texas, New Mexico, Arizona, and Colorado.

There are many splits in the black movement. But there's something the American Negro knows for sure—he's black. He can easily define his problems as a race which make him part of a cohesive force. This is what has forged the beginning of black power in the United States. As yet, most Mexican Americans seem not to identify with any one single overriding problem as Americans. Though they know they're somehow different, many still cling to the idea that Mexican Americans are Caucasian, thus white, thus "one of the boys".

Many prove it: by looking and living like white Americans, by obtaining and keeping good jobs and by intermarrying with Anglos who rarely think of it as a "mixed marriage," to these people, Mexican Americans are assimilating well into white American society. They felt uncomfortable about the Commission's hearing because in their eyes it would merely tend to continue the polarization of Anglos and Mexican Americans at a time in which they felt it was disappearing.

To many other Mexican Americans, especially the young activists, Mexican Americans have for too long been cheated by tacitly agreeing to be Caucasian in name only. They say they would rather be proud of their Indian blood than uncertain about their Caucasian status. They feel they can achieve greater dignity by identifying with pre-Anglo Mexican Indian civilizations and even the Conquistadores than by pretending that they can truly relate to the *Mayflower* and early New England Puritanism.

This division of feeling will continue and perhaps widen. The hearing, however, clearly showed that people who are indigenous to the Southwest seem sometimes strangers in their own land and certainly in many ways curiously alienated from their fellow Americans.

1 AQUÍ NO SE HABLA ESPAÑOL

You know it almost from the beginning: speaking Spanish makes you different. Your mother, father, brothers, sisters, and friends all speak Spanish. But the bus driver, the teacher, the policeman, the store clerk, the man who comes to collect the rent—all the people who are doing important things—do not. Then the day comes when your teacher—who has taught you the importance of many things—tells you that speaking Spanish is wrong. You go home, kiss your mother, and say a few words to her in Spanish. You go to the window and look out and your mother asks you what's the matter?

Nada, mama, you answer, because you don't know what is wrong. . . .

Howard A. Glickstein, then Acting Staff Director of the Commission asked witness Edgar Lozano, a San Antonio high school student, whether he has ever been punished for speaking Spanish at school. Yes, in grammar, in junior high, and in senior high schools, he answers.

". . . they took a stick to me," says ·Edgar. "It really stayed in your mind. Some things, they don't go away as easy as others."

Edgar relates with some bitterness and anger the times he was beaten by teachers for speaking Spanish at school after "getting a lecture about, if you want to be an American, you have got to speak English."

Glickstein tries to ask Edgar another question and the boy, this this time more sad than angry, interrupts and says:

"I mean, how would you like for somebody to come up to you and tell you what you speak is a dirty language? You know, what your mother speaks is a dirty language. You know, that is the only thing I ever heard at home.

"A teacher comes up to you and tells you, 'No, no. You know that is a filthy language, nothing but bad words and bad thoughts in that language.'

"I mean, they are telling you that your language is bad. . . . Your mother and father speak a bad language, you speak a bad language. I mean you communicate with dirty words, and nasty ideas.

". . . that really stuck to my mind."

Edgar, like many Mexican Americans before him, had been scarred with the insults of an Anglo world which rejects everything except carbon copies of what it has decreed to be "American." You start being different and you end up being labeled as un-American. An Anglo-oriented school in a Mexican American barrio can do things to the teachers, too. Bad communication can sorely twist the always sensitive relation between teacher and pupil.

Under questioning from David Rubin, the Commission's Acting General Counsel, W. Dain Higdon, principal of San Antonio's Hawthorne Junior High School, 65 percent Mexican American, asserted that he felt there was something in the background or characteristics of the Mexican Americans which inhibits high achievement.

Mexicans or Mexican Americans, Higdon told the Commission, have a "philosophical concept" in dealing with life which says *lo que dios quiera*, "what God wishes."

An Anglo, on the other hand, Higdon continued, says "in God we trust," not "this is how it shall be and you are limited."

". . . you have unlimited horizons," Higdon explained to the Commission. "And whenever some situation befalls me [as an Anglo], I say it is my fault. Whenever some situation befalls a Mexican American, he may say it is his fault, but more generally and from a heritage standpoint he would be inclined to say, *lo que dios quiera*."

Rubin: Would it be fair to say that you feel there are genetic factors involved which account for the differences in achievements, that mixture of genes causes differences in people?

Higdon: Well, when you were in my office, I made that statement to you and I will stick by it. . . .

The Mexican American child learns early that he is different. Then he learns that speaking Spanish prevents his becoming a good American. It's at this time, perhaps, when he most needs sensitive guidance. Yet, how do some teachers see the role of their profession?

Rubin: Did you state in an interview with me and with another staff member that the obligations of the teacher were first to complete paperwork and secondly to maintain discipline?

Higdon: Yes, sir, I did.

Rubin: And thirdly, to teach?

Higdon: Yés, sir.

What can a school, in which teacher and student speak not only different languages but are also on different emotional wave lengths. do to a Mexican American child?

This kind of school, Dr. Jack Forbes of Berkeley's Far West Laboratory for Educational Research and Development, told the Commission:

"Tends to lead to a great deal of alienation, a great deal of hostility, it tends to lead also to a great deal of confusion, where the child comes out of that school really not knowing who he is, not knowing what he should be proud of, not knowing what language he should speak other than English, being in doubt as to whether he should completely accept what Anglo people have been telling him and forget his Mexican identity, or whether he should listen to what his parents and perhaps other people have said and be proud of his Mexican identity."

The word "Mexican" has been and still is in many places in the Southwest a word of contempt. Mexican Americans refer to themselves as Mexicanos or Chicanos with the ease of those who know and understand each other. But when some Anglos talk about "Mexicans" the word takes on a new meaning, almost the counterpart of "nigger."

The Mexican Americans' insistence on keeping the Spanish language is but one aspect of cultural differences between Anglos and Mexican Americans.

Values differ between these two groups for a variety of historical reasons. Mexicans have deep rural roots which have produced a sense of isolation. Spanish Catholicism has given Mexicans an attitude of fatalism and resignation. Family ties are extremely important and time, or clock-watching, is not.

Luis F. Hernandez, assistant professor of education at San Fernando Valley State College in Los Angeles, has described the differences this way:

"Mexican American values can be said to be directed toward tradition, fatalism, resignation, strong family ties, a high regard for authority, paternalism, personal relations, reluctance to change, a greater orientation to the present than to the future and a greater concern for being than doing.

"The contrasting Anglo-American values can be said to be directed toward change, achievement, impersonal relations, efficiency, progress, equality, scientific rationalization, democracy, individual action and reaction, and a greater concern for doing than being."

Distortion of or deletion of Mexicans' contribution to the Southwest in history books can inhibit a Mexican American child from the beginning of his schooling.

State Senator Joe Bernal of Texas told the Commission that the "schools have not given us any reason to be proud" of being Mexican Americans. People running the schools "have tried to take away our language," the senator continued, and so Mexican American children very early are made to feel ashamed of the Spanish language and of being Mexican.

The children start building up defenses such as insisting on being called "Latin" or "Hispano" or "Spanish American" because, said Bernal, "they want no reference made to being Mexican." One of the reasons for this, Bernal told the Commission, is that "it has been inculcated" in the minds of grammar school children that the Mexican "is no good" by means of, for instance, overly and distortedly emphasizing the Battle of the Alamo and ignoring all contributions made by Mexicans in the Southwest.

To be Spanish, of course, is something else. Spanish has a European connotation and Europe is the motherland.

Carey McWilliams in his "North From Mexico" explains that "the Hispanic heritage of the Southwest has two parts: the Spanish and the Mexican-Indian. Originally one heritage, unified in time, they have long since been polarized. Carefully distinguished from the Mexican, the Spanish heritage is now enshrined throughout the Southwest. It has become the sacred or templar tradition of which the Mexican-Indian inheritance is the secular or profane counterpart . . . ."

Dr. Forbes noticed on his arrival in San Antonio for the hearing that things have not changed.

". . . the San Antonio greeter magazine which I picked up in a hotel lobby and which had the statement about the history of San Antonio said nothing about the Mexican heritage of this region, talking only about the glorious Spanish colonial era and things of this nature. . . ."

To be Spanish is fine because white is important and Spain is white.

Dr. Forbes reminded the Commission that "first of all, the Mexican American population is in great part a native population in the Southwest. It is not an immigrant population. Now this nativity in the Southwest stems not only from the pre-1848 period during the so-called Spanish colonial and Mexican periods, but it also stems from the fact that many people who today identify as Mexican Americans or in some areas as Hispanos, are actually of local Indian descent. . . ."

Aurelio Manuel Montemayor, who taught in San Felipe High School at Del Rio, Texas, explained to the Commission how in his view all this is ignored in the school curriculum.

Quoting from a State-approved textbook, Montemayor said the book related how "the first comers to America were mainly Anglo-Saxons but soon came Dutchmen, Swedes, Germans, Frenchmen, Africans, then the great 19th century period of immigration added to our already melting pot. Then later on, it [the textbook] said, the Spaniards came."

"So my students," continued Montemayor, "had no idea where they came from" and wondered whether "they were part of American society." This frustrated Montemayor so much, he said, that he told his students "let's see if we can write our own textbook." He instructed them to write papers on the subject, "Who Am I?"

"They told me in their words," Montemayor said, "that they were inferior to the standards of this country. That no matter how much they tried they could never be blonds and blue-eyed."

San Felipe High School is located in the San Felipe Independent School District of the city of Del Rio which also contains the Del Rio Independent School District. San Felipe High School has about 97 percent Mexican Americans and the Del Rio High School has about 50 percent Anglos and 49 percent Mexican Americans. Though the Laughlin Air Force Base is located in the San Felipe Independent School District, the base children are bused to the more affluent and less Mexican American Del Rio High School.

Some of Montemayor's students, prompted by the teacher's concern with self-identity, decided to work on a project called: Does San Felipe Have an Inferiority Complex?

"They studied the schools, they studied the discontent in the San Felipe Community," Montemayor told the Commission. A boy and a girl interviewed parents at the air base and asked them what they thought of the San Felipe schools and whether they would allow their children to attend there.

The boy and girl told Montemayor that base officials had them escorted to the gate when they discovered what they were doing. But not before a base mother told the young pollsters what she thought of San Felipe.

Montemayor: . . . [a woman told my students] that she wouldn't send her children to [San Felipe] district schools. They had them there for a semester, the neighborhoods were so dirty and all of that, and that the schools were falling down. And, of course, the students were finding this out on their own and, of course, as far as morale, it couldn't have been lower.

Many Mexican American youths, despite their low morale, continue on their business as best they can even though lamenting, as some of Montemayor's students, that no matter how much they try they will never be blond and blue-eyed.

Others become ultramilitant as did David Sanchez, prime minister of the Brown Berets in Los Angeles, who told a newsman: "There are very few gabachos [Anglos] who don't turn me off. To the Anglo, justice means 'just us'."

And many others, as did some 1,500 Mexican Americans from throughout the Southwest who last March attended a "Chicano Youth Liberation Conference" in Denver, will adopt, in their anger, frustration, and disillusion, a resolution which condemns the "brutal gringo invasion of our territories".

2 LA FRONTERA

The marchers, followers of farm labor leader Cesar Chavez, finished their 100-mile trek across the blazing hot desert from Indio, California, to the border town of Calexico on Sunday, May 18, 1969. According to the plan, Chavez' people were supposed to hold a solidarity rally with Mexican national farm workers at the international line. But the rally never took place.

The official explanation was that the Mexican Government did not want its people to get involved in an American labor dispute, the California table grape strike-boycott. Actually, the Mexican workers who live in Mexico's border towns and work in American borderland farms and in American border cities are very much involved in a unique American labor controversy. As commuters, the Mexican workers are the unwitting pawns of an international labor dispute without precedence. The 1,800-mile United States-Mexico border stretches from the coast of California to the Gulf of Mexico in an irregular line which orators like to describe as the only such unfortified frontier in the world. This does not mean that "armies" do not crisscross this border every day.

Perhaps the most telling contrast between the two countries is that while an army of fun-seeking American tourists crosses the border into Mexico, another army of job-hungry Mexicans crosses the line into the United States.

The American tourists, for the most part, have a good effect on the Mexican economy and this army is welcomed with good will. The army

of job-hungry Mexicans which commutes across the international line
has an adverse effect on American labor. For many years this was
passively taken for granted. But now, in the age of activism, a confrontation seems inevitable.

The situation is a highly complicated and sensitive one because it
involves mostly Mexicans against Mexican Americans. That is, the
poorest of the poor Mexican nationals vying for jobs with Mexican
Americans who are striving to attain U.S. economic standards. Result:
Mexican nationals, because they're understandably willing to work for
less, take jobs away from Mexican Americans.

Even in their resentment, Mexican Americans find it difficult to
condemn these commuters. They, their parents, or grandparents were
in the same boat not too long ago. The fact remains that Mexicans are
pitted against Mexican Americans for the lowest paid jobs in America.

The problem is further complicated by the fact that U.S. borderland
businessmen fear that any effort to terminate the commuter program
would result in a retaliatory refusal by Mexico to allow its citizens to
carry on their extensive trade in American border towns.

(Cheap labor on the Mexican side of the border attracts industrialists
as much as it does growers. A free industrial zone program in Mexican
border towns was started in 1965, whereby American industrialists
can set up factories there under a special program which exempts them
from all import duties. Mexican workers reportedly earn as little as
$2 a day in these American factories. The American labor movement,
which helped kill the bracero [Mexican farm labor] program, claims
that in effect under this new plan—since braceros are no longer available
in the United States—the work is now being taken to the braceros.)

Former Secretary of State, Dean Rusk, in commenting on a court
suit concerning the commuter problem, voiced his concern over United
States-Mexico diplomatic relations should the commuter system be
stopped.

"[If] as a result of a substantial reduction in the commuter traffic
across the border between Mexico and the United States, a significant
number of Mexican nationals would be deprived of their earning power,
the trade between the two countries would be substantially reduced,"
the Secretary said. "We would expect that this would have an immediate depressing effect on the economy of the region on both sides
of the border. Moreover, the loss of gainful employment and dollar
earnings by 30,000 to 50,000 Mexican nationals, estimated at over $50
million annually, might compel the Government of Mexico to consider
compensating steps, which would further damage the economic life of
the region."

This led a Commission staff report to conclude that:

"The Mexican American in the border area is thus charged with
the responsibility of protecting our diplomatic relations. The economic

burdens involved in this charge, he may justifiably feel, should be borne by the Nation as a whole, not thrust upon a minority of its citizens."

The Commission staff report notes that: "The commuter system has deep roots. People have commuted to work across the United States-Mexico border since the border's inception. Up until the 1920's this traffic was unrestricted."

Since then, the law has been changed so that a Mexican national wishing to cross the border to work in the United States must obtain immigrant status. When he does, he is issued an alien registration card and in the vernacular of those concerned with the problem becomes a "green carder" after the color of the card.

There is nothing in the law which says the green carder, though technically an immigrant, must live in the United States. Because the green carder usually performs agricultural work in the U.S. border-lands or menial jobs in the U.S. border cities, he prefers to live on the Mexican side to save money.

The result is that these commuters, not really immigrants at all, use their green card merely as a working pass which permits them to cross the border. Basically then, the traffic of commuters is almost as unrestricted as it was in the twenties. But more to the point, as long as the Mexican commuter can live on the Mexican side he can afford to work for less than his Mexican American brother. (The Mexican American, of course, must also compete against the Mexican worker who crosses the border illegally.)

The commuter system will be much harder to abolish than the bracero program which, until its demise, was another burden on the backs of the Mexican American farm and unskilled workers.

The bracero program, initiated during World War II when farm labor was genuinely scarce, was a formal program whereby two Governments, the United States and Mexico, made an agreement to bring Mexican farm laborers [braceros] to the United States until American farm workers were again available. Though farm workers feel the bracero program lasted too long after the war, the program was success-fully phased out when unemployed farm workers in the United States were able to convince authorities that such an agreement between the two countries was having an adverse effect on them. The green card commuter, on the other hand, is a bracero, who, it might be said, made his contract individually with the U.S. Government by becoming an "immigrant" in name if not in fact.

Unlike the bracero, who came here under a special temporary arrangement, a commuter as an "immigrant" has virtually a permanent status, even though he has no intention of living permanently in the United States—as does the genuine immigrant.

One of the ideas behind the march to Calexico was to recruit com-muters for Chavez' union. Commuters, as the Commission report shows.

have been used as strike-breakers notably in farm labor disputes in Delano, California, and in Starr County, Texas.

Knowing that commuters are forced by poverty to be commuters, the union knew the system would continue. So Chavez extended an invitation to join the union so that commuters would not work for less than Mexican Americans along the border. Though it looks like a simple solution, it must be seen from the context of a rich economy [the United States] living next door to a poor one [Mexico].

To the Mexican commuter, joining the union is not as attractive as it looks on the surface. For one thing, he knows that besides his labor, it's his docility which the employer appreciates, and he is aware that joining the union will only alienate him from his employer. He also reasons that if he joins the union, then it will be of little value for the employer to hire him [a unionized commuter] when he can hire local unionized workers, both of whom he would have to pay the same amount.

Domingo Arredondo, strike chairman of the United Farm Workers Organizing Committee, who participated in the labor dispute at Starr County, discussed his attempt to recruit commuters in testimony before the Senate Subcommittee on Migratory Farm Workers.

"The problem about these green carders is that they come to work from Mexico every day. They will come in the morning and they will go back at night."

After claiming that growers had raised the pay of commuters so they would not join the union, Arredondo testified that "we went and talked to these people [commuters] at the bridge, international bridge. We told them to cooperate with us for better wages and working conditions, but they always say that . . . they would sign but they would probably get laid off their jobs. So, really we couldn't get nowhere convincing them that a union is something that a worker needs."

As the Commission's staff report points out, there is also, but to a smaller extent, commuter traffic across the American-Canadian border. However, the report continues, "Canadian commuters do not depress local economic conditions, as do Mexican commuters, because they live in a substantially identical cost-of-living economy, work in highly unionized occupations, and are highly unionized themselves. Being well assimilated into the labor force, they offer no undue competition to American labor."

The Commission staff report notes that "there is wide disagreement about the actual extent of the commuter traffic. An Immigration and Naturalization Service survey on January 11 and 17, 1966, counted a total of 43,687 commuters. The United Farm Workers Organizing Committee, AFL-CIO, on the other hand, has estimated the number to be closer to 150,000. While the former estimate includes only daily commuters working along the border, the latter includes aliens remaining here for periods of weeks or months, usually working in areas farther north."

Because the people involved in this commuter controversy are used to dealing with each other on a friendly basis for generations, and think of the border as an artificial line drawn by latecomers, the issue is one not only of great economic import but also of cultural significance.

Between the two countries, writes J. Fred Rippy in his "The United States and Mexico," "there have been no natural barriers, the two nations being separated by an imaginary line, a barbed wire fence, an easily forded river, an undergrowth of mesquite or chaparral. Citizens of both nations have passed back and forth with little difficulty or interruption, or have settled in neighboring states amidst natural surroundings which have not repelled them by their unfamiliar aspects. . . ."

There's only one catch. On one side of the border, or *frontera,* is a rich Nation with the highest standard of living in history. On the other side is a poor Nation with a seemingly inexhaustible supply of cheap labor.

"The Mexican aliens, as a group, are a readily available, low-wage work force which undermines the standards American workers generally enjoy throughout the rest of the country," said the 1968 Report of the Senate Migratory Labor Subcommittee. "More importantly, the normal play of free enterprise principles is subverted and prevented from operating to develop standards along the border commensurate with the American standards. So long as Mexican aliens are allowed indiscriminately to work in the American economy, and take their wages back to the low-cost Mexican economy, the growth of the American standards will continue to be stultified."

Senator Edward M. Kennedy of Massachusetts, speaking on a proposed amendment to the Immigration and Nationality Act, said:

"In El Paso [an urban Texas city], where unemployment is currently some 35 percent greater than the State average, the estimated number of commuters in 1966 was more than double the number of unemployed. In El Centro, California, [a rural area city], where the unemployment rate is currently 13.1 percent, the estimated number of commuters in 1966 was nearly double the number of unemployed."

When talking about themselves or about each other, Mexicans and Mexican Americans refer to themselves simply as "Mexicanos." The commuter problem is beginning to cut a wedge into this traditional term. When poor Mexican Americans have to compete for low-paying jobs against very poor Mexican nationals only the poor suffer. But resentment builds up between the poor and the very poor.

And when that happens, the border becomes a real dividing line.

3 LOS POBRES

For the Mexican American in the Southwest, poverty is often experienced part of the time in the city and the rest of the year in the
country. But no matter where he might be living at the moment,
Mexico and its poverty hover over him like an ominous cloud.

The closer the Mexican American is to the border, the lower his wages are—whether in the field or in the city.

Sometimes it's just a matter of a few miles.

Luis Chavez, 55, a father of nine children, who lives near Edinburg, Texas, in the border county of Hidalgo, explained this phenomenon under questioning from Cruz Reynoso, special legal consultant to the Commission.

Reynoso: Now tell me, during the time that you are in the south of Texas, approximately how much do you earn in your work as an agricultural worker?

Chavez: There are times, let's speak of certain areas, if from where I live going North, for instance, up to about 15 miles, they pay $1.15 an hour. In other places in the other direction, say, going South [toward the border] . . . they pay $1 an hour . . . . There are other areas [closer to the border] where they are paying less than a dollar.

But traveling 15 miles north from his Rio Grande Valley is not enough for Chavez to make ends meet. It is not far enough from the border and the cheap labor offered by his Mexican brothers across the line.

So Chavez must go part of the year to the most un-Mexican of places, Michigan.

"Due to the lack of sufficient economic development and the declining state of agriculture . . . poverty is most acutely felt in the fields of the Rio Grande Valley," the social action department of the Texas Catholic Conference told the Senate Subcommittee on Migratory Labor. "The overwhelming majority of hired farm workers in this State are Mexican American. Because of the lack of opportunities in this area, 88,700 Texas farm workers (not including their families) are forced to migrate from their homes every year in search of employment. Unfortunately, because of the vast supply of 'green carders', that is, people who have been granted immigrant status but who live in Mexico and work in the United States, the domestic workers are unable to compete with the depressed wages that result from the availability of cheap labor to the growers. This accounts for the fact that almost one-half of the Texas migrant workers come from the four counties of the Lower Rio Grande Valley."

Chavez, who told the Commission he went to school only 1 day in his whole life and speaks no English, wants a better life for his nine children. At the time he testified, he, his wife Olivia, and their children, lived in a two-bedroom shack near Edcouch, Texas.

Turning to Mrs. Chavez, Reynoso asked how a couple with nine children can live in a two-bedroom house.

Mrs. Chavez: Well, in the children's room there is four sleeping there and in our room five girls sleep together with us.

Chavez explained that some of his neighbors in his barrio have better houses than his because some families sacrifice the schooling of their children for material benefits.

Chavez: . . . As far as I am concerned, the little that I have been able to get, to earn in one place or another, outside even the State of Texas, has been with the purpose of giving an education to my children.

After explaining that work is hard to get in the summer in the Rio Grande Valley, Chavez told the Commission he migrated about the second week in July.

Reynoso: Why did you wait until then?

Chavez: We wanted to wait for the children to finish school. . . .

Though work was relatively good in the North, Chavez continued, he sent his two older sons back to Texas in time for the beginning of school even though "the rest of the family, the small ones, we remained in order to work a little longer."

Living conditions for the Chavezes while migrating to the North are even worse than at home in Texas, Mrs. Chavez' testimony to the Commission showed. While traveling, everyone from 8 years on up works and the Chavez family usually lives in a one-room shack in labor camps, where, according to Mrs. Chavez, it is not unusual to have only one bathroom for 200 to 250 people.

Describing how the family lives in a one-room shack while migrating, Chavez told the Commission:

". . . you put some partitions and you put some cots on one side and some cots on this side and then you cook your meals on the edge where the door is, that is where the small kitchen is. And on the table we put a hot plate on top of that."

Reynoso: And the whole family lives there?

Chavez: Yes, we have to manage . . . the ceiling isn't high enough to put three cots on the top of each other, so we put cots on one side and two on the other side and two here, and two across and two criss-crossed, we sort of complete the entire family.

And how much does the Chavez family of 11 earn while migrating for about 4 months out of the year?

Chavez: Approximately when we come back home . . . the most we are able to keep [after expenses on the road] is about $1,200 to $1,300 free when we come back home.

Reynoso: And during the time, all told, how much did you earn approximately?

Chavez: Between $2,500, thereabouts . . . this is the entire family that makes those earnings, those earnings are for the entire family.

Reynoso asked one of Chavez' sons, José, 19, whether counselors at his school in Texas, which is about 90 percent Mexican American, encourage students to continue their schooling.

José: Most of the time when a student has a problem in school, he tried to go to the counselor, but she always tells you that she is too busy, she will get back to you later. Instead of going back again you just stay with it. . . .

Reynoso: How many counselors do you have at this school?

José: One.

Reynoso: How many students are there?

José: About 1,100.

Reynoso: Has there been some concern with respect to getting advice as to going to college and that sort of thing in addition to plain counseling at the high school?

José: Most of the time students that I have talked with say that the teacher says the opportunities are there to go to college which she doesn't talk about it too much to us.

Reynoso: So the young people in high school don't know anything about the opportunities?

José: Most of them don't.

Reynoso: Do you yourself hope to go on with your education if you make it through high school okay?

José: Yes, I do. . . . I would like to be a mathematics teacher.

Like the Chavezes, Jesus Garcia, 36, his wife Manuela, and their 13 children live their poverty both in the country and in the city. The difference is that Garcia lives, when not migrating, in a large urban city, San Antonio, and understands well how it is to be poor in small farming towns and in the metropolis.

While in San Antonio, the Garcias, whose children's ages range from 8 months to 15 years, live in a two-room house: a bedroom and a kitchen. Asked by Reynoso how the family of 15 sleeps, Mrs. Garcia answered: "In the bedroom I have four [beds], and I have another one in the kitchen, and that is it." Mrs. Garcia related that they have no bathroom, no shower, no television set, no telephone, and no radio set.

The summer before the hearing, Garcia migrated to Michigan and other Northern States and after 3½ months in the fields was able to bring back to San Antonio $300, after expenses. Asked what he did with the $300, Garcia answered that much of it went to paying off debts in San Antonio, where he is making payments on his two-room house.

Reynoso: And you are able to keep up with the payments?

Mrs. Garcia: No, we are not keeping up with the payments.

Turning to the husband, Reynoso asked him where he works in San Antonio.

Garcia: . . . I am working for a company, an oil company.

Reynoso: . . . and how much do you make?

Garcia: $1.35 an hour I am making now.

Reynoso: How long have you been working for this oil company?

Garcia: I have been working for them about 3 weeks . . . .

Reynoso: And before that where were you working?

Garcia: In a restaurant.

Reynoso: How much did they pay there?

Garcia: $1.15 an hour.

In the months before the hearing, Garcia, who had gone to school only 2 months in his life, had worked at what he could from the Rio Grande Valley to the Northern States, but never made more than $1.35 an hour and never for long.

Directing his questioning to Mrs. Garcia, Reynoso wanted to know whether the family participated in the food stamp program [a plan which permits poor families to buy food cheaply through the purchase of Government stamps].

Mrs. Garcia: No.

Reynoso: Why not?

Mrs. Garcia: We don't have enough money to buy the stamps.

Later, Reynoso asked the woman's teenage daughter, Maria, "Your mother said that you do not participate in the [school] program for free lunches, is that right?"

Maria: Yes.

Reynoso: And why haven't you talked to the principal about [the free lunches]?

Maria: Because I am ashamed.

Reynoso: And if you wouldn't have to ask or beg for food, if it were just offered, would you take it?

Maria: Yes, I would.

Father Ralph Ruiz, a Catholic priest who works in the barrios of San Antonio, told the Commission that even though there are many families like the Chavezes and Garcias, too many people prefer to close their eyes to the problem.

Father Ruiz: . . . They [public officials] deny hunger. You see, we have to preserve an image of San Antonio . . . people can starve and people can be hungry and poor, but let's not tell the Nation this, you know, because we suffer, our reputation suffers. We are more concerned with images than with people.

The priest told the Commission that the exposure of extreme poverty in San Antonio, by citizens' committees and a television program brought into the area FBI agents "asking questions, taking my time to prove that what we claim [poverty and hunger in the San Antonio area] is not true. I can handle these guys myself, they don't [frighten] me and they don't intimidate me. But when they go and bother people who are no match for them, I think this is a crime myself."

Father Ruiz: They [FBI agents] invade the privacy of the poor. They ask them if they are hungry, how much money they make, they go into their kitchens and into their living rooms. . . . They say they want to find out if there are hungry people in San Antonio. What do they want? These FBI agents, what do they know about hunger, about the poor? . . .

Locally, the priest told the Commission: "The welfare system intimidates our people, harasses them, asks them unnecessary questions. The family practically has to go to confession to them in order to get some help. . . ."

As for the food stamp program, Father Ruiz told the Commission that he has seen store signs saying to separate the food that can be purchased with stamps from the rest before going to the cashier.

"This is a public insult," Father Ruiz said. "Why must they have stamps? If stamps equal money, then send them money. All they do is tell the whole store there that they are under welfare. . . ."

Welfare itself, the priest continued, "has become a master over the lives of these people. They fear it."

Rubin asked him to explain.

Father Ruiz: Their total life depends [on it], what other income do they have? When characters like the FBI agents come around asking this kind of questions . . . about how much money you get, does your husband work, what do you eat, are you telling the truth. Their very existence is at stake. Their very existence depends on a paternalistic type and very inadequate type of welfare. It is the master. They get their livelihood from there, and the welfare knows it.

The priest said that the Federal Government, despite his anger with the FBI, should run the welfare programs and that the system should be changed so that people on welfare be given an incentive to work.

After pointing out that some families of four or more members have to survive on $123 a month, Father Ruiz proposed one solution:

". . . I would put a minimum according to the families, say this family should get $300 per month. If somebody works in the family and makes $100, well, then the Government would supplement $200. The way it is right now, let's say, if the mother works, a mother on welfare works, say she irons clothes or washes clothing for somebody else, to make extra dollars, she has to report that. If she lives in a housing project . . . if she reports this to the housing project her rent will come up. And if the welfare agent knows about this, her check comes down. So it is best for her not to work at all. She endangers what she is getting.

"I know a case where this lady refused to take her social security increase in money because her rent would come up and she would be losing more money than otherwise. So the person is enslaved in this circle. . . . I would give an opportunity to the people to do some work, not to be afraid of work, fearing their check will come low, or the housing rent will come up. To guarantee a monthly income, not to enslave them but to free them."

4
LA EDUCACIÓN
DE MEXICANOS

When the Mexican American in the Southwest complains about having nightmares instead of the American dream, he's usually told: "Education is the answer, amigo. Get an education and your problems will be solved."

Who can argue with that? At the San Antonio hearing, however, the Commission heard experts in the field of educating bilingual and bicultural children argue with the premise behind this alleged panacea. The premise, of course, is that the Mexican American child can receive a meaningful education merely by wanting it.

Dr. George I. Sanchez of the University of Texas told the Commission that in his State "persons of Spanish surname . . . 17 years of age or older averaged 4.7 years of school, whereas the Negroes averaged 8.1, and the average of the population averaged 10 plus."

In California, that State's Advisory Committee to the Commission reported that the median school years completed for Mexican Americans was 8.6, for Negroes, 10.5, and for Anglos, 12.1.

Why is Juanito so far behind?

One of the reasons is that many Mexican American children enter school speaking little or no English because, generally, only Spanish is spoken at home. About the first thing that Juanito encounters at school is an IQ [intelligence quotient] test—in English. Usually, he makes a bad showing because of his limited knowledge of English. This means that at best he will be considered a "slow learner" and treated accordingly; at worst he will be placed in classes for the mentally retarded. Either way, the child begins his school career with a stigma which will remain for the rest of his life. Though many educators have recommended abolishing IQ tests in the early grades—as has been done by the Los Angeles School District—others have recommended that the tests be made more realistic.

In California, Mexican American students once labeled mentally retarded showed dramatic increases in their IQ scores after taking Spanish-language tests. The report of the tests, submitted to the California Board of Education in May 1969, said that some children have been victims of a "retarding influence" by being left in the mentally retarded classes for long periods of time. The children who took part in the study were in such classes on the basis of English-language IQ tests. When they were retested in the Spanish language, the children's IQ scores jumped by as much as 28 points.

Unfortunately, such studies, as enlightening as they are, do not change other realities. Reforms, which cost money, must be implemented to change the shabby education which many Mexican Americans receive. In Texas, although State allotments to school districts are determined by the average daily attendance, also considered are the level of academic attainment and the length of teachers' experience. Consequently, inequities are created between wealthier "Anglo districts" and less affluent Mexican American districts.

A Commisson staff study of nine school districts in the San Antonio area showed that in the Northeast School District [predominantly Anglo] expenditures per pupil from all revenue sources in 1967–68 amounted to $745.07. In the Edgewood School District [predominantly Mexican American] expenditures per pupil, also from all revenue sources, amounted to $465.54. The staff report showed that 98 percent of the noncollege degree teachers employed in the nine San Antonio districts are concentrated in the predominantly Mexican American districts.

An Edgewood district student told the Commission that a teacher admitted to a class that he was not qualified to teach the course and asked the students to bear with him. Another student testified that Mexican Americans are counseled away from college and into vocational training. A high school senior said Armed Forces representatives go to the schools before graduation to induce boys to enter the service. Commissioner Hector Garcia wanted to know whether any scientists, doctors, lawyers, or businessmen ever visited the schools to encourage graduating students to enter these fields. No, the boy answered.

Edgewood's financial situation could be improved, for example, by merging with the San Antonio Independent School District. Edgewood has unsuccessfully petitioned for merger several times to equalize Edgewood's property tax base with that of San Antonio's. But political realities are at work to make this impossible. Indeed, districts are often created to avoid integration of Anglo and Mexican American students. In one case in Texas, the students residing at Laughlin Air Force Base [89 percent Anglo] are bused through the 97 percent Mexican American San Felipe School District (in which the base is located) to the Del Rio School District [51 percent Anglo].

As a result, Federal funds are awarded the Del Rio district for the education of military dependents. For example, in 1966 Del Rio received more than $200,000 in Federal impacted aid funds, while San Felipe, whose district boundaries encompass the Air Force installation, received less than $41,000.

In an impassioned plea to the Commission, Homero Sigala, school superintendent at San Felipe, called this situation "unfair" and asked that the Commission advise the President, Congress, and the Air Force "to direct the Commander at Laughlin Air Force Base to send the students residing at Laughlin to the San Felipe schools."

Unfair though it may be, the political reality of the situation is that even though Val Verde County, where San Felipe is located, is about 50 percent Mexican American, there are no Mexican Americans on the five-member county school board. In other words, Mexican Americans have no political muscle to make much of an impression on Washington.

This might be attributed to what Dr. Jack Forbes of Berkeley's Far West Laboratory for Educational Research and Development described to the Commission as the "conquered population" syndrome. The indigenous people of Mexico, who included those in what is now the American Southwest, first experienced the Spanish conquest, followed by a long period of colonialism, Dr. Forbes explained. This was followed by the Anglo-American conquest of the Southwest, at the end of the Mexican-American War.

To understand the significance of this syndrome, Dr. Forbes continued, "one must of course get past the romance and mythology of the supposed westward movement of the pioneers and look at the Anglo-American conquest of the Southwest as we might look at the German march eastward against the Poles or as we might look at the Franco-Norman conquest of England, in other words, in a purely detached and objective manner."

And if we are to do this, continued Dr. Forbes, "we would see the U.S. conquest of the Southwest as a very real case of aggression and imperialism, that it involved not only the military phase of immediate conquest, but the subsequent establishment of a colonial society, a rather complex colonial society because there was not one single colonial office to administer Mexican American people. Instead, there were many institutions that were created to control and administer Mexican American people and also to enable the dominant population to acquire almost complete control of the soil and the other forms of wealth, of the social institutions, cultural institutions, and so on.

"Now the conquest in the colonial period can be further understood if we think about a community such as the city of Los Angeles in California which has long had a large Mexican American population but in which no major institution of any kind is controlled even proportionately to numbers by the Spanish-speaking population."

The concept of conquest, the Berkeley historian told the Commission, is very often ignored but "I can't emphasize it too much because we're beginning to learn the process of conquest," particularly the "tremendous effect upon people's behavior."

"For example," Dr. Forbes continued, "a conquered population tends to exhibit certain characteristics such as apathy, apparent indifference, passivity, and a lack of motivation in relation to the goals of the dominant society."

Another dimension of the Mexican American educational quandary was posed by Dr. Manuel Ramirez, an assistant professor of psychology at Rice University, Houston, who spoke of the conflict of cultures between the Anglo and the Mexican American.

"My research has identified two different kinds of conflict," he stated. "The first type arises as a result of the fact that [the Mexican American] is led to believe that he cannot be identified with two cultures at the same time. There is one message that is given by his parents, his relatives, and other Mexican American students, who tell him that if he rejects Mexican American culture and identifies with the Anglo culture, he may be considered a traitor to his ethnic group." Dr. Ramirez went on to say: "The other message comes from teachers, employers, and Anglo friends, who tell him that if he doesn't reject the Mexican American culture, he will be unable to reap the educational and economic benefits that are in the Anglo culture.

"The second type is really a series of conflicts which come about because the Mexican American student is bringing with him a series of behaviors, perceptions, methods of viewing the world, of doing things . . . and this conflicts with the value system of the Anglo middle class." Then he concluded:

"The big problem that we face as Mexican Americans is, how can we have our children maintain as many of the Mexican American values as possible and still be a success in the Anglo world? . . . And if we could have people who are sensitive to our culture, people who understand our problems and don't take this as a criticism to some teachers, I think that people like myself and others in Texas and other parts of the Southwest are living testimony that there were some Anglo teachers who work, but there aren't enough of them."

Giving another view, Dr. Sanchez told the Commission that one of the barriers to educational reform in Texas was "the poverty of Mexican Americans and their lack of effective statewide political organization."

"[Mexican Americans] have not been heard yet as an effective political force," Dr. Sanchez said. "We number some 2½ million in the State of Texas and that political weight has not been effectively harnessed to bring about reforms."

Nevertheless, testimony at the San Antonio hearing indicated that young activists are beginning to stir in the "conquered" Mexican American community.

Homer Garcia, a student at San Antonio's Lanier High School, told the Commission how a group of students and parents fought for a change in curriculum in the predominantly Mexican American school to include such studies as chemistry, physics, algebra, trigonometry, calculus, and computer programing. According to Homer, about 500 parents and 500 students turned out to a meeting in a community hall to hear the student demands for a better education. At another Mexican American school, Edgewood High, students demanded better qualified teachers.

Howard A. Glickstein, then Acting Staff Director of the Commission, asked Homer how the turnout of parents to the Lanier High School meeting compared to the number of parents who usually attend PTA meetings.

Homer: Nobody comes to PTA meetings. For one thing, the parents really don't know what a PTA is, because they're held during the daytime when—well, my parents, for instance, can't go to the PTA meeting because they are held during the day for the convenience of the teachers. My dad works during the daytime. My mother has to take care of my brothers. I mean, it is not to their convenience at all. It's a teachers' organization, not a parent-teacher organization.

The concern of students and parents for better education at San Antonio's Mexican American schools brought about positive results, according to student testimony. Much credit was given to parents who backed the students in their demands for curriculum reforms. Community participation in implementing school reforms is essential, the Commission was told, if the powerlessness and alienation felt by the Mexican American community is to be corrected. Ignoring the community while planning reforms is not only an insult to parents, the Commission was told, but it also indicates that groups of elite educational reformers seem to think they are the only ones who know what's best for the children.

In at least three instances, Anglo educators in their testimony to the Commission revealed that cultural differences and the involvement of the Mexican American community were not even considered in preparing studies or proposing school reforms. The director of the Texas Governor's Committee on Public Education admitted that Mexican

American parents were not consulted during a 3-year study on improving education in Texas; a member of the Governor's committee related that not one top-notch Mexican American educator was consulted during this same 3-year study, and the State commissioner of education said he was not familiar with studies which indicate that Mexican Americans experience culture conflict when they enter an Anglo-oriented school system.

If regular education for Mexican Americans is inadequate and unrealistic, the education of migrant children is a national scandal.

Dr. Joseph Cardenas, director of Migrant Education for the Southwest Educational Development Laboratory and now superintendent of the Edgewood School District, estimated that the dropout rate for migrant children is about 90 percent. But more "startling," said Dr. Cardenas, is the fact that "one-fifth of migrants are school dropouts at the preschool age. That is, one-fifth of all migrant children never enroll in any school in spite of the State's compulsory attendance laws. So by the time they [migrant children] start the first grade, or they are 6 years old, you have already lost 20 percent of your population."

Of the 65,000 migrant students in Texas, less than 14 percent are in the upper six grades, Dr. Cardenas disclosed. The average income of the Texas migrant, he continued, is $1,400 a year and a "person with this amount of money will have a lot of difficulty in educating his children adequately."

The only solution, Dr. Cardenas said, is a multi-State educational program geared especially for migrant children, to follow them wherever the parents are following the crops. After agreeing that this would cost a great deal of money, Dr. Cardenas asserted that actually the only real solution is to stop migration altogether. This last drew the applause of the audience. But the perennial question loomed:

How can Mexican Americans in the border States afford to stop migrating as long as armies of cheap labor are allowed to cross the international border?

While this part of the hearing was intended to probe into the educational problems of Mexican Americans in the Southwest, something just as important emerged from the testimony: the Anglo children (and for that matter, the Negroes) had been cheated also—they had not been permitted to take advantage of the Southwest's cultural and language heritage. This became clear when Harold C. Brantley, superintendent of the United Consolidated School District of Webb County, Texas, explained his district's bilingual program.

It should be noted that the United States' first full-fledged bilingual program in public schools was not initiated in the Southwest, where its need had been apparent for generations, but in Florida—following the Cuban crisis. It was in Florida that Brantley got some ideas for the bilingual program in his school district.

The philosophy behind his approach, Brantley told the Commission, was that "I don't feel like a kid's ability to speak Spanish is a detriment. I think that it is an asset. . . . It is merely our responsibility as educators to turn this asset that these kids bring to us, where it not only becomes an asset to them, but can become an asset to the little blue-eyed, blond-haired Anglo."

Brantley's district is made up of the larger part of the rural area of border Webb County—some 2,400 square miles—and does not include the county's largest city, Laredo. The district has 987 students, 47 percent of them Mexican American and 53 percent Anglo. Without waiting for more research, specialized teachers, bilingual instructional materials, or substantial financial resources, Brantley in 1964 persuaded his staff, Anglo and Mexican American parents, and the Texas Education Agency to begin a bilingual program in his bicultural district.

Today, in the district's three elementary schools, instruction is 50 percent in Spanish and 50 percent in English in the first through fifth grades.

"I am not a linguist," Brantley explained to the Commission. "My sole service is creating [an] atmosphere where things can happen."

Brantley said his program does not ignore the fact that it is very important for schools to facilitate Mexican American children "getting into the mainstream of the dominant culture and the dominant language of the country." By the same token, Brantley continued: "We also try to stress to that child who comes from this other culture, speaking this other language [that] we want to provide him with the opportunity to improve upon his knowledge of his culture and his ability to function in his vernacular."

As for the Anglo child, Brantley said, his district tries "to create an atmosphere in the classroom where the children who come to us from the dominant culture, speaking the dominant language . . . recognize that here this little kid [Mexican American] has got something that he [Anglo] doesn't have, and that he ought to be interested in getting what this little kid can teach him."

Warming up to the subject, Brantley asked the Commission: "Now, can you begin to see what this does for the stature of this little kid that comes from this other culture with this other language? Where he is made to feel like he can do something that somebody can't do, and that he has something that this other little kid wants to learn about?"

The Commission understood.

5
NO HAY TRABAJO

When Mexico lost the Southwest to the United States, the Treaty
of Guadalupe-Hidalgo specifically guaranteed the property and
political rights of the conquered native population. The treaty, exe-
cuted on February 2, 1848, also attempted to safeguard the Mexican
culture and language.

Throughout the San Antonio hearing, it became clear that Mexican
Americans in the Southwest cling tenaciously to their ancestors' culture
and language. But it also became evident that the spirit of the treaty
has been violated.

Though Mexican Americans persist in retaining the Spanish language,
they do so at the price of obtaining a second rate education because
bilingualism has been suppressed and has never been accepted as an
asset. Though they have kept their culture, they have had to pay for it
by being stereotyped as backward or, at best, quaint. Nowhere is this
more evident than in the jobs Mexican Americans have traditionally
held in the Southwest and the jobs they hold now. It is almost the rule
that only Mexican Americans who have been willing to sacrifice their
culture and language have succeeded in an Anglo society.

Carey McWilliams in "North From Mexico" says that the "basic
factor retarding the assimilation of the [Southwest Mexican], at all
levels, has been the pattern of his employment.

"With few exceptions," says McWilliams, "only a *particular class*
of employers has employed Mexican labor in the Southwest: large-scale
industrial enterprises, railroads, smelters, copper mines, sugar beet re-
fineries" and, of course, agriculture. . . . "Traditionally," continues the
author, "Mexicans have been paid less than Anglo Americans for the
same jobs. These invidious distinctions have reenforced the Mexican
stereotype and placed a premium on prejudice . . . the pattern of employment . . . dictated the type and location of residence. Segregated

residential areas have resulted in segregated schools, segregated schools have reenforced the stereotype and limited opportunities for accultura-tion.

"In setting this merry-go-around in motion, the pattern of employ-ment has been of crucial importance for it has stamped the Mexican as 'inferior' and invested the stereotype with an appearance of reality. . . ."

It was revealed at the San Antonio hearing that in some industries Mexican Americans are not even employed as laborers.

Under questioning, Ralph Allen, director of employee relations, El Paso Natural Gas Company, told the Commission that in the com-pany's Permian division no Mexican Americans are employed as un-skilled laborers. Working for the company is considered unusually beneficial because it does not offer the dead-end jobs Mexican Americans often get. Allen said the company's Permian division laborers must be high school graduates "because they advance from that on up through."

Commissioner Hector P. Garcia noted that in part of the operating area of the El Paso Natural Gas Company, the percentages of Mexican Americans by county are the following: Jeff Davis, 56 percent; El Paso, 44 percent; Brewster, 42.6 percent; Presidio, 40.5 percent; and Hud-speth, 29.4 percent.

In the city of El Paso, where the company makes its headquarters and is about 50 percent Mexican American, Allen testified that out of 1,150 employees only 13 percent were Mexican American.

Commissioner Garcia noted that El Paso was "practically the first settlement north of the Rio Grande that was colonized by Spaniards and Mexican Americans" and that Spanish-speaking people have been in the area for "hundreds of years." "And yet," Garcia said, ". . . you haven't been able to find one single Mexican American that you could . . . employ as a laborer . . .?"

Working for the telephone company can be advantageous because of good wages and opportunities for advancement. Telephone com-panies, as well as any other firms having contracts with Federal agencies, must comply with Executive Order 11246 which requires affirmative action in seeking out members of minority groups for employment.

Joe Ridgway, employment manager for the San Antonio metropolitan sector of the Southwestern Bell Telephone Company, was questioned about the Executive order by the Commission's Acting General Counsel David Rubin.

Rubin: You still haven't answered my question as to whether you have ever received a communication which has directed you to take affirmative action to seek out members of minority groups for employ-ment.

Ridgway: Yes, sir, we have and are following an affirmative action program that has been presented to me.

Rubin: When was that done?

Ridgway: In November.

Rubin: Of this year?

Ridgway: Of this year.

In other words, though Executive Order 11246 was issued in 1965, Ridgway testified that a program of affirmative action in employing members of minority groups was not initiated until November of 1968, a month before the Commission hearing.

Ridgway added, however, that the program was meant to "continue" to "pursue the things that we have historically done in this area."

This exchange followed:

Rubin: Prior to speaking with staff members of the Civil Rights Commission, were you aware that less than 15 percent of your employees were members of minority groups?

Ridgway: As I remember, there was some question as to exact percentages, and that 15 percent mentioned was a little on the low side.

Rubin: Were you aware of the percentage of the total number of employees constituted by minority groups at that time?

Ridgway: Yes, I was conscious that there would be a percentage.

Rubin: But you didn't know what the percentage was?

Ridgway: The actual percentage, I did not know what it was and had no way of knowing it at that time.

Rubin: Now, your 1968 [Equal Employment Opportunity—1] form shows that out of 626 craftsmen, only 12, or under 2 percent have a Spanish surname. How do you account for this in a city that is close to 40 percent Mexican American?

Ridgway: Though I would like to answer your question, I am at a loss as to how to historically go back. It predates what I am personally acquainted with and could answer to. . . .

Yet, a couple of minutes before, Ridgway had testified that the company's new program for affirmative action in employing members of minorities was merely "to pursue the things that we have historically done in this area." Despite Ridgway's seeming confusion over the historical practice of employment discrimination, it became apparent at the hearing that historically the Mexican American and other minorities had been victims of discrimination in employment.

It was put quite bluntly when Rubin questioned Robert A. Wallace, Deputy Assistant Secretary of the Treasury.

Rubin: Mr. Wallace, the banking industry has been said to have been traditionally—and I am quoting, "a white man's industry." Would you agree with that characterization?

Wallace: Until about 2 years ago, I would have to agree with that, yes. . . .

Wallace's reference to "2 years ago," coincides with a 1966 Treasury Department ruling that all banks receiving Federal deposits are covered by Executive Order 11246, and therefore are required to undertake affirmative policies to recruit minority group persons.

A Commission staff report, however, showed that though all banks visited reported that they had Federal deposits, only two said they had been informed of this requirement by the Treasury Department. And, only one bank reported the establishment of an affirmative program to recruit minorities. The staff report also revealed that in San Antonio, where almost half of the population is Spanish-speaking, only 5.6 percent of all bank officials were Mexican Americans, and nearly half of them were found in one bank, the Frost National Bank. Seven banks reported that none of their officials were Mexican American and five others reported that they had only one Mexican American official.

Of the clerical and office workers, 16.4 percent were Mexican American and 1.4 percent were Negro. The percentage of Mexican American office workers ranged from 100 percent in one bank (located in the predominantly Mexican American area) to less than 1 percent in two banks.

In the schools, a staff report indicted that in the San Antonio Independent School District there were 14 Mexican American administrators out of a total of 132 administrators. In the Bexar County [where San Antonio is located] Welfare Department, Mexican Americans held close to 50 percent of all jobs and nearly one-third of the supervisory and administrative positions. But, the report notes, though Mexican Americans comprised 75 percent of all welfare recipients in Bexar County, only 20 of 91 social workers, or less than 22 percent, were Mexican Americans.

In nine restaurants surveyed by the Commission staff, less than 15 percent of the customer-contact positions were held by minorities, while minorities held 93 percent of the noncustomer contact positions. The staff report showed that at the Texas Employment Commission, the State agency responsible for aiding persons in obtaining employment, Mexican Americans held less than 7 percent of the nonclerical and custodial positions in the State of Texas.

In emphasizing that the Commission was not trying to condemn one section of the country or any one industry, Commissioner Theodore M. Hesburgh said that in its 11-year history, the Commission has found that "there isn't a single city, North, South, East or West, where we have gone to, where it doesn't appear very difficult for minority groups to have some kind of adequate representation in all kinds of businesses and professions and trades.

"As a matter of fact," continued Commissioner Hesburgh, "I could say quite openly, the most difficult task we have had is with the construction trades where the minorities find it very difficult to become members of the unions."

The historical pattern of employment for Mexican Americans was perhaps best dramatized by the controversy over employment practices at Kelly Air Force Base, one of San Antonio's major employers.

There is so much argument on the subject, that between June 1966 and December 1968, there were six surveys of equal employment practices conducted at Kelly.

One of the reports, that of the Texas State Advisory Committee to the Commission, issued in June 1968, found that at Kelly Field there "are broad and glaring inequities in the distribution of supervisory and higher grade positions among Mexican Americans and Negroes. . . ."

The Advisory Committee said that among Mexican American white-collar employees at Kelly, 68.9 percent were in grades 1–5, for which the initial per annum salaries in 1966 were $3,609 to $5,331.

In the higher pay scales, the committee reported, even though Mexican Americans comprise about 44 percent of the total work force, only 8 percent of them were in the $9,221 per year and up white-collar jobs and only 5 percent were in the $7,000 and up blue-collar jobs.

The Advisory Committee also asserted that "there exists at Kelly Air Force Base and in the San Antonio community, among a significant number of Mexican American citizens and leaders, a lack of confidence in the base's management and equal employment opportunity program. The Mexican American community feels that it does not receive equal treatment and that Kelly Air Force Base management has failed to remedy this situation, despite the community's protestations. This fact takes on greater significance when it is recognized that Kelly Air Force Base is one of the largest employers of Mexican Americans in the Nation."

Dennis Seidman, Air Force Deputy Chief of Staff Personnel, on the other hand, curiously concluded, after his staff conducted a study, that there was a "lack of credibility" on the part of the Mexican American community, but asserted that there did not seem "to be a significant number of employees who felt that the employment opportunity program was a negative kind of program." Seidman also told the Commission that he himself was not personally at Kelly during this particular study but drew his conclusions from reports by 12 personnel management experts who spent 6 weeks at Kelly.

Howard A. Glickstein, then Acting Staff Director of the Commission, reminded Seidman that the Commission's Texas State Advisory Committee report showed that in 1966, Mexican Americans held 11.6 percent of the starting high grade jobs at Kelly. And that in 1967 that figure was 12.3 percent.

"And your report," Glickstein continued, "I believe shows that in 1968 it was 13.7 percent.

"Now the Mexican Americans represent about 30 percent of the [higher category] employees, and about 44 to 45 percent of the total work force. Would you consider that a broad and glaring inequity?"

Seidman: I think we have considered that in the report to be an imbalance in the number of people in each of these grades as related to their proportion in the population.

Glickstein: Mr. Seidman, there is one overriding impression that I receive by reading your report, and I wonder if you would care to comment on it. It seems as though the word discrimination, or the word inequity, is just a dirty word that will not be used. Is there any reason why that is so?

Seidman: . . . We put no value either positive or negative on those words. We have no evidence to indicate that there is discrimination. We have no empirical evidence that there has been discrimination and therefore the word discrimination does not appear.

Glickstein wanted to know whether Seidman disputed a report issued by the subcommittee of the equal opportunity committee at Kelly before the hearing which asserted that "minority group members employed at Kelly during the period 1917 to 1966 did not have equal employment opportunities."

Seidman: I think the phrase . . . which projected, as it were, a historical discrimination, is just that, a projection. I don't believe there are any—there are any empirical evidence in our report to indicate that there has been discrimination, by organization, by grade, or by individuals.

Glickstein: Do you think it is possible to find out if there has been discrimination? Do you think that is a relevant consideration?

Seidman: I think it is possible. I wouldn't know at the moment how to find out, historically.

Later, Glickstein pointed out that at the rate Mexican Americans were obtaining higher grade level jobs at Kelly it would take about 17 more years to equalize the situation. "And if they were to attain a proportionate number of jobs in proportion to their representation in the entire work force, it will take until about 2000."

Seidman answered that he thought "there are many, many factors that impinge on predicting the rate of movement," and that minorities had made good progress in moving up to the higher levels especially in the past 12 months.

Later, Matt Garcia, a Mexican American attorney who had handled job discrimination cases, told the Commission he felt the Air Force survey team, headed by Seidman, had come to San Antonio, "only in an effort to negate the Texas State Advisory Committee's report." Seidman had earlier testified that it was just a "coincidence" that his team made the study just after the Advisory Committee's and just before the Commission met in San Antonio.

Attorney Garcia also charged that Seidman's contention that members of minorities were obtaining more higher paid jobs at Kelly was misleading because Seidman did not mention that more higher level positions had been created in 1968. It's true, he said, that in 1966 there were 142 Mexican Americans in the beginning category of the higher paying jobs but the number had increased to 208 in 1968.

Furthermore, he continued, Seidman did not mention the fact that in 1967 there were 1,434 such jobs while in 1968 there were 1,520.

Maj. Gen. Frank E. Rouse, Commander of Kelly Air Force Base, told the Commission he didn't believe "there was any necessity for Mr. Seidman and his [surveying] team in the first place," but he agreed that there is "an ethnic imbalance" in the number of good jobs Mexican Americans have at Kelly. However, he agreed with Seidman that this was not caused by "discriminatory acts either in the recent past, or the fairly distant past."

I must believe what I see, can touch, and prove. And I think the conclusion I come to is that under the merit promotion system, rightly or wrongly, the opinion is that the best people were promoted."

Despite General Rouse's contention that discrimination must be seen and touched to be proven, Mexican Americans have long noted that racial prejudice against them has been perpetrated in a more subtle way than against blacks but that it has been just as effective.

Prof. Daniel P. Rodriguez of Trinity University in San Antonio, who also conducted an employment opportunity study at Kelly, explained to the Commission how this subtle discrimination works.

During his investigation, Rodriguez told the Commission, he got the impression that Kelly management "were complying with the requirement of the [equal employment opportunity] regulation without complying with the spirit of it."

Some of management's remarks, Rodriguez said, "led me to believe that among some of these men, even though they felt there was no prejudice or bias on their part, they were not even aware of it."

Rodriguez: I had one supervisor tell me that when a Mexican American was promoted you had to be careful to insure that the Anglo group there was going to accept him as a supervisor. What he left unsaid of course—and I casually pointed it out to him—was that when an Anglo was being promoted that there was never any question about whether he could handle minority group people working under him.

Glickstein: Did you think that he thought he was discriminating?

Rodriguez: I am positive that he didn't feel that he was discriminating, or that the statement he made to me was—that there was anything wrong with it. I think he was a little bit surprised when he realized what he had said.

The historical pattern of Mexican American employment can be changed abruptly for the better with imagination, know-how, sensitivity, and money. This was the message conveyed to the Commission by Joseph B. Andrasko, director of industrial relations for the aeronautics division of the Ling-Temco-Vought Aerospace Corporation of Dallas, in one of the hearing's most positive presentations.

Andrasko said that in 1965, his company, which builds airplanes, foresaw the need for about 14,000 semi skilled and skilled workers for its expansion program. Dallas, where the company is located, could not be a main source of labor because that city had a less than 2 percent unemployment rate. It was suggested that the Rio Grande Valley, whose unemployment rate is very high as a result of the cheap labor available just across the border, be considered as a source for workers.

"This came as much of a shocker," Andrasko said, "as the Rio Grande Valley is approximately 450 to 500 miles from our plant. . . ."

Nevertheless, the company took the plunge and after 2½ years of negotiations with local, State, and Federal agencies, the company reached an agreement to train 750 persons in the Rio Grande Valley in a period of 12 months. Of the 750 persons who entered the training program, 684 finished the course and 622 were still on the payroll at the time of the hearing. The trainees, 97 percent of them Mexican Americans, who could not have hoped to earn more than $1,200 to $1,500 a year in the Valley, started making $5,000 to $6,000 a year after 5 weeks' training.

It was quite an undertaking, considering the workers had to be uprooted from the Rio Grande Valley to live in a Dallas suburb, where they would have to look for housing and schools for their children. These problems were solved, Andrasko said, by assigning company counselors to help the workers get settled in Dallas.

"The counselors were Mexican American," Andrasko said, "all of them. And we did it by design."

Federal and State funds provided wages for the trainees while they trained, salaries for instructors, rent for equipment that had to be taken to the Valley, and transportation for the workers from the Valley to Dallas. It cost the State and Federal Government about $1,200 per trainee.

Was the money well spent?

Andrasko told the Commission that the company made a survey which showed that when the trainee started working full-time it took about 18 months for the newly trained worker to pay $1,200 in taxes.

"As a taxpayer I'd say you're darn right [the money was well spent]," Andrasko said.

The trainees, Andrasko added, turned out to be "conscientious, hard workers and followed instructions." As a matter of fact, he continued, the first two wing panels which they built after training were found to have no defects by the inspectors.

The team of Mexican Americans who were brought to Dallas from the Valley broke the myth that Mexican Americans can do only certain types of work, Andrasko said. All they needed was an opportunity to prove themselves.

6 LA LEY

Justice is the most important word in race relations. Yet too many Mexican Americans in the Southwest feel with David Sanchez, Los Angeles Brown Beret leader, that "to Anglos justice means 'just us'."

La Ley or The Law, as Mexican Americans call the administration of justice, takes forms that Anglos—and even Negroes—never have to experience. A Mexican American, though a third generation American, for instance, may have to prove with documents that he is an American citizen at border crossings while a blue-eyed blond German immigrant, for example, can cross by merely saying "American."

Besides the usual complaints made by racial minorities about police brutality and harassment, Mexican Americans have an added problem: sometimes they literally cannot communicate with the police. A Commission report told of a young Mexican American, who, while trying to quell a potentially explosive situation, was arrested because the police officers, who did not understand Spanish, thought that he was trying to incite the crowd to riot.

In another case, the Commission report told of a Mexican American in Arizona who was held in jail for 2 months on a charge of sexually molesting his daughter. As it turned out, he had been mistakenly charged with this offense, but he did not voice any objections at the time because he did not understand the proceedings and no interpreter was provided for him. A probation officer, who spoke Spanish, talked to the defendant later and upon learning the facts explained the situation to the local magistrate, who dismissed the case.

One of the many reasons a Mexican American cannot relate well to *La Ley* is that he doesn't see many of his own in positions of authority serving on agencies which administer justice. The 1960 census indicated that Mexican Americans represent about 12 percent of the Southwest's population. In 1968, only 7.4 percent of the total uniformed personnel in law enforcement agencies in the Southwest were Mexican Americans, according to those agencies answering a Commission questionnaire.

As for policymaking positions, the Commission learned in its survey that only 10 law enforcement agencies are headed by Mexican Americans and eight of these are in communities of less than 10,000 in population.

(A Commission study of the grand jury system of 22 California counties concluded that discrimination against Mexican Americans in juror selection is "as severe—sometimes more severe—as discrimination against Negroes in grand juries in the South.")

In East Los Angeles, which is the largest single urban Mexican American community in the United States, "friction between law enforcement and the Mexican American community" is on the increase, according to a psychiatric social worker, Armando Morales.

Morales is State chairman of the California Unity Council, Police Community Relations Committee, which is composed of members from five statewide Mexican American organizations—the Community Service Organization, the League of United Latin American Citizens, (LULAC) the Mexican American Educators, the American GI Forum, and the Mexican American Political Association.

One of the reasons for this increasing friction, Morales told the Commission, was that "gradually the Mexican American community is becoming much more aggressive as to its social demands, its social needs. It is becoming more active. And, at the same time, law enforcement is becoming much more suppressive, hence creating that much more friction between the two." Morales also contended that police aggressive behavior seems to be condoned by high level government.

Morales charged "indifference and apathy to the justice and needs of the Mexican American" by the Federal Government. He said his council investigated 25 cases of alleged police brutality, five of which were submitted for consideration to the FBI. The FBI referred them to the U.S. Department of Justice, which in turn ignored the matter, according to Morales.

The Reverend John P. Luce, rector of the Epiphany Parish in East Los Angeles, agreed with Morales that communication between Mexican Americans and the Los Angeles police had broken down and said he feared "we are on a collision course in Los Angeles" along the lines of a "police-barrio confrontation." Rev. Luce charged that the Los Angeles police and sheriff departments "refuse to talk with militant and political leaders with whom they might disagree, with young people, with a whole variety of activist people who want change."

The Anglo clergyman told the Commission that the indictment of 13 Mexican American leaders in the March 1968 East Los Angeles High School walkouts has led to the strong feeling that "the [Los Angeles] district attorney has singled out the Mexican community because he thought they were weaker than some other communities" but that he "miscalculated on this point, because the Mexican is organizing even that much more."

A Commission staff report said that "one of the most common complaints (throughout the Southwest) was that Anglo juvenile offenders are released to the custody of their parents and no charges are brought, while Mexican American youths are charged with offenses, held in custody, and sent to a reformatory."

A counselor for the New Mexico State Employment Office told the Commission's Advisory Committee:

". . . I was very shocked when I became involved in working with young [Mexican American] people . . . and found that charges were made against them, such as stealing cantaloupes out of a farmer's field, curfew violations, being truant from school, and things like this. These would all be on record and they all have quite extensive juvenile records. Among the Anglo people I work with, this just [isn't] done. I don't think the Anglo children are this much better."

The Commission's report further stated that it is felt throughout the Southwest that "the most serious police harassment involves interference with attempts by Mexican Americans to organize themselves in order to assert their collective power."

To the advocates of brown or Chicano power, the Texas Rangers, or *"Los Rinches,"* are the symbols of this repression. The Texas Rangers is an elite 136-year-old statewide law enforcement agency under the Texas Department of Public Safety. At the time of the hearing there were 62 Texas Rangers, none of them Mexican Americans.

To the Mexican American, especially the poor, such as the farm worker in the Rio Grande Valley, the Rangers in their Stetson hats, fancy boots, hand tooled revolvers, and holsters personify everything they fear: tough-talking, rancher-grower types who can run you out of town at the slightest suspicion that the Mexican Americans want to assert themselves.

"The Rangers are the cowboys and we're the Indians," say Mexican Americans.

Farm workers, labor organizers, and civil rights workers testified before the Commission that the Texas Rangers break agriculture worker strikes in the Rio Grande Valley through force and intimidation. The unionization of farm workers is seen as a holy war in Texas where farm hands get no workmen's compensation, no State minimum wage, no unemployment and disability insurance, and where there are no mandatory standards in farm worker housing. (In contrast, California requires by law all of these things.)

Reynaldo de la Cruz, 26, a farm worker and father of six children, who had been arrested six times for union activities, told the Commission he joined the union because of "what every Mexican American farm worker faces, that they have been cheated too long . . . because I had been cheated too many times. [I joined the union] so that we could fight for our rights and for the rights of other people that don't know how to defend themselves."

Asked what the feeling of Mexican Americans is toward the Texas Rangers, José M. Martinez, a farm worker, told the Commission:

"Many people hate them, many people are afraid, because the majority of the Mexicans are not armed. They [Rangers] are armed. And when the Rangers are coming, then the people are afraid. They are afraid of being hit, or being pushed around. . . . The minute that you hear the Rangers are coming, everybody hides. If you are on strike, if you know the Rangers are coming, then they don't want to strike. This is the feeling of the people in the Valley. They are afraid."

Trying to determine what Mexican Americans thought of Government as an administrator of justice, Howard A. Glickstein, then Acting Staff Director of the Commission, asked farm worker de la Cruz whether in his work as a union organizer he saw the State government and State officials as friends or enemies.

De la Cruz: Well, considering that the Rangers are State officials, I think they are our enemies.

Glickstein: How do you view the Federal Government? What do you think of the role the Federal Government has played or hasn't played?

De la Cruz: Well, I am not too sure about the Federal Government. But if they were really our friends, then something would have been done when the Texas Rangers were messing with the strike.

Earlier, Pete Tijerina, executive director of the Mexican American Legal Defense and Educational Fund, had noted that the U.S. Attorney General had intervened on behalf of Negro cases throughout the South but that "not once, not once, has the Attorney General . . . intervened in any Mexican American case."

The Reverend Edgar A. Krueger, an ordained minister whom the Texas Council of Churches sent to the Rio Grande Valley as an observer during a long farm workers' strike, told the Commission of his experiences with the Texas Rangers, including his arrest.

He said he went to Mission, Texas, one night, in the lower Rio Grande Valley, where he heard farm workers would be picketing. When he, his wife, and their 18-year-old son arrived at Mission he learned that 12 farm workers had been arrested. He spotted Ranger Captain Alfred Y. Allee and other Rangers in their parked cars in the drive-in bank on the other side of the railroad tracks. The Reverend Krueger said that since it was Friday night, "when people just gather, visit, and watch the cars go by," there were about 200 people on both sides of the tracks. But no one was trying to gather a crowd, no one was talking to the group, or trying to convince anyone to become a union member," the Reverend Krueger said. "No one was trying to stop the train, nor was anyone carrying a picket sign at that particular time. All we wanted to do was to find out where the persons had been taken that were arrested."

When the train arrived, the Texas Rangers with very long flashlights signaled the train to pass, the minister said, and he decided to take a picture with his wife's small camera from a hundred feet away. "About that time Captain Allee walked right straight down the west side of the street toward me," recalled the Reverend Krueger, "and said, as he was walking up, 'Krueger, I am sick and tired of seeing you around.'

He grabbed me by the collar and the seat of the pants and lifted me practically to the center of the street."

Mrs. Krueger then took a picture of what was happening, the Reverend Krueger said.

"And then Captain Allee yelled, 'Grab that woman.',", the minister told the Commission. "Another Ranger grabbed my wife, and I didn't see it when it happened, but he grabbed her. But I did see later on that he had her arm twisted behind her back."

Captain Allee then turned the minister over to another Ranger and walked up to a farm worker, Magdaleno Dimas, who was eating a hamburger, the Reverend Krueger said.

"Captain Allee slapped the hamburger out of his hand," the Reverend Krueger continued, "and then with double hands slapped him in the face. . . . And then they took me [and Dimas] to the passing train. Since they were running around so rapidly there in something of a frenzy, I was very fearful when they held Dimas, it seemed like his head was just a few inches from the metal that was sticking out from the passing train, and held us there beside the train while it was passing."

After manhandling Dimas some more, the minister, his wife, Dimas, and a friend were thrown into the back seat of a Ranger car and searched, the Reverend Krueger said. Seeing that the pipe of one of the men had bounced off the car doorway, the minister said: "It seemed like a very natural thing sitting on the edge of the seat like that to reach down and pick up his pipe. At that time Ranger Jack Van Cleve, with tremendous force, slapped me in the cheek." The Reverend Krueger, his wife, and friends were arraigned for unlawful assembly. This was a year and a half before the Commission hearing and up to then their case had not come to trial. In charging that the Texas Rangers and sheriff's deputies were "strike breakers," and completely partial to the growers, the Reverend Krueger told the Commission that a sheriff's deputy told him [Krueger] that if he really wanted to help "these people" he should tell them to go back to work.

"And there was an occasion when Captain Allee did say that if the [striking] farm workers wanted jobs he would see that they would get jobs," the Reverend Krueger told the Commission. "And he also said that if they didn't go to work that it would have a depressing effect on the whole Valley, and they would suffer and the whole Valley would suffer if they didn't get the cantaloupes out."

But perhaps the Reverend Krueger's most serious charge was that mass arrests by Rangers and other law enforcement officers usually followed any success the strikers or union had. "For example," said the minister, "the night when my wife and 114 other persons were arrested. This was on the same day, I believe, that the Texas Advisory Committee to the U.S. Commission on Civil Rights finished their hearing in Starr County, in Rio Grande City, and it seemed that that hearing

gave some support to the union's cause, and that same night people
were arrested."

Arnulfo Guerra, a Rio Grande Valley attorney, charged that local
and State government openly opposed the strike and the farm workers'
right to organize and he said that the Rangers in particular "were entirely and completely partial to the growers. And I say this because
the people who called them [Rangers] in was the county administration,
and the county administration was completely and totally partial to
the growers. It was a one-sided affair, and they [Rangers] were exces-
sively partial. . . ."

Ranger Captain Allee, a 36-year veteran of the Texas Rangers, appeared before the Commission on the closing day of the San Antonio
hearing.

Commission Acting General Counsel Rubin asked him why the
Texas Rangers were sent to Starr County during the farm workers'
strike.

Captain Allee: To keep peace and order and to protect the lives and
property and to assist the sheriff's department.

Rubin: What was occurring at that time to warrant [the Rangers
going to Starr County]?

Captain Allee: It is my understanding that it had been going on a
good while and the United Farm Workers Organizing Committee was
trying to organize the employees there.

Rubin: And that was the reason why . . . why . . . the Rangers [were]
sent?

Captain Allee: That's right. There had been trouble, there was a
railroad trestle had been burned and I had my sergeant down there
before then and had one or two Rangers there. . . . [the Rangers] were
sent . . . to make [an] investigation. . . .

Asked why he had arrested the Reverend Krueger, Captain Allee
said "he came up and talked to me, and he got pretty arrogant about it,
and he was poking me on the chest with his finger and accused me of
putting his men in jail. My people, he called them, my people. And he
was loud and abusive.

"And I got Reverend Krueger by the belt and the collar and took
him over to the car. On the way over there Mrs. Krueger, she had a
camera and she was with him, and about that time I heard someone say,
look out, captain. And he said, give me that camera, Mrs. Krueger, and
he was Ranger Jack Van Cleve, and he said she attempted to hit me
over the head with it."

Rubin wanted to know why the minister was arrested.

Captain Allee: I just got through telling you this, for [being] loud
and abusive, and disturbing the peace. Language, of course, one thing
and another is why I arrested him.

Rubin: What charge was placed against him?

Captain Allee: I don't know. I didn't file the complaint. I can get
that for you and send it to you, if you wish.

Rubin: Did Reverend Krueger resist arrest?

Captain Allee: No, he didn't resist arrest.

Rubin: What did he do? You said that you lifted Reverend Krueger by the seat of his pants?

Captain Allee: No, I didn't lift him by the seat of the pants, I said I got him by the belt.

Rubin: By the belt?

Captain Allee: Yes, sir.

Rubin: Why was it necessary to do that?

Captain Allee: Well, I don't know why it was necessary to do it. . . . I usually grab a fellow by the belt if I am going to take him somewhere. Of course, he didn't especially want to go after I talked to him there a little while.

Later, Rubin wanted to know about the arrest of farm worker Dimas and whether the captain had slapped him.

Captain Allee: I slapped a hamburger out of his hand.

Rubin: Why did you do that?

Captain Allee: Well, he was trying to tell me something, I don't know what it was, and he was spitting that mustard. . . .

Asked what reputation the Texas Rangers have among Mexican Americans, Captain Allee said: "Among Mexican Americans I think they have a good reputation. I worked around the Mexican people all my life. I had a big percentage of the people of Starr, Texas, of Mexican American people send a petition into Austin and I didn't request it, asking the Rangers to stay there because they feared violence and bloodshed. And that petition is on file. . . ."

Questioned whether there were workers in the fields during the strike, Captain Allee responded: "Oh, yes, there were workers in the fields, lots of people working in the fields. I couldn't tell you whether they were from Starr County or not. Some of them were and some of them from across the border, the green card workers.

Glickstein: There were a lot of green card workers?

Captain Allee: I don't know how many.

Glickstein: They come across [the border] in the morning and go home at night?

Captain Allee: That's right.

It was as if Captain Allee was reminding Mexican Americans what they have known for many years: If they rock the boat, they can always be replaced by cheaper Mexicans from across the border.

CONCLUSION

In restrospect, perhaps the most positive result of the hearing was that barrio Mexican Americans came out of it with a feeling that the Government does care about them.

This was no small accomplishment. To Mexicans *el gobierno*, the Government, has traditionally been a natural enemy. Until the Revolution of 1910, which at last made Mexico a free country, Mexicans experienced foreign dictatorships—Spanish colonialism and the French imposed Emperor Maximilian, for example—and domestic dictatorships, Santa Anna and Porfirio Diaz.

It is not surprising therefore that Mexican Americans have an inherent distrust of Government. The older ones remember that during the depression of the 1930's, the Government "incited" Mexican resident aliens to leave the United States to what was almost certain worse poverty in Mexico. Many Mexican Americans over 30 in the border areas can remember unpleasant moments at the hands of the U.S. Immigration and Customs agents at border crossings. They remember learning to live with the fear of deportation posed by *el gobierno* which at any moment might demand proof that they're American citizens and not Mexican nationals.

To many Mexican Americans, dealings with *el gobierno* have always been unpleasant. The contacts with teachers, employment officials, social workers, police, and other representatives of *el gobierno* have, in many instances, left behind memories of mistreatment and insensitivity.

With the San Antonio hearing there was a breakthrough for Mexican Americans who have felt neglected, if not persecuted, in the past by their Government. They had been studied many times before San Antonio, but at the hearing, for the first time on a national platform, the problems of the Mexican American were explored not only in the general sense but also in the specific.

The obvious challenges of discrimination in employment, competition of cheap labor from Mexico, inadequate education, police harassment, and cultural conflicts were again aired with a monotonous consistency, but there was a difference. This time the investigators talked face to face with members of the "establishment" involved in the areas indicated above and the Commission dealt in precise names, organizations, and systems accused of insensitivity toward the Mexican American.

The hearing did not end in a tone of: "Look, we've got problems and something must be done." Instead, it ended saying in effect: "Look, these people and these situations are keeping us back and this has to be done."

Something else very valuable came out of the hearing—an underscoring of the gravity of the problems that are now bubbling to the surface in the Mexican American community. Only the most insensitive spectator could miss the sense of urgency of the problems of the Mexican Americans and the realization that delay in reaching solutions could only exacerbate those problems.

Following the hearing, though not necessarily because of it, the State of Texas appropriated money for its first bilingual education program, passed a minimum wage law for farm workers, raised the ceiling on money to be made available for welfare benefits, and enacted legislation to prevent confiscation of property outright for a missing delinquent house payment.

The hearing represented another step in a trend toward understanding of the Mexican American which started a few years ago. The creation of the Inter-Agency Committee on Mexican American Affairs in June of 1967, by President Lyndon B. Johnson, showed a growing awareness by Washington of the Spanish-speaking population.

Making the Committee a permanent agency under President Nixon further indicated that the National Government recognized that the Mexican American had unique problems that required separate consideration from the seat of power.

The formation of the Southwest Council of La Raza and the Mexican American Legal Defense and Education Fund with the help of Ford Foundation money showed that the private sector was also interested.

But what probably has most warmed the Mexican American to *el gobierno* is the Government's growing concern for the uneducated and rural Mexican American.

Congress' refusal to extend the bracero program was a significant victory for the Mexican American farm workers who claimed braceros were taking jobs away from them.

The Federal Government's funding of the California Rural Legal Assistance through the Office of Economic Opportunity was further proof that Washington cared about Mexican Americans, who comprise about 67 percent of the State's agriculture workers.

The CRLA was founded on the philosophy that the poor, like the rich, are entitled to good lawyers who take the time to serve their needs.

Mexican American farm workers who, with their fellow black and Anglo colleagues, are the only major occupational group excluded from unemployment insurance coverage and other federally conferred benefits such as collective bargaining legislation, had now someone to represent them in court.

At least technically, the Mexican American farm worker could now defend himself not only from powerful growers but from the Government itself.

As for education, the passing of the Bilingual Education Act of 1967 recognized the absurdity of punishing children for speaking Spanish in the school grounds.

It also showed that the time would come when the knowledge of a second language would become an asset instead of a liability.

A stirring has occurred in the Mexican American community itself. New groups are emerging, older ones are moving in new directions. There is a sense of mobility, typified by expressions of solidarity and demands for change. Not untypical of the mood was the gathering, several months after the San Antonio hearing, of some 1,000 Mexican Americans in Del Rio, Texas, to protest the termination of a VISTA program.

The hearing can be described as a piece of a mosaic, and it provided the groundwork for an even better understanding by the Government of the Mexican American. The information from the hearing was also extremely valuable in the comprehensive studies on Mexican American education and the administration of justice in the Southwest undertaken by the Commission.

So stark was the picture of the Mexican American in the Southwest drawn by the words of the witnesses, so evident was the need for additional resources, that the Commission subsequently approved the conversion of its temporary field office in San Antonio to a permanent installation.

Despite all this, and because change takes time, those attending the hearing could easily come to the conclusion that Mexican Americans have been victims of fraud.

Much of the testimony showed how Mexican Americans have been cheated of things most Americans take for granted: their right to their language, their culture, their color.

This was perhaps most poignantly expressed when Commissioner Hector P. Garcia asked Irene Ramirez, a San Antonio high school girl, whether she wanted to have "nice things."

"Of course," answered Irene, "but from the very beginning we are taught . . . I mean, this is an impossible dream."

"What is impossible, dear?" Garcia asked.

"Going to college and achieving something . . . ," she answered.

This exchange dramatized to those attending the hearing that though lip service has always been paid to the theory that Mexican Americans "are like any other Americans," in reality they are not.

The hearing showed that the Mexican American has been made to feel negatively about his Mexican background—to the point where even the word "Mexican" has become a liability.

As a result, Mexican Americans have tried to assimilate into Anglo society as quietly as possible. Some have succeeded. But, if the testimony is to be believed, the attempt at assimilation has failed for too many.

The feeling among activist Mexican Americans—who prefer to call themselves Chicanos—is that Spanish-speaking people should resist any attempt to become American at the expense of their language and culture.

Chicanos also emphasize that assimilation for assimilation's sake has been oversold and that it must be learned once and for all that you can't turn a brown child into a white child through patriotic rhetoric.

The hearing may also have helped kill the myth that with time Mexican Americans will assimilate as have the Irish, Italians, Polish, and other ethnic groups. This argument crumbles with the obvious fact that the United States and Mexico share a 1,800-mile open border, and not an ocean as do the United States and Ireland.

The influence of Mexico on the Mexican American will continue as long as Mexico is there.

The Americanization of the Mexican American has too often meant that he must shun his background and assume a ridiculous role of being what has been described as a "tanned Anglo".

The hearing may have helped bring home an obvious historical fact: Mexicans are not strangers to this land, especially in the Southwest. They are indigenous to it.

The hearing may have focused a growing feeling among Mexican Americans. That is, that they understand the importance of becoming Anglicized but that in the process they insist that Anglos become Mexicanized, if the melting pot theory of America is to have value.

EL PLAN DE AZTLAN

The Plan de Aztlan, which was written at the
First Chicano National Conference in Denver,
Colorado in 1969, is the ideological framework
and concrete political program of the Chicano
Movement because of its emphasis on national-
ism and the goal of self-determination.

Source: Documents of the Chicano Struggle,
Pathfinder Press, Inc. 1971.

El Plan Espiritual de Aztlan

In the spirit of a new people that is conscious not only of its
proud historical heritage but also of the brutal "gringo" invasion
of our territories, *we,* the Chicano inhabitants and civilizers of
the northern land of Aztlán from whence came our forefathers,
reclaiming the land of their birth and consecrating the determination of our people of the sun, *declare* that the call of our blood
is our power, our responsibility, and our inevitable destiny.

We are free and sovereign to determine those tasks which are
justly called for by our house, our land, the sweat of our brows,
and by our hearts. Aztlán belongs to those who plant the seeds,
water the fields, and gather the crops and not to the foreign Europeans. We do not recognize capricious frontiers on the bronze
continent.

Brotherhood unites us, and love for our brothers makes us
a people whose time has come and who struggles against the
foreigner "gabacho" who exploits our riches and destroys our
culture. With our heart in our hands and our hands in the soil,
we declare the independence of our mestizo nation. We are a bronze
people with a bronze culture. Before the world, before all of North
America, before all our brothers in the bronze continent, we are
a nation, we are a union of free pueblos, we are *Aztlán.*

Por La Raza todo. Fuera de La Raza nada.

Program

El Plan Espiritual de Aztlán sets the theme that the Chicanos
(La Raza de Bronze) must use their nationalism as the key or
common denominator for mass mobilization and organization.
Once we are committed to the idea and philosophy of El Plan
de Aztlán, we can only conclude that social, economic, cultural,
and political independence is the only road to total liberation
from oppression, exploitation, and racism. Our struggle then must
be for the control of our barrios, campos, pueblos, lands, our
economy, our culture, and our political life. El Plan commits all
levels of Chicano society—the barrio, the campo, the ranchero,
the writer, the teacher, the worker, the professional—to La
Causa.

Nationalism

Nationalism as the key to organization transcends all religious, political, class, and economic factions or boundaries. Nationalism is the common denominator that all members of La Raza can agree upon.

Organizational Goals

1. UNITY in the thinking of our people concerning the barrios, the pueblo, the campo, the land, the poor, the middle class, the professional — all committed to the liberation of La Raza.

2. ECONOMY: economic control of our lives and our communities can only come about by driving the exploiter out of our communities, our pueblos, and our lands and by controlling and developing our own talents, sweat, and resources. Cultural background and values which ignore materialism and embrace humanism will contribute to the act of cooperative buying and the distribution of resources and production to sustain an economic base for healthy growth and development. Lands rightfully ours will be fought for and defended. Land and realty ownership will be acquired by the community for the people's welfare. Economic ties of responsibility must be secured by nationalism and the Chicano defense units.

3. EDUCATION must be relative to our people, i. e., history, culture, bilingual education, contributions, etc. Community control of our schools, our teachers, our administrators, our counselors, and our programs.

4. INSTITUTIONS shall serve our people by providing the service necessary for a full life and their welfare on the basis of restitution, not handouts or beggar's crumbs. Restitution for past economic slavery, political exploitation, ethnic and cultural psychological destruction and denial of civil and human rights. Institutions in our community which do not serve the people have no place in the community. The institutions belong to the people.

5. SELF-DEFENSE of the community must rely on the combined strength of the people. The front line defense will come from the barrios, the campos, the pueblos, and the ranchitos. Their involvement as protectors of their people will be given respect and dignity. They in turn offer their responsibility and their lives for their people. Those who place themselves in the front ranks for their people do so out of love and carnalismo. Those institutions which are fattened by our brothers to provide employment and political pork barrels for the gringo will do so only as acts of liberation and for La Causa. For the very young there will no longer be acts of juvenile delinquency, but revolutionary acts.

6. CULTURAL values of our people strengthen our identity and the moral backbone of the movement. Our culture unites and educates the family of La Raza towards liberation with one heart and one mind. We must insure that our writers, poets, musicians, and artists produce literature and art that is appealing to our people and relates to our revolutionary culture. Our cultural values of life, family, and home will serve as a powerful weapon to defeat the gringo dollar value system and encourage the process of love and brotherhood.

7. POLITICAL LIBERATION can only come through independent action on our part, since the two-party system is the same animal with two heads that feed from the same trough. Where we are a majority, we will control; where we are a minority, we will represent a pressure group; nationally, we will represent one party: La Familia de La Raza!

Action

1. Awareness and distribution of El Plan Espiritual de Aztlán. Presented at every meeting, demonstration, confrontation, courthouse, institution, administration, church, school, tree, building, car, and every place of human existence.

2. September 16, on the birthdate of Mexican Independence, a national walk-out by all Chicanos of all colleges and schools to be sustained until the complete revision of the educational system: its policy makers, administration, its curriculum, and its personnel to meet the needs of our community.

3. Self-defense against the occupying forces of the oppressors at every school, every available man, woman, and child.

4. Community nationalization and organization of all Chicanos: El Plan Espiritual de Aztlán.

5. Economic program to drive the exploiter out of our community and a welding together of our people's combined resources to control their own production through cooperative effort.

6. Creation of an independent local, regional, and national political party.
A nation autonomous and free — culturally, socially, economically, and politically — will make its own decisions on the usage of our lands, the taxation of our goods, the utilization of our bodies for war, the determination of justice (reward and punishment), and the profit of our sweat.

El Plan de Aztlán is the plan of liberation!

CHICANO MILITANTS: ASSERTIONS AND AIMS*
by Richard A. Garcia

This article gives a panoramic and programatic
view of the different major Chicano organizations
in the Southwest. It captures the essence and development of Chicano political thought and activity
in the late 1960s and early 1970s by outlining the
growth of the "new" ideology of nationalism.

Source: Political Ideology: A Comparative Study
of Three Chicano Youth Organizations. Unpublished
master's thesis by Richard A. Garcia.

CHICANO MILITANTS: ASSERTIONS AND AIMS

Wherever interests are vigorously pursued, an
ideology tends to be developed also to give meaning, re-enforcement and justification to these interests. An this ideology is as "real" as the real
interests themselves, for ideology is an indispen-
sable part of the life process which is expressed
in action.

                                        -- Otto Hintze

There is a militancy among Chicano youths in 1970 reminiscent of the
Chicano activities of the 1920's, 1930's and 1940's but the pace is acceler-
ated, the demands more pronounced, and the participation more extensive.
There is a ground swell movement of Chicano solidarity throughout the
Southwest comprised of a loose fellowship of some two to three hundred
civic, social, cultural, religious and political groups. The vanguard is the
Chicano youth. The movement, which encompasses various degrees of militancy, many viewpoints and many objectives, can be placed in five different
categories. These do not include the older organizations such G.I. Forum,
LULAC, PASO, MAPA and the Community Service organizations. The categories consist of the pinto groups (prisoners and ex-convicts), barrio youth
groups, the university youth groups, the campesino groups (farm workers),
and the adult groups that attract many youths, such as Tijerina's Alianza.
        From these five areas of participation come such organizations as the
Brown Berets, Mexican American Youth Organization (MAYO) of South Texas,
Moviemiento Estudiantil Chicano de Aztlan (MECHA), the Crusade for Justice, Alianza Federal de las Mercedes (Aliana), National Farm Workers
Organizing Committee, and El Mexican Preparado Listo Educado y Organizado (EMPLEO), League of United Citizens to Help Addicts (LUCHA), Mexi-

---

* This is a chapter from a larger study done by the author in 1970.

can-American Youth Organization of Los Angeles (MAYO), which are pinto
organizations. These organizations, though quite different, exhibit ideological postures which are quite similar but broad enough to attract many
youths.

The emergence of these ideological postures, predicated on the conditions already described, make for an explosive situation. In fact, the same
basic causes that the National Advisory Commission on Civil Disorders
describes as being responsible for the Black disorders are present in the
Southwest barrios of the Chicano: white racism, pervasive discrimination,
segregation, frustrated hopes, legitimation of violence, feelings of powerlessness, incitement and encouragement of violence, and the police.[1]
These conditions are documented by the 1970 Civil Rights Commission report entitled Mexican Americans and the Administration of Justice in the
Southwest which clearly shows that Chicanos face police oppression and
brutality, unfair judicial processes, the probability of biased juries, repri-
sals by law enforcers if Chicanos raise their voices about these injustices,
frequent unjust arrests especially among the youth, unfair jury selection
processes, unfair bail practices, a lack of appointed counsels for misdemeanor cases, and many other injustices.

That racism and discrimination are embedded in the social fabric of
the United States is undeniable, and that racism discrimination, inequality
and injustices have plagued Chicanos throughout their history is also undeniable. Therefore, in a society where racism and discrimination permeate
the atmosphere, a member of a minority group usually has two alternatives
in maintaining his personal dignity and feeling of human worth. First, he
can "by personal effort . . . make himself sufficiently useful to the in-race
to gain approval . . . or second, by group effort, an out-race can create
a culture and ideology that affirms, independently of in-race attitudes,
their human worth."[2] This second alternative is a collective effort rather
than an individual one and this is what Chicanos are emphasizing today.
Thus, there is this continuation of Brown militancy which had appeared to
lie dormant during the 1950's but in fact was simmering in the Chicano
barrios.

The cry of "Chicano Power!" is now constantly being heard and as the
Brown Berets state,

> Chicano power is not white reform, but is a thought that
> cries for a self-determined community. So far, the cries
> of "Chicano Power" are being prostituted by politicians
> and poverty programs. Chicano power is not American
> politics, and does not mean more poverty programs . .
> . . Chicao power is a direct power, through a source
> of community action. Community power is a thought that
> cries for a self-determined community.[3]

The underlying motive of the Brown Berets and other barrio groups is illus-

trated by a comment from David Sanchez, the prime minister of the Los
Angeles Brown Berets, "I hate the white ideal."[4]

The Brown Berets trace their history back to the pachucos of the 1930's,
1940's and 1950's. The pachucos were the Chicanos who suffered injustices
and ostracism from American society, but who nevertheless developed their
own mannerisms, their own ways of dress and their own way of rebelling.
In addition, the spirit of the pachuco is evident in the Brown Berets, a spirit
to be different, to be non-assimilated, to be strong-willed. As Octavio Paz
states, this spirit belongs to a person who "does not want to become a Mexican [citizen] again; and at the same time does not want to blend into the
life of North America."[5]

Many of these Brown Berets are former gang members who have developed the concept of "political pachuquismo" into a viable political organization. As Eliezer Risco, the Editor of La Raza, an East Los Angeles Chicano
newspaper, states, these

> . . . methods of barrio organization . . . are our own
> survival techniques. It is difficult for the culture of a
> minority to survive in the larger society. If we can util-
> ize them the barrio organizations for social action, now
> that we are stronger, we will surprise the country. The
> country won't know where our strength is coming from
> or how we organize.[6]

Much of the organization of the barrio is coming from the youths in the barrios themselves and these youths deny it is coming from the university.
The spirit of pachuquismo and sense of self-organization is the same found
in Chicano youths whether they are from the barrios of San Antonio, El Paso,
Los Angeles, San Jose, Denver, or any other barrio where there are Chicano youths.

The Brown Berets, with chapters extending across the Southwest, but
particularly in California, resemble a paramilitary organization. Their
motto is to serve, observe and protect. Their insignia, a holy cross em-
braced by two crossed rifles, is a reflection of their philosophy, which is
to use peaceful means to achieve their goals, but the crossed rifles sym-
bolize the fact that they may have to use extreme means to attain them.
They have a militant devotion to the protection of their barrio. More specifically, their purpose is:

> . . . to serve the Chicano community, by all means,
> necessary, so that it will be able to determine its own
> destiny; and to observe all city, county, state and fed-
> eral agencies which deal with and/or affect our com-
> munity, especially law enforcement agencies; and to
> protect the Chicano community, by all means necessary,
> from an individual or agency which threatens the life,
> actions, or goals of the Chicano community.[7]

The Brown Berets have justifiably taken it upon themselves to be the
law enforcement arm of the Chicano movimiento since they believe that injustices, discrimination, and violence are "still happening today . . .
[wherever] there is RAZA . . . by the white aggressor; in every barrio--
the people are being terrorized by the marano police."[8] The Brown Berets
advocate the replacement of the police department, which they say is racist,
by a people's department which will then initiate investigations into the cor-
ruption, bribery, brutality and other violations perpetrated by the police
department. Furthermore, they want to establish community review boards
which will allow individuals in the community to have a voice in the formu-
lation and administration of policy by the various agencies in the barrio.

Although the Brown Berets chapters are decentralized and autonomous,
the ten-point program of the Sacramento Brown Berets is the following:

1. UNITY of our people regardless of age, income, religion or political philosophy.
2. WE DEMAND the right to Bi-lingual Education as guaranteed by
   the Treaty of Guadalupe-Hidalgo of 1848.
3. WE DEMAND that the true history of the Chicano be taught in all
   schools of the five (5) Southwestern states.
4. WE DEMAND a civilian police review board made up of people who
   live in our community.
5. WE DEMAND that all police officers in the Chicano community
   must live in the community and speak the Spanish language.
6. WE DEMAND that all Chicanos whose homes get removed by
   Urban Renewal be given job training to acquire employment
   that will enable them to live in the new homes built in their
   barrios.
7. WE DEMAND a guaranteed annual income of $5,000 for all Mexi-
   can American families.
8. WE DEMAND that all juries that try our people be composed of an
   equal number of people of each race - Chicanos, Blacks, Orientals,
   Whites, and the jury must be of the same economic and social
   status as the defendant.
9. WE DEMAND that the literacy test for voting be given in Spanish
   language, and that persons who speak only Spanish have the same
   voting rights as any other person.
10. WE will keep and bear arms and use them against any threatening
    elements from outside our community such as the police or right-
    wing extremist groups.[9]

In addition to their preoccupation with their own barrios, the Brown
Berets have now turned their attention to two "external" influences which
affect the barrio--the Vietnam war and the political system. David Sanchez,
the prime minister of the Berets, has said that the "Chicano death rate in
Vietnam is . . . the most direct form of genocide against La Raza. It is
just part of a systematic destruction and degradation of La Raza."[10] The

Berets have lead the Chicano moratorium marches of December 20, 1969, and February 28, 1970, in which contingents from all areas of California participated, including farm workers from Delano and MECHA students from San Jose, San Diego, Oakland and San Francisco. Moreover, there were representatives from the Crusade for Justice in Denver, the Alianza in Albuquerque, New Mexico, and MAYA from Texas. The rhetoric at these marches emphasized the need for political action. As one Chicano speaker stated:

This social system is killing our brothers in Vietnam. We have one enemy, the capitalist system and their agents in the Democratic and Republican parties. We must organize independent political parties along with Puerto Ricans including poor whites in a political coalition. The Third World must lead the way because it is the most oppressed. We must control every aspect of our lives.

The Chicano community responded favorably to the march and over 2,000 youths and adults marched in Los Angeles, California.[11]

Concerning the second 'external force"--the political party system-- the Brown Berets have stated that they,

...do not recognize any party that is affiliated with white traditions and white history. The left wing, the right wing, the socialist, the democratic and any other damn foreign ideology has attempted to prostitute the Chicano movement for their own purpose of perpetuating cacosoid (sic) madness. We are Chicanos and we denounce all white foreigners who try to put any other jacket on us. We must denounce all white history and creations in order to create La Vida Nueva de la Raza.[12]

The Brown Berets, as many other youths of high school age who are in the movimiento, favor the concept of a third party in politics--La Raza Unida Party--which would operate within the geographical area of Aztlan (Aztec name for the Southwest).

But the main preoccupation of Chicano high school youths, whether they belong to the Brown Berets or not, has been with "blowouts" (school walk-outs) instead of political activity per se. In fact, the cry of "Blowouts, Baby, Blowouts!" has been the cry which indicates the underlying resentment and discontent that Chicanos have toward the American education system. As one student put it, "It's time for a Mexican Revolution. We've got to stand up and talk straight to the gabachos saying, 'Hell, no! I won't go to your white lousy [school] system.'"[13]

Within the last two years, Chicano youths have staged unprecedented high school demonstrations and walkouts in Los Angeles, Denver, San Antonio, South Texas and other various parts of the Southwest. The objectives of these walkouts are usually demands ranging from wanting Mexican food served in the cafeteria to better sanitary conditions, to more vocational courses, to Chicano studies programs and courses, to bi-lingual education, to more Chicano teachers, to the dismissal of racist teachers and the end of punishment after school for speaking Spanish during school hours. In general, the students protest against the Anglo-orientation of the school system which is irrelevant to them and does not take into account the cultural differences of the Chicano student.[14] Chicano youths, who have been involved in walkouts, including the Brown Berets, have made it clear that education is important to them, but that it is relevant to them mainly as a means to obtain credentials in order to help their community rather than themselves. They do not want to become part of the establishment. They realize that the skills and technical knowledge to help their community must come from those who return from the colleges and universities with a sense of responsibility and commitment. There are those, however, in the barrio who say that "an educated Chicano will be counseled into the white status quo by [his] oppressed wife who believes that advancement and success are only regulated by material property."[15]

The realization that many Chicanos who have completed their university education have not been responsive and committed to helping the community has been acknowledged by Chicanos who are now in college. And they, like the Chicanos at the high school level, are saying "Chale con el sistema gabacha de educacion public." These students believe that it must be realized that the

. . .function of the public and private institutions supported by federal and state monies is not to change Chicano culture as it has turned out in practice . . . [Moreover] education has a social responsibility which links it intimately to the community and to the political scene. The Chicano perspective challenges the Anglo misconceptions of education, of degrees, and of the entire academic scene.[16]

In many of the universities and colleges in the Southwest where Chicanos study, Chicano organizations have been formed. At present most Chicano campus organizations have changed their name to MECHA. This was the first step toward uniting the Chicano campus youth movement. MECHA's function, according to the Plan de Santa Barbara which is the plan for Chicano higher education programs, is "to provide socialization and politicization of Chicano students who are at different levels of awareness on campuses throughout the Southwest."[17] MECHA also has the function of recruiting Chicano students and thereby giving them the opportunity of furthering their education. Moreover, Gaspar Oliviera, Chairman of MECHA at San Diego State College points out that MECHA members

. . . adhere to the concept of self-determination and local control of our communities. . . . We are an extension of the community . . . . Throughout the community MECHA is represented and respected as the voice of the Chicano people at San Diego State College . . . . We cannot separate our ties with the community.[18]

Luis Nogales, special assistant to the president at Stanford University, also stresses the importance of a close working relationship between the MECHA groups and the community. He states,

If the Chicano students, and in fact, the Chicano academic community is to be effective in promoting social change beyond the
university, it must also maintain its identity with the community,
thereby making their efforts more credible. The problem of credibility is not that our communities are anti-intellectual; that is,
a belief of negative opposition to the use of reason and knowledge
to confront social problems, but rather scepticism that so-called
educated persons do not share a concern in the welfare of the
community. There is certainly a need to continue to cultivate
the non-rational, emotional and sentimental aspects of CHI-
CANISMO, the feeling of brotherhood, but there is also a need
for knowledge and analysis; they are not mutually exclusive. It
is clear that Romanticism is not enough to change institutions.
It would be a great loss,however, if in the effort to effectuate
social change we lost or did not cultivate simultaneously our
emotional and sentimental bonds. [19]

These MECHA groups have been and continue to be the essential elements in establishing and maintaining the Chicano studies departments and
programs that now extend throughout the Southwest, and especially in California. The Chicano student, states Rudy Acuna, a historian who is chairman of the Chicano Studies Department at San Fernando State, must be the
controlling factor in the Chicano studies program. [20] But the barrio input
is essential. Community members should serve on the important committees, especially the Chicano Affairs Committee which is usually the governing body of the Chicano program at the university. The idea "that the people own the schools and the schools and their resources are at their service" must clearly be established. [21]

In essence, Chicano studies programs are to educate (politicize) Chicanos, provide them with the skills and techniques needed to manipulate
the economic and political system, preserve the Chicano life style, and
serve as a resource for the Chicano community. In addition, MECHA as
well as the Chicano studies program has the responsibility to show Chicano
students that "the liberation of their people from prejudice and oppression
is more meaningful than personal achievement and advanced degrees especially if they are earned at the expense of their idenity and cultural integ-
rity." This dedication and commitment to the Chicano community can be
developed through a sense of Chicanismo. [22]

Chicanismo is the philosophical base of Mecha. It is the tie that
binds all members of Mecha. Chicanismo implies Carnalismo (fraternity), responsibility, and commitment to all Chicano brothers
and sisters at the University and at the barrio. It further implies
a respect for ourselves as Chicanos, for our history,our culture,
and our values. Chicanismo is the philosophical tie between Chicanos throughtout the Southwest regardless of socio-economic
level. It is a philosophy that is the essence of self-identity, fra-

ternity, and self-determination, a self-determination that is both a basis and an objective in the Chicano movement.

Specifically, Mecha holds to the following principles:

1. All Chicanos are equal whether they are at the barrio or at the university.
2. Self-determination is vital for the existence of the Chicanos.
3. All Chicanos must have commitment and responsibility not only to themselves but to their brothers and sisters whether at the university or the barrio.
4. All Chicanos must work toward ending the social, economic problems and educational inequalities.
5. Unity (with diversity) through organization is vital.
6. Allegiance to the organization is imperative if the Chicano is to accomplish his goals.
7. All Chicanos--rich or poor--must share with their comrades until the struggle is ended. Chicanos must share what they can--time, money, influence, or any other material or intellectual resources available.
8. The people are more important than the government or the organization. The organization exists for the people. Let us work for the people. Policy is made by the leadership, but always with the consent, advice, and concurrence of the membership. The people are the power: policy reflects the needs of the people. Therefore, the most important element in the organization is the people--the membership.
9. While there exists a Chicano who is hungry, while there remains a Chicano who is uneducated, while there remains a Chicano who is discriminated against, the struggle . . . the movimiento will continue--both at the university and the community.[23]

The above principles are from the MECHA organization at the University of Texas at El Paso, but they are very similar to the stated principles and objectives stated in the Plan de Santa Barbara which introduced the concept of MECHA organizations. Therefore, the ideology expressed is valid for the most part to all MECHA organizations.

Although by principle and ideology, the MECHA groups have committed themselves to work in the Chicano barrios, there have been problems, as Luis Nogales pointed out. Chicanos at the university, especially in the Chicano studies programs; are trying to project the idea that the university is only an extension of the Chicano community and not an elevated, superior community. An attempt is also being made by Chicanos in the barrio to rid themselves of the feeling that the Chicano university student is nothing more than a "would-be intellectual patron" or "the new conservative" as Corky Gonzales calls him. Stan Steiner in his book La Raza: Mexican Americans states,

Now the Chicano university students have begun to climb down

from their lonely success to the streets of the barrios and the
fields of the campesinos. They come as on a pilgramage, seeking an identity. Los Angeles Community leader Eduardo Perez
says, "I find that many Mexicans-turned-Spanish are coming
back into the fold and are being identified for what they are:
Mexicans! They now have a 'pride in being Mexican.'"[24]

Besides the Brown Berets and the MECHA university organizations,
there is the powerful MAYO organization (Mexican American Youth Organization) of South Texas. It is an organization which plans to correct Chicano
problems non-violently through politics, education and the establishment of
Chicano-owned businesses. At first this organization was financed by the
Ford Foundation until former MAYO chairman Mario Compean cut off its
ties after Ford Foundation officials asked the group to refrain from political activity.[25] MAYO came into existence in 1967 and most of its work is
in South Texas, but it now has chapters in Minnesota, Illinois, and Michigan. Therefore, according to Compean, it is now a national organization
in scope. One of MAYO's objectives has been to persuade the Catholic
Church to become responsive to the poor since today the Church has neglected La Raza.[26] As Jose Angel Gutierrez, a former MAYO chairman
stated recently,

> As long as it's [the Catholic Church] a business and a corpora-
> tion, there is no hope for social justice. They'd go out and cut
> their own necks if they went in for social justice. Poor people
> can't build cathedrals and support the air-conditioning in those
> guys' [priests'] houses and their new cars. They'd have to go
> out and eat tamales and frijoles and things, and I don't think the
> priests are ready for that even though they've made all kinds of
> vows.[27]

This indictment of the Catholic Church by MAYO is an indication of the
feelings of other Chicano youths in the Southwest who are now demanding
that the Church practice what it preaches--social justice, poverty and
equality. It was for these reasons that a group in California entitled Catolicos Por La Raza recently confronted the Archdiocese of Los Angeles and
demanded: First, the creation of a Commission on Mexican American Affairs, within the hierarchy of the Church, composed of members of the
community, nuns, and priests; second, the use of this commission to obtain
funds for educational programs, housing programs, health programs and
leadership and orientation classes for the Chicanos in the community; third,
the use of Church facilities and "the total power of the Church . . . to implement the aims and policies of the Chicanos involved in their struggle for
liberation against forces of repression." This would involve such struggles
as the farmworkers' strike, the war in Vietnam, the educational struggle
of the Chicanos and the "racist" grand jury of Los Angeles.[28]

Concerning the responsibility of the Church, Cesar Chavez also spoke out. He said, "We do not want more cathedrals, but ask the Catholic Church to sacrifice with the people for social change." The Catolicos Por La Raza added, "The Church must be returned to the people. In the past the bureaucracy of the Church hierarchy has not addressed itself to the grinding poverty of the barrios. To be responsible to the people one serves is one of the most significant of Christian doctrines."[29]

For MAYO, the problem of the Church was minor compared to the task it was going to perform -- to organize an independent political party. MAYO moved toward an independent party position because as Mario Compean stated:

> In Texas, the only viable political strategy is to form an inde-
> pendent Chicano party. It has to be a party that is responsive to
> Chicanos only. In essence, we are pushing an independent politi-
> cal party to lead us to community control of those political insti-
> tutions in areas where we predominate. Educationally, we are
> pushing those school districts toward community control . . .
> [and] we are pushing [certain religious congregations] to turn
> over complete control of the [community] centers which they
> run to the [Chicano] communities which they serve.[30]

MAYO established La Raza Unida Party (the United Chicano People's Party) thereby disassociating itself from the political system it considered oppressive and hypocritical. Then in 1969 Mario Compean, then chairman of MAYO, ran for mayor in San Antonio, Texas, and finished only 200 votes short of a runoff. The fact that he had run on La Raza Unida ticket and on a community control platform and received 56,000 votes out of a total of 165,000 was encouraging especially when it is considered that he was expected to receive only 3,000 votes.[31] Encouraged by this, La Raza Unida Party under the astute leadership of Jose Angel Gutierrez, began registering voters in South Texas with the help of every Chicano available. Then, on April 4, 1970, the slate of La Raza Unida party won the school board elections in Crystal City, Texas. On April 7, 1970, the Chicano party again emerged victorious. This time La Raza Unida candidates won city council elections in three cities. In Carrizo Springs, Rufino Cobello was elected the first Chicano mayor of the city. In Cotulla, Alfredo Zamora was also elected mayor. In both of these cities, La Raza Unida candidates also won city council positions. In Crystal City two La Raza Unida candidates were elected to city council positions.[32]

But, according to Gutierrez, political power must be accompanied by economic power. Complete political control cannot occur without economic control. This can be obtained by organization--organizando la familia Mexicano--(organizing the Mexican families) and this occurs through constant conflict and crisis. Only through community control, via a third party, can the Chicano improve himself because then "you don't have to talk about community control because you are the community."[33]

MAYO therefore, like the Brown Berets, and MECHA seek community participation, community control and emphasize, above everything else, the people. Basically, MAYO seeks political and economic power; MECHA, educational politicalization and the ultimate provision of university-trained Chicanos with a sense of responsibility and commitment, as well as a sense of cultural identity; the Brown Berets seek to protect the barrio from further exploitation by all agencies and institutions and demand, for the Chicanos in the barrio, community control. However, in addition to these three groups, there is Reis Lopez Tijerina and the Alianza.

The Alianza Federal de Los Mercedes (Federal Alliance of Land Grants) or as it was later renamed Alianza de los Pueblos Libres (Alliance of Free City-States) which was incorporated on October 7, 1963, is basically an organization of New Mexico land grant heirs. The Alianza movement is not something new; it was preceded by the Mano Negra (Black Hand) which was a very loosely structured organization of the late 1900's. Its members raided Anglo properties which they felt still belonged to them. Actually, long before Tijerina arrived in New Mexico, individuals and land grant organizations had been testing their claims through the courts. One of these organizations was the Abiquire Corporation, an organization of Tierra Amarilla land grant heirs.[34]

Tijerina, who no longer is president of the Alianza and is serving a prison term, was catapulted into national prominence in 1967 when he and some of his followers became involved in a courthouse gun battle in Tierra Amarilla. The central demand of the Alianza is a call for a thorough investigation of the violations of the guarantees of the Treaty of Guadalupe Hidalgo. The Alianzistas believe that these violations have denied the Hispanos of New Mexico personal and cultural rights as well as property rights.[35] In fact, there have been property losses of over four million acres from which stem many of the problems of the Hispano in New Mexico today.[36]

Specifically, the Alianza charges the United States on two grounds: first, that the United States violated the rights of the land grant heirs by not protecting their property as guaranteed by the Treaty of Guadalupe, Hidalgo; second, that the United States used "questionable" methods to acquire large tracts of the disputed land.[37] In reparation, the Alianza expects group compensation not only for the lands but for all of the profits acquired by the "new owners." This includes payment for all profits and benefits acquired through the addition of livestock, mining, construction, water, and minerals.[38]

But, Tijerina is more than just an advocate of land grant restoral and his movement is more than the nativistic movement Nancie Gonzales claims in her book, The Spanish-Americans of New Mexico. Tijerina, according to Tobias and Woodhouse in their book Minorities in Politics, represents a new style of politics for Hispanos--confrontation--rather than the traditional style of localized politics. It is a style which is transcending the demand for the restoration of lands, and is now a demand for unity--a pan-

ethnic appeal--to Blacks, poor whites and Indians. The Alianza is providing .
a sense of unity based upon an appeal for recognition of a distinctive cultural identity.[39] This is new for Hispanos.

Thus, other Chicanos, especially the youth, have responded to Tijerina's movement because it not only calls for restoration of the Chicano lands,
compliance by the United States with the Treaty of Guadalupe Hidalgo, political confrontations with the establishment, as well as emphasis on cultural identity. In fact, Tijerina is so popular that the Brown Berets of Albuquerque, together with the California Brown Berets, introduced a resolution on the floor of the Chicano youth convention in Denver asking for the
release of Tijerina from jail and, furthermore, making Tijerina the first
official hero of Aztlan.[40]

Reis Lopez Tijerina rivals Rudolfo (Corky) Gonzales, the leader of the
Denver-based Crusade for Justice, who often boasts that he can put together
a protest march "at the drop of a hat."[41] And often he can. He assembled
a crowd estimated at 5,000 for the 16th of September celebration of Mexico's independence in Denver, Colorado.[42]

Gonzales heads the first organization in Denver which is willing to use
militant means to achieve the social and economic improvement of more
than 75,000 Chicanos who now reside in Denver, Colorado. Corky Gonzales
seeks to develop cultural nationalism among Chicanos as the first step toward economic and political control of their own destinies. He claims "the
cause of the Cuban Revolution as his; the slogan venceremos is as much
his as Castro's."[43]

The political system, Gonzales believes, castrates Chicanos; the educational system perverts Chicanos into thinking they are Anglo by giving
them middle class aspirations. In spite of these problems Gonzales believes that the best way to unify Chicanos is through nationalism. To foster this sense of nationalism, the Crusade for Justice has sponsored two
National Chicano Youth Liberation Conferences in Denver. These two conferences, in addition to many speaking tours, have served to spread Gonzales' fame and ideas among the youth of the Southwest.

The first conference, at Denver, Colorado in 1969, was attended by
about 1,000 young Chicanos from the five southwestern states who represented the complete ideological spectrum.[44] From this first conference
emerged two very basic concepts. The first was the concept of Aztlan.
Aztlan was the Aztec name for the five southwestern states where the majority of Chicanos live. Aztlan was the home of the Chicanos before the
conquest by Spain and the United States. In effect, Aztlan is the utopian
state and provides an intellectual framework for liberation. Together with
this concept came the second idea--El Plan Espiritual de Aztlan. The pre-
face read as follows:

El Plan Espiritual de Aztlan sets the theme that the Chicanos (La
Raza Bronze) must use their nationalism as the key or common
denominator for mass mobilization and organization. Once we
are committed to the idea and philosophy of El Plan de Aztlan,

we can only conclude that social, economic, cultural and political
independence is the only road to total liberation from oppression,
exploitation and racism. Our struggle then must be for the control of our barrios, campos, pueblos, lands, our economy, our
culture and our political life. El Plan commits all levels of Chicano society--the barrio, the campo, the ranchero, the writer,
the teacher, the worker, the professional--to La Causa. [45]
The plan then proceeds to outline three main points. First, nationalism is stated to be the key to organization transcending all differences between Chicanos. Then, unity in thought among all Chicanos and economic
control are delineated as organizational goals. Moreover, it is pointed
out that education and control over education are as essential as the control of basic political, social and economic institutions by Chicanos. The
merits of community self-defense and the retention of cultural values are
pointed out. In addition, certain prescribed actions are proposed. One
specific objective listed a call for school walkouts on the 16th of September. Only a mention is made of the establishment of a La Raza political
party. [46]

The second National Chicano Youth Liberation Conference, also at
Denver, was even better attended than the first. Youths from over four-
teen states were present there in 1970. There were Chicanos from the
Southwest and also from such states as Wisconsin, Michigan, Wyoming and
Oregon. In addition, there were Puerto Ricans and Dominicans from New
York and Chicago. Most of the organizations attended: MECHA, UMAS,
MAYO, La Raza Unida Party, Brown Berets, Black Berets, MAPA, Alianza
from El Paso, MAYA. From New York and Chicago came the Young Lords,
the Latin Kings, and the 18th Street Gang. [47]

Out of the conference came certain resolutions that were very impor-
tant--ideologically speaking. The two most important were the resolutions
establishing the nation of Aztlan and an independent La Raza Unida political party with El Plan Espiritual de Aztlan being the platform. Additions
were made to the plan which reflected the ideas of the socialist Chicanos.
(See the plan and additions in the Appendix.) A Congress of the nation of
Aztlan was selected and it was to be the governing body for the party as
well as the body to handle all policy for the Nation of Aztlan. It was further
resolved that the Nation of Aztlan and La Raza Unida party would maintain
- at least for the present time - all of its activities within the United States'
political framework. [48]

Additional resolutions passed: first, that the artists of Aztlan would
establish a national information center (on the arts) in the Crusade for Justice hall and also would hold a National Conference of Los Artistos de
Aztlan. The women (Chicanas) also passed a resolution stating that they
would not separate (pursue women's liberation ideology) but remain and
strengthen Aztlan and the family. Two other resolutions were passed, one
calling for the liberation of all political prisoners in the United States,
Mexico and Latin America, and the other strengthening and affirming ties

between Chicanos and other Latinos. Definite action was also taken in calling for a Chicano Moratorium in August of 1970. In fact, Vietnam was a constant issue during the conference. [49]

El Plan de Aztlan has had quite an impact on Chicano youths, expecially as a rationale and a plan for action. This plan, while it is not totally acceptable to all Chicanos, is still an ideological framework providing for a utopian nation and a program which activates as well as motivates. One of the most important aspects of this ideological construct is the provision of a philosophical basis for unity. This need for a philosophical base or ideological framework is expressed in the following statement issued by a group which called itself the Revolutionary Caucus at Denver's Chicano Youth Liberation Conference:

> We, a non-conquered people living in a conquered land, come together hoping that a plan of liberation, a concrete revolutionary program acceptable to the entire Southwest, will come from this conference. Subjected to a system that has denied our human dignity, our rights are also being denied under a constitution which we have had no part in formulating, but more fundamentally the rights protected under the Gualalupe Hidalgo Treaty which grants the right to cultural autonomy have been violated. [50]

For youths seeking a modus operandi El Plan de Aztlan seemed to be the answer.

In addition to Tijerina and Gonzales, who have had much national exposure, perhaps the symbol best known to thousands in the Chicano movement is the head of the United Farm Workers Organizing Committee, Cesar Chavez. Chavez has organized thousands of farm workers in California and his cause has gained supporters ranging from United States senators to religious groups.

Human dignity and the right of farm workers to organize are the basic issues of the California grape strike, which began in 1965. Farm workers under Chavez' leadership are striking for the right to build a community union of their own. But they must have the basic right of collective bargaining. In order to obtain their demands, the United Farm Workers Organizing Committee has employed the tactic of a consumer boycott. That is, farm workers are asking consumers not to buy grapes and not to shop at stores that sell grapes.

To date, Chavez' Union, the UFWOC, has obtained contracts with over 30 growers guaranteeing that over 44,000 grape acres are now under the union label. The boycott is an international one and is supported by civic and religious groups, trade unions, political leaders, students and consumers all over the world. Such groups and organizations as the AFL-CIO, the United Automobile Workers, the Canadian Labour Congress, the International Confederation of Free Trade Unions, the Consumer Federation of America, the National Consumers League, the World Council of Churches, the National Council of Churches, the Union of American Hebrew Congregations and numerous Catholic bishops have endorsed the boycott. [51]

The United Farm Workers Organizing Committee is committed to the
principles of non-violent change as espoused by Gandhi and Martin Luther
King. Chavez points this out when he says,

Our struggle is not easy. Those who oppose our cause are rich
and powerful and they have many allies in high places. We are
poor. Our allies are few. But we have something the rich do
not own. We have our bodies and spirits and the justice of our
cause as our weapons.

I am convinced that the truest act of courage, the strongest act
of manliness, is to sacrifice ourselves for others in a totally
non-violent struggle for justice. [52]

The strike in Delano is more than a labor struggle. It is more than
an economic struggle. It is a struggle of unification under the banner of
the Virgin of Guadalupe, the cry of raza and the patria (country). Luis
Valdez, founder of the teatro compesino, a guerilla theater group, believes,

Delano is only the beginning of our active search. For the last
hundred years our revolutionary progress has not only been frustrated, it has been totally suppressed. This is a society largely
hostile to our cultural values . . . . The NFWA National Farm
Workers Association is a RADICAL union because it started
and continues to grow. Its store, cafeteria, clinic, garage,
newspaper and weekly meetings have established a sense of
community the Delano farmworker will not relinquish. After
years of isolation in the barrios of Great Valley slum towns
like Delano, after years of living in labor camps and ranches
at the mercy and caprice of growers and contractors, the
Mexican-American farm worker is developing his own ideas
about living in the United States. He wants to be equal with
all the working men of the nation, and he does not mean by the
standard middle class route. We are repelled by the human
disintegration of peoples and culture as they fall apart in this
Great Gringo Melting Pot, and determined that this will not
happen to us . . . Listen to these people farm workers , and
you will hear the first murmurings of revolution. [53]

Although symbolically the center of the Chicano movement, Chavez
has not attempted to be the voice of the urban Chicano. When asked why
he has not tried to be the rallying point for all Chicanos in the Southwest,
Chavez stated that his main problem and preoccupation was the grape strike,
and until that was settled, he would not have any time for other things.
But perhaps, he says, when the grape strike is over . . . . [54]

Unfortunately, may youths will not wait and for them the non-violence
of Chavez is not attractive. As several Chicano youths state,

I see the barrios already full of hate and self-destruction. I see
an educational system doing psychological damage to the Mexican-
American creating a self-identity crisis by refusing to recognize
his rich cultural heritage and by suppressing his language. And

therefore to me, burning a building and rioting is less violent than
what is happening to our youth under a school system that classes
as "retarded and inferior" those with a language difficulty.
Another states,
Basically, people are tired of talking. A confrontation is inevitable. It's not unusual to see people going around with
grenades and TNT. The tension is here; the weapons are here.
The new organizations of ex-cons, addicts and dropouts make
the Brown Berets look like the Boy Scouts.[55]

And so the militants are being pressed on by even more militant youths
while the problems of the Chicano remain basically unchanged.

But even when an observer looks beyond the rhetoric the Chicano community is becoming more interested, more vocal, less patient and more
politically aggressive as Chicano youths push their elders to help them do
what Corky Gonzales has said is of primary importance--making the Chicano community politcally aware, beginning with the family.[56]

Awareness and politicalization are becoming goals for young Chicanos
in an institution few would suspect of interest--the prison. The Chicanos
have always been well represented in two institutions--the armed services,
and the prisons. Today there are Chicano organizations for prisoners
themselves inside the prisons as well as for ex-pintos (ex-convicts) such
as MAYO, outside the prisons.

MAYO is an organization which provides detoxification centers and
half-way houses for ex-pintos in order to enable them to be productive Chicanos working within society for the betterment of their Chicano brothers.[57]
LUCHA (League of United Citizens to Help Addicts) is doing similar work.
LUCHA seeks to provide an organization in which Chicanos help Chicanos
overcome drug problems. LUCHA's basic assumption is that the techniques
of group therapy are not effective for Chicanos. Instead, LUCHA feels that
Chicanos would be more responsive to psycho-drama, counseling, jobs,
reading and writing workshops, and confidence-building clinics. By becoming intensely involved, former addicts would have no time for drugs.[58]

In addition to these two organizations, the pintos also have started
EMPLEO (El Mejicano Preparado, Listo, Educado y Organizado - The
Mexican Prepared, Ready, Educated and Organized) to bring reform to
California's treatment of over 7,000 Spanish-surnamed prisoners.
EMPLEO is philosophically guided by the proposition that Chicano prisoners
will look after their own interest, both inside and outside the prison, by
providing employment, education, better family relations and civic responsibilities. EMPLEO plans to have a comprehensive program within the
prison to prepare Chicano convicts for successful employment upon their
release. The program will be structured and implemented by the pintos
themselves and all of their programs will be bilingual.[59]

The pintos do not only seek to help themselves, but are cognizant of
helping the Chicano community. They hope to "open direct lines of communication with the Chicano community and gain their support in our en-

deavors. We will attempt to influence the Chicano movement with special effort made to influence the Chicano youth from following our footsteps."[60]

Ruben P. Perez, writing in El Noticiero, the EMPLEO newspaper, elaborates on the relationship between the pintos and the Chicano youths:

The Chicano youth, for the post part, demonstrates an acute awareness and sense of having a mission to carry out and a vital and intense concern about his future and the future of this country. He has a questioning mind and spirit and an unquenchable thirst for justice. He welcomes and embraces the brothers and sisters in prisons or on parole. He wants to know why there are so many of us who are enslaved to heroin and in prison. . . . those of us here in prison can learn from those outside and, they in turn, can learn from us.

. . . Our movimiento can be the decisive and determinant factor towards a creative contribution in our lives and for the lives of others as well. Our "Chicanismo" may be "nationalistic in character, but it is humanistic in its fundamental aim and aspiration . . . . We (pintos and non-pintos) must move on to learn and educate ourselves in the political, social, religious and economic structure in which we live. We must move on to learn to distinguish and differentiate between those structures which would oppress and those that would meet our needs." We must learn and become convinced that heroin addiction and being in prison is counter-movement, counter-progress and counter-our cause.[61]

Basically the pintos are trying to unite, better themselves educationally, communicate with the Chicano community in order to prepare themselves and be able to contribute to the Chicano movimiento. As is stated in the EMPLEO newspaper, El Noticero,

We, the Chicanos of the Penal Institutions have but one cuase, the advancement and betterment of our people. Since our efforts can only be limited, because of our incarceration, we must pursue any effort, no matter how small toward our goal. We feel that our chief goal at present is to better ourselves in training and education, so that we may be more of an asset to our cause when we are released from custody.[62]

The Chicano movement with its constellation of groups has given birth to an ideology. In the future this ideology may incorporate other ideologies, but the importance is that in the movimiento, especially from within the groups that have been discussed, a belief system or value system is clearly evident. This ideology includes a program for the defense or reform or abolition of important social institutions, definite major values, a normative relationalization of group interest, a body of social documents, heroes, and a definite theory of the nature of man.

REFERENCES

1. Report of the National Advisory Commission on Civil Disorders (Washington, D.C.: Government Printing Office, 1968), pp. 203-61.

2. A.K. Bierman and James A. Gould, Philosophy for a New Generation (London: The Macmillan Company, 1970), p. 260.

3. La Causa, December 16, 1969, p. 4.

4. Newsweek, June 29, 1970, pp. 22-28.

5. Octavio Paz, Labyrinth of Solitude: Life and Thought in Mexico (New York: Grove Press, 1961), p 14.

6. Stan Steiner, La Raza: The Mexican Americans (New York: Harper and Row, 1970), p. 235.

7. Brown Beret Newsletter, January, 1969, Sacramento, California

8. La Causa, May 22, 1970, p. 6.

9. Brown Beret Newsletter, January, 1969, Sacramento, California.

10. La Causa, May 22, 1970, p. 6

11. El Gallo, Denver-Aztlan, 1970, p. 9.

12. La Causa, May 22, 1970, p. 7

13. John Rechy, "No Mananas for Today's Chicano," Saturday Review, March 14, 1970, pp. 31-34.

14. Denver Post, May 14, 1969, p. 4AA; San Jose Mercury News, August 24, 1969, p. 1F; and El Machete, July 5, 1968, San Jose, California, p. 7.

15. Bronze, March, 1969, Oakland, California, p. 5.

16. Chicanismo, April 9, 1970, Mecha, Stanford University, p. 4.

17. Plan de Santa Barbara, Chicano Plan for Higher Education (Oakland: La Causa, 1969), p. 54.

18. La Raza Habla, San Diego State College, MECHA Special Issue, April 27, 1970, p. 1.

19. Luis Nogales, "Chicanismo and Education: Building a Better World," Chicanismo, MECHA, Stanford University, June, 1970, p. 4.

20. Rudy Acuna, Lecture at Stanford University, July 10, 1970.

21. Plan de Santa Barbara, p. 60.

22. Ibid, pp. 54-57.

23. MECHA Constitution, University of Texas at El Paso, El Paso, Texas.

24. Stan Steiner, La Raza, p. 236.

25. San Jose Mercury News, August 24, 1969, p. 4F.

26. The Militant, March 27, 1970, p. 8.

27. The Militant, June 5, 1970, p. 4.

28. Catolicos Por La Raza Newsletter (n.d.): and La Causa, December 16, 1969, p. 4.

29. La Causa, December 16, 1969, p. 4.

30. The Militant, March 27, 1970, p. 8.

31. Ibid., p. 9.

32. Ibid., June 19, 1970, p. 9.

33. Jose Angel Gutierrez, Lecture at Soledad Prison, July 3, 1970; and The Militant, June 19, 1970, p. 13.

34. Michael Jenkinson, Tijerina: Land Grant Conflict in New Mexico (Paisano Press: Albuquerque, New Mexico, 1968), pp. 41, 50.

35. Francis L. Swadesh, "The Alianza Movement in New Mexico," in Minorities and Politics, Henry J. Tobias and Charles E. Woodhouse (eds.) (Albuquerque: University of New Mexico Press., 1969), p. 55.

36. John H. Burma, Spanish Speaking Groups in the United States (Durham, North Carolina: Duke University), p. 16.

37. The Socio-Economic Studies Foundation, Pre-Conditions for Social Unrest: A Special Survey of Northern New Mexico for the Office of the Governor (unpublished report), p. 7.

38. "Constitucion Nacional de la Alianza Federal de Mercedes, " Capitulo VI, Article VI, pagina 9 in Nancie Goncales' The Spanish-American of New Mexico: A Heritage of Pride (Albuquerque: University of New Mexico Press, 1967), p. 100.

39. Tobias, Minorities and Politics, pp. 10-11.

40. La Causa, May 22, 1970, p. 3.

41. San Jose Mercury News, August 24, 1969, p. 4F.

42. Denver Post, September 17, 1969, p. 20.

43. Ramon Eduardo Ruiz, "Another Defector from the Gringo World, " New Republic, Vol. CLIX, No. 4, July 27, 1968, p. 11.

44. Denver Post, May 14, 1969, p. 4AA.

45. The Program of El Plan Espiritual De Aztlan (mimeographed), p. 1.

46. Ibid., pp. 2, 3.

47. The Militant, April 10, 1970, p. 4; and People's World, April 4, 1970, pp. 1, 2.

48. Resolution Sheet, Chicano Conference, Politics Workshop Chairman, Liz Montoya, March 26, 1970. (Mimeographed.)

49. Los Artistas De Aztlan, Workshop Report of the National Liberation Conference, March 27, 1970 (mimeographed); El Grito Del Norte, April 29, 1970, p. 6; and People's World, April 4, 1970, pp. 1, 2.

50. Statement of the Revolutionary Caucus at Denver's Chicano Youth Liberation Conference, p, 1. (Mimeographed.)

51. El Malcriado: The Voice of the Farm Worker, January 1-31, 1970, Vol. III, No. 18, Delano California, pp. 5, 11. (The grape strike has terminated and Chavez has now turned to organizing the workers in other fields, for example, lettuce workers.

52. El Malcriado: The Voice of the Farm Worker, "Our Commitment to Non-Violence, " January 1-31, 1970, Vol. III, No. 18, p. 17; and Vol. III, No. 23, April 15, 1970, Delano, California, pp. 7, 9.

53. Luis Valdez, "Quien es La Raza," Bronze, November 25, 1968, Oakland. (Italics in quote are Valdez's.)

54. Interview with Cesar Chavez, by Richard Garcia, December 5, 1969, in El Paso, Texas.

55. Denver Post, May 14, 1969, p. 5AA

56. Corky Gonzales, speech at Stanford University, April 15, 1970.

57. Conversation with ex-pinto who was a MAYA member, June 6, 1970, El Paso, Texas.

58. "Convictos Latinos Reforman Prisiones," Bronze, April, 1969, p. 14.

59. Ibid.

60. La Voz Del Chicano, June 29, 1970, Latin American Culture Group, North Soledad Prison, Soledad, California, p. 1.

61. Ruben P. Perez, "Chicano Nationalism: Positive or Negative," El Noticiero, EMPLEO por La Unidad, Inc., Department of Correction, Vacaville, California, Vol. I, No. 5, January, February and March, pp. 4-7.

62. Ibid, p. 12.

WOMEN: NEW VOICE OF LA RAZA
by Mirta Vidal

Mirta Vidal's article postulates that Chicanas are oppressed as women, as part of an ethnic group and as workers. Consequently, they have responded with a feminist and nationalist consciousness, although, not yet with a worker's consciousness. Following her article are the Resolutions of the First National Chicana Conference which provides "empirical" evidence in support of Vidal's premises.

Source: Reprinted by permission of Pathfinder Press, Inc., and reprinted by permission of the International Socialist Review, copyright 1971 International Socialist Review.

At the end of May 1971, more than 600 Chicanas met in Houston, Texas, to hold the first national conference of Raza women. For those of us who were there it was clear that this conference was not just another national gathering of the Chicano movement.

Chicanas came from all parts of the country inspired by the prospect of discussing issues that have long been on their minds and which they now see not as individual problems but as an important and integral part of a movement for liberation.

The resolutions coming out of the two largest workshops, "Sex and the Chicana" and "Marriage — Chicana Style," called for "free, legal abortions and birth control for the Chicano community, controlled by *Chicanas*." As Chicanas, the resolution stated, "we have a right to control our own bodies." The resolutions also called for "24-hour child-care centers in Chicano communities" and explained that there is a critical need for these since "Chicana motherhood should not preclude educational, political, social and economic advancement."

While these resolutions articulated the most pressing needs of Chicanas today, the conference as a whole reflected a rising consciousness of the Chicana about her special oppression in this society.

With their growing involvement in the struggle for Chicano liberation and the emergence of the feminist movement, Chicanas are beginning to challenge every social institution which contributes to and is responsible for their oppression, from inequality on the job to their role in the home. They are questioning "machismo," discrimination in education, the double standard, the role of the Catholic Church, and all the backward ideology designed to keep women subjugated.

This growing awareness was illustrated by a survey taken at

the Houston conference. Reporting on this survey, an article in the Los Angeles magazine *Regeneración* stated: "84% felt that they were not encouraged to seek professional careers and that higher education is not considered important for Mexican women . . . 84% agreed that women do not receive equal pay for equal work." The article continued: "On one question they were unanimous. When asked: Are married women and mothers who attend school expected to also do the housework, be responsible for childcare, cook and do the laundry while going to school, 100% said yes. 88% agreed that a social double standard exists."[1] The women were also asked if they felt that there was discrimination toward them within La Raza: 72% said yes, *none* said no and 28% voiced no opinion.

While polls are a good indicator of the thoughts and feelings of any given group of people, an even more significant measure is what they are actually doing. The impressive accomplishments of Chicanas in the last few months alone are a clear sign that Chicanas will not only play a leading role in fighting for the liberation of La Raza, but will also be consistent fighters against their own oppression as Chicanas, around their own specific demands and through their own Chicana organizations.

Last year, the women in MAPA (Mexican-American Political Association) formed a caucus at their annual convention. A workshop on women was also held at a Latino Conference in Wisconsin last year. All three Chicano Youth Liberation Conferences — held in 1969, 1970, and 1971 in Denver, Colorado — have had women's workshops.

In May of this year, women participating at a Statewide Boycott Conference called by the United Farm Workers Organizing Committee in Castroville, Texas, formed a caucus and addressed the conference, warning men that sexist attitudes and opposition to women's rights can divide the farmworker's struggle. Also in May, Chicanas in Los Angeles organized a regional conference attended by some 250 Chicanas, in preparation for the Houston conference and to raise funds to send representatives from the Los Angeles area.

Another gathering held last year by the Mexican American National Issues Conference in Sacramento, California, included a women's workshop that voted to become the Comision Feminil Mexicana (Mexican Feminine Commission) and function as an independent organization affiliated to the Mexican American National Issues Conference. They adopted a resolution which read in part: "The effort of Chicana/Mexican women in the Chicano movement is generally obscured because women are not accepted as community leaders either by the Chicano movement or by the Anglo establishment."

In Pharr, Texas, women have organized pickets and demonstrations to protest police brutality and to demand the ousting
of the city's mayor. And even in Crystal City, Texas, where La
Raza Unida Party has won major victories, women have had
to organize on their own for the right to be heard. While the men
constituted the decision-making body of Ciudadanos Unidos
(United Citizens) — the organization of the Chicano community
of Crystal City — the women were organized into a women's auxiliary — Ciudadanas Unidas. Not satisfied with this role, the women
got together, stormed into one of the meetings, and demanded
to be recognized as members on an equal basis. Although the vote
was close, the women won.

The numerous articles and publications that have appeared recently on La Chicana are another important sign of the rising
consciousness of Chicanas. Among the most outstanding of these
are a special section in *El Grito del Norte,* an entire issue dedicated to and written by Chicanas published by *Regeneración,*
and a regular Chicana feminist newspaper put out by Las Hijas
de Cuahtemoc in Long Beach, California. This last group and
its newspaper are named after the feminist organization of Mexican women who fought for emancipation during the suffragist
period in the early part of this century.

These developments, by no means exhaustive of what Chicanas
have done in this last period, are plainly contradictory to the
statement made by women participating in the 1969 Denver Youth
Conference. At that time a workshop held to discuss the role of
women in the movement reported to the conference: "It was the
consensus of the group that the Chicana woman does not want
to be liberated." Although there are still those who maintain that
Chicanas not only do not want to be liberated, but do not *need*
to be liberated, Chicanas themselves have decisively rejected that
attitude through their actions.

In part, this awakening of Chicana consciousness has been
prompted by the "machismo" she encounters in the movement.
It is adequately described by one Chicana, in an article entitled
"Macho Attitudes":

> When a freshman male comes to MECHA [Movimiento Estudiantil
> Chicano de Aztlan — a Chicano student organization in California],
> he is approached and welcomed. He is taught by observation that
> the Chicanas are only useful in areas of clerical and sexual activ-
> ities. When something must be done there is always a Chicana
> there to do the work. "It is her place and duty to stand behind
> and back up her Macho!" . . . Another aspect of the MACHO at-
> titude is their lack of respect for Chicanas. They play their games,
> plotting girl against girl for their own benefit. . . . They use the
> movement and Chicanismo to take her to bed. And when she re-

fuses, she is a *vendida* [sell-out] because she is not looking after the welfare of her men.[2]

This behavior, typical of Chicano men, is a serious obstacle to women anxious to play a role in the struggle for Chicano liberation.

The oppression suffered by Chicanas is different from that suffered by most women in this country. Because Chicanas are part of an oppressed nationality, they are subjected to the racism practiced against La Raza. Since the overwhelming majority of Chicanos are workers, Chicanas are also victims of the exploitation of the working class. But in addition, Chicanas, along with the rest of women, are relegated to an inferior position because of their sex. Thus, Raza women suffer a triple form of oppression: as members of an oppressed nationality, as workers, *and* as women. Chicanas have no trouble understanding this. At the Houston conference 84 percent of the women surveyed felt that "there is a distinction between the problems of the Chicana and those of other women."

On the other hand, they also understand that the struggle now unfolding against the oppression of women is not only relevant to them, but *is* their struggle.

Because sexism and male chauvinism are so deeply rooted in this society, there is a strong tendency, even within the Chicano movement, to deny the basic right of Chicanas to organize around their own concrete issues. Instead they are told to stay away from the women's liberation movement because it is an "Anglo thing."

We need only analyze the origin of male supremacy to expose this false position. The inferior role of women in society does not date back to the beginning of time. In fact, before the Europeans came to this part of the world women enjoyed a position of equality with men. The submission of women, along with institutions such as the church and the patriarchy, was imported by the European colonizers, and remains to this day part of Anglo society. Machismo — in English, "male chauvinism" — is the one thing, if any, that should be labeled an "Anglo thing."

When Chicano men oppose the efforts of women to move against their oppression, they are actually opposing the struggle of every woman in this country aimed at changing a society in which Chicanos themselves are oppressed. They are saying to 51 percent of this country's population that they have no right to fight for their liberation.

Moreover, they are denying one half of La Raza this basic right. They are denying Raza women, who are triply oppressed, the right to struggle around their specific, real, and immediate needs.

In essence, they are doing just what the white male rulers of this country have done. The white male rulers want Chicanas to accept their oppression because they understand that when Chicanas begin a movement demanding legal abortions, child care, and equal pay for equal work, this movement will pose a real threat to their ability to rule.

Opposition to the struggles of women to break the chains of their oppression is not in the interest of the oppressed but only in the interest of the oppressor. And that is the logic of the arguments of those who say that Chicanas do not want to or need to be liberated.

The same problem arose when the masses of people in this country began to move in opposition to the war in Vietnam. Because Black people did not until recently participate in massive numbers in antiwar demonstrations, the bourgeois media went on a campaign to convince us that the reason Blacks were not a visible component of these demonstrations was because the antiwar movement was a "white thing." Although, for a while, this tactic was successful in slowing down the progress of the Black nationalist movement, for whom the question of the war is of vital importance, Black antiwar activity is now clearly rising.

But once again the white males who run this country are up to their old tricks. Only this time around it is the women's liberation movement which is a "white thing." Again, the bourgeois media is a key tool for perpetrating this myth. As one Chicana explains, in an article entitled "Chicanas Speak Out" in *Salsipuedes,* published in Santa Barbara, California: "The real issue of the women's liberation movement is fighting the established female role in society which has kept women enslaved as human beings. But the news media portrays women's liberation people as karate-chopping, man-hating hippies."3

Among the many distortions about the feminist movement is the argument that women are simply fighting against men. One such statement appeared in an article by Enriqueta Vasquez some months ago in *El Grito del Norte.* Vasquez wrote:

> In looking at women's lib [sic] we see issues that are relevant to that materialistic, competitive society of the Gringo. This society is only able to function through the sharpening of wits and development of the human instinct of rivalry. For this same dominant society and mentality to arrive at a point where there is now a white women's liberation movement is *dangerous* and *cruel* in that that social structure has reached the point of fracture and competition of the male and female.

Thus, since the feminist movement is "antimale," when Chicanas attempt to organize against their own oppression they are accused of trying to divide the Chicano movement.

The appeal for "unity" based on the continued submission of women is a false one. While it is true that the unity of La Raza is the basic foundation of the Chicano movement, when Chicano men talk about maintaining La Familia and the "cultural heritage" of La Raza, they are in fact talking about maintaining the age-old concept of keeping the woman barefoot, pregnant, and in the kitchen. On the basis of the subordination of women there can be no real unity.

This attitude is vividly illustrated in an article entitled "El Movimiento and the Chicana" which explains:

> The political and economical struggle of the Chicana is the universal question of women. The difference between the liberation of Chicana women and other Third World women is cultural. The Chicano culture has very positive effects and very bad ones. We have to fight a lot of Catholic ideas in our homes and in the movement. For example, the idea of large families is very Catholic. The Pope says no birth control, abortions, lots of kids (and make me richer). So what do the guys say in the movement, have lots of kids, keep up the traditional Chicano family. [4]

The point is made even clearer by Francisca Flores in the issue of *Regeneración* cited earlier when she says: "The issue of birth control, abortions, information on sex and the pill are considered 'white' women's lib issues and should be rejected by Chicanas according to the Chicano philosophy which believes that the Chicana women's place is in the home and that her role is that of a mother with a large family. Women who do not accept this philosophy are charged with betrayal of 'our culture and heritage.' OUR CULTURE HELL!"[5]

Far from turning their anger and frustrations against individual men, what Chicanas, and all women, are saying is that men should support their struggles. This, too, has been repeatedly expressed by Chicanas. For example, an editorial in *Regeneración* says in part:

> It is hoped that women who disagree with any aspect of the new role of the Chicana will be willing to discuss the issue or the difference of opinion within the group. This is the only way many of the questions will be dealt with. Primarily . . . that the Chicana feminist movement is not antimen! The Comision Femenil Mexicana in California welcomes men members — but the men who have joined to date are men not threatened by women. Rather, they represent a small but growing nucleus who recognize and appreciate the power of women in action. [5]

The only real unity between men and women is the unity forged in the course of struggle against their oppression. And it is by supporting, rather than opposing, the struggles of women that Chicanos and Chicanas can genuinely unite.

Stripped of all rationalizations, when Chicanos deny support to the independent organization of Chicanas, what they are saying is simply that Chicanas are not oppressed. And that is the central question we must ask: are Chicanas oppressed?

All other arguments aside, the fact is that Chicanas *are* oppressed and that the battles they are now waging and will wage in the future, are for things they need: the right to legal abortions, the right to adequate child care, the right to contraceptive information and devices, the right to decide how many children they do or do not want to have. In short, the right to control their own bodies. As Flores points out:

> Mexican women who bear (large) families beyond the economic ability to support them, suffer the tortures of damnation when their children die of malnutrition, of tuberculosis and other illnesses which wipe out families in poverty stricken or marginal communities in the Southwest. . . . IF A WOMAN WANTS A LARGE FAMILY . . . NO ONE WILL INTERFERE WITH HER RIGHT TO HAVE ONE . . . even if they cannot personally afford it . . . that is their right. However, to stipulate this right as a tenet of La Causa for all women of La Raza is to play a dangerous game with the movement. It means — stripped of its intellectual romanticism — that Chicanas are being condemned to wash diapers and stay home all of their youth. 6

She goes on to say, "As stated before, the question of large families is the choice each person or family will make for themselves. That is their inalienable right. A woman who wants a large family should not be denied. *What we are saying is that the woman should have the right to participate in making that decision.*"7

At the National Abortion Action Conference held in New York in July, a Third World Women's Workshop, attended by close to fifty Blacks, Asian-Americans, Chicanas, and Latinas, voted unanimously to support the national abortion campaign and passed a resolution which reads in part:

> There is a myth that Third World women do not want to control our bodies, that we do not want the right to contraception and abortion. But we know that Third World women have suffered the most because of this denial of our rights and will continue to suffer as long as the antiabortion laws remain on the books. We know that more Third World women die every year from illegal back-street abortions than the rest of the female population. We know that Third World women are the first victims of forced sterilization. And we know that we intend to fight for our freedom as women.

Coupled with this campaign to repeal all abortion laws, women are fighting to end all forced sterilizations, a campaign in which

Chicanas will play a central role. This demand is of key importance to Chicanas who are the victims of forced sterilizations jus-
tified by the viciously racist ideology that the problems of La
Raza are caused by Raza women having too many babies.

In line with other brutal abuses of women, Chicanas have been
used as guinea pigs for experimentation with contraception. This
was done recently in San Antonio by a doctor who wanted to
test the reaction of women to birth control pills. Without inform-
ing them or asking their opinion, he gave some of the women
dummy pills (placebos) that would not prevent conception, and
as a result some of the women became pregnant. When questioned
about his action, his reply was: "If you think you can explain
a placebo test to women like these you never met Mrs. Gomez
from the West Side."

The feminist movement today provides a vehicle for organizing
against and putting an end to such racist, sexist practices. And
that is what women are talking about when they talk about wom-
en's liberation.

Another essential fight that Chicanas have begun is around
the need for adequate child care. While billions of dollars are
spent yearly by this government on war, no money can be found
to alleviate the plight of millions of women who, in addition to
being forced to work, have families to care for.

The following figures poignantly demonstrate the seriousness
of this problem and the pressing need for adequate child-care
facilities. Nancy Hicks, writing in the November 30, 1970, *New
York Times,* reports: "There are more than 11.6 million working
mothers in the country today, more than 4 million of these with
children under 6 years old. However, only 640,000 licensed day-
care spaces are available. More than one-third of these are pri-
vately run." These figures do not include the women who, because
of lack of child care, are unable to work and are therefore pushed
onto the welfare rolls. In addition, although such figures are not
available for Raza women specifically, it is safe to assume that
they are much higher.

Demands such as twenty-four hour child-care centers financed
by the government and controlled by the community, are the kinds
of concrete issues that Chicanas are fighting for. As Chicanas
explain in "A Proposal for Childcare," published in *Regeneración,*
"Child care must be provided as a public service, like public
schools, unemployment insurance, social security, and so forth.
The potential for a mass movement around this initiative is clear."[8]

An important aspect of the struggles of Chicanas is the demand
that the gains made through their campaigns be *controlled by
Chicanas.* The demand for community control is a central axis
of the Chicano liberation struggle as a whole. Thus, when Chicanas, as Chicanas, raise demands for child-care facilities, abor-

tion clinics, etc., controlled by Chicanas, their fight is an integral part of the Chicano liberation struggle.

When Chicanas choose to organize into their own separate organizations, they are not turning away from La Causa or waging a campaign against men. They are saying to Chicanos: "We are oppressed as Chicanas and we are moving against our oppression. Support our struggles." The sooner that Chicanos understand the need for women to struggle around their own special demands, through their own organizations, the further La Raza as a whole will be on the road toward liberation.

It is important to keep in mind that many of the misunderstandings that have arisen so far in the Chicano movement regarding Chicanas are due primarily to the newness of this development, and many will be resolved through the course of events. One thing, however, is clear — Chicanas are determined to fight. As Flores states, the issue of equality and freedom for the Chicana "is *not negotiable*. Anyone opposing the right of women to organize into their own form of organization has no place in the leadership of the movement. FREEDOM IS FOR EVERYONE."9

In the spirit of Las Adelitas, Las Hijas de Cuahtemoc, and all the unrecognized Mexican women who fought valiantly for their rights, who formed their own feminist organizations, and who fought and died in the Mexican revolution, Chicanas in this country will take the center stage in the advances of La Raza.

The struggle for women's liberation is the Chicana's struggle, and only a strong independent Chicana movement, as part of the general women's liberation movement and as part of the movement of La Raza, can ensure its success.

FOOTNOTES

1. *Regeneracion,* Vol. I, No. 10, 1971, p. 3.
2. *Las Hijas de Cuahtemoc,* unnumbered edition, p. 9.
3. *Salsipuedes,* Vol. I, No. 5, p. 4.
4. *La Raza,* Vol. I, No. 6, p. 41.
5. *Regeneracion, op. cit.,* p. 1.
6. *Ibid.*
7. *Ibid.,* p. 2.
8. *Ibid.,* p. 11.
9. *Ibid.,* inside cover.

Statement by Elma Barrera*

I have been told that the Chicana's struggle is not the same as the white woman's struggle. I've been told that the problems are different and that . . . the Chicana's energies are needed in the barrio and that being a feminist and fighting for our rights as women and as human beings is anti-Chicano and anti-male.

But let me tell you what being a Chicana means in Houston, Texas. It means learning how to best please the men in the Church and the men at home, not in that order.

You know, it's really funny the way that the Church has . . . grasped onto this "sinful" thing about abortion and birth control. It's really funny how the laws only apply to the woman and not to the man. . . . Chicano men . . . fool around, have mistresses, and yet, when it comes to abortion or birth control with their wives, it's a sin. . . .

I will take just one minute to read the two resolutions which came out of the Sex and the Chicana workshop: "Free, legal abortions and birth control for the Chicano community, controlled by the Chicanas. As Chicanas, we have the right to control our own bodies."

And then out of the workshop on Marriage: Chicana style . . . : "We as *mujeres de La Raza* recognize the Catholic Church as an oppressive institution and do hereby resolve to break away and not to go to them to bless our union. So be it resolved that the national Chicana conference go on record as supporting free and legal abortions for all women who want or need them."

*Organizer of First National Chicana Conference, Houston, Texas, May 1971.

Workshop Resolutions—
First National Chicana Conference

May 1971

SEX AND THE CHICANA

We feel that in order to provide an effective measure to correct
the many sexual hangups facing the Chicano community the following resolutions should be implemented:

I. Sex is good and healthy for both Chicanos and Chicanas
and we must develop this attitude.

II. We should destroy the myth that religion and culture control
our sexual lives.

III. We recognize that we have been oppressed by religion and
that the religious writing was done by *men* and interpreted by
men. Therefore, for those who desire religion, they should interpret their Bible, or Catholic rulings according to their own feelings, what they think is right, without any guilt complexes.

IV. Mothers should teach their sons to respect women as human
beings who are equal in every respect. *No double standard.*

V. Women should go back to the communities and form discussion and action groups concerning sex education.

VI. Free, legal abortions and birth control for the Chicano community, controlled by *Chicanas.* As Chicanas we have the right
to control our own bodies.

VII. Make use of church centers, neighborhood centers and any
other place available.

"Liberate your mind and the body will follow. . . ."

*"A quitarnos todos nuestros complejos sexuales para tener una
vida mejor y feliz"* (Let's cast off all our sexual complexes to
have a better and happier life).

MARRIAGE-CHICANA STYLE

Reaffirmation that Chicano marriages are the beginnings of Chicano families which perpetuate our culture and are the foundation of the movement.

Points brought up in the workshop:

1. Chicano Marriages are individual and intimate and solutions to problems must be primarily handled on an individual basis.
2. A woman must educate and acquaint herself with outside issues and personal problems (sexual hangups, etc.).
3. It is the responsibility of Chicanas with families to educate their sons and thus change the attitudes of future generations.
4. Chicanas should understand that Chicanos face oppression and discrimination, but this does not mean that the Chicana should be a scapegoat for the man's frustrations.
5. With involvement in the movement, marriages must change. Traditional roles for Chicanas are not acceptable or applicable.

RESOLUTIONS:

I. We, as *mujeres de La Raza,* recognize the Catholic Church as an oppressive institution and do hereby resolve to break away and not go to it to bless our unions.

II. Whereas: Unwanted pregnancies are the basis of many social problems, and

Whereas: The role of Mexican-American women has traditionally been limited to the home, and

Whereas: The need for self-determination and the right to govern their own bodies is a necessity for the freedom of all people, therefore,

BE IT RESOLVED: That the National Chicana Conference go on record as supporting free family planning and free and legal abortions for all women who want or need them.

III. Whereas: Due to socio-economic and cultural conditions, Chicanas are often heads of households, i. e., widows, divorcees, unwed mothers, or deserted mothers, or must work to supplement family income, and

Whereas: Chicana motherhood should not preclude educational, political, social, and economic advancement, and

Whereas: There is a critical need for a 24-hour child-care center in Chicano communities, therefore,

BE IT RESOLVED: That the National Chicana Conference go on record as recommending that every Chicano community promote and set up 24-hour day-care facilities, and that it be further resolved that these facilities will reflect the concept of La Raza as the united family, and on the basis of brotherhood (La Raza), so that men, women, young and old assume the responsibility for the love, care, education, and orientation of all the children of Aztlán.

IV. Whereas: Dr. Goldzieher of SWRF has conducted an experiment on Chicana women of westside San Antonio, Texas, using a new birth control drug, and

Whereas: No human being should be used for experimental purposes, therefore,

BE IT RESOLVED: That this Conference send telegrams to the American Medical Association condemning this act. Let it also be resolved that each Chicana women's group and each Chicana present at the conference begin a letter writing campaign to:

> Dr. Joseph Goldzieher
> c/o SW Foundation for Research
> & Education
> San Antonio, Texas
> and
> Director
> SW Foundation for Research and
> Education
> San Antonio, Texas

RELIGION

I. Recognize the *Plan de Aztlán*

II. Take over already existing Church resources for community use, i.e., health, Chicano awareness — public information of its resources, etc.

III. Oppose any institutionalized religion.

IV. Revolutionary change of Catholic Church or for it to get out of the way.

V. Establish communication with the barrio and implement programs of awareness to the Chicano movement.

OAKLAND AREA RAZA UNIDA PARTY PROGRAM
Raza Unida Parties have been organized throughout the Southwest since 1969. While these political parties differ in each locality, the essence of
their political direction and demands are captured
within the Oakland, California party program.

Source: Documents of the Chicano Struggle
Pathfinder Press, Inc.

Oakland Area
RAZA UNIDA PARTY PROGRAM
Preamble

I. When we begin to illuminate and examine the so-called "dark
chapters" in the history of this nation, the most affluent and powerful nation in the world, we see that the history of La Raza is to
be found therein, and that from the beginning, the United States
used the labor of our people to build not only the Southwest but
this entire country and to amass fortunes for the Anglo exploiters
of our people.

We examine further. We see that our lands were stolen from us.
We see that the only payment was in poverty, starvation, disease,
racist mockeries made of our language and culture and race.
This was the payment for the labor which our people put into
the building of this country, for the lands that were unjustly stolen
from us. This country has seen fit to use and brutalize our people
and to attempt at the same time to trick us into thinking that
it bears no responsibility for our oppression and that its greatest
desire is to help us. The two political parties in this country, and
particularly the Democratic Party, have been the primary tools
of our oppression.

Because we see through the trickery of the Democratic and Republican politicians and see that these two political parties have
completely failed us in their promises and understand that in reality they have been working for the benefit of the wealthy Anglos
by furthering and perpetuating the oppression of our people;

Because our people are still starving, are still being miseducated,
are being increasingly brutalized by police authority;

Because poverty and death from curable diseases are still ram-
pant among our people;

Because our people are not given the benefit of the justice that
is due them as citizens of this land and therefore fill the jails in
outrageous numbers;

Because the denial of education and job opportunities to our
women has placed them in an even more oppressed situation than
the men of La Raza;

And because this total, racist oppression of our people is an
integral part of an economic system which uses as its political

arm the two-party system, two parties working for the same wealthy few, two parties between which there is no significant difference in our eyes;

Given that these factors of oppression form the common denominator that unites us, THEREFORE, WE THE PEOPLE OF LA RAZA, have decided to reject the existing political parties of our oppressors and take it upon ourselves to form LA RAZA UNIDA PARTY, which will serve as a unifying force in our struggle for self-determination.

We understand that our real liberation and freedom will only come about through independent political action on our part. Independent political action, of which electoral activity is but one aspect, means involving La Raza Unida Party at all levels of struggle in actions which will serve to involve and educate our people. We recognize that self-determination can only come about through the full and total participation of La Raza in the struggle.

Because of the cultural genocide committed against our indigenous population by an outside invader and in full recognition of the daily oppression, humiliation, degradation, psychological and spiritual assassination, economic exploitation and the continuing misery of our people in violation of their basic constitutional and human rights, we consider it not only our right but our obligation to struggle for our full and complete liberation by any means necessary.

These oppressive conditions that form the common denominator that unites us give rise to a spiritual cohesiveness, a collective consciousness, that forms the basis of RAZA NATIONALISM.

We further specify that although the protection of our culture and the continuing maintenance of it will be a necessary part of our struggle, we recognize that our culture alone cannot produce our freedom and that only an organized and protracted struggle, confronting our oppressors at every level and involving the greatest number of our people, can bring about our goal of complete self-determination and total freedom.

II. La Raza Unida Party will not support any candidate of the Democratic or Republican Party or any individual who supports these parties.

III. Membership: Any person of La Raza registered in La Raza Unida Party and/or who works actively to support the program and activities of the party will be considered a member with the right to participate in all decision-making processes of the party on the basis of one person, one vote.

By "La Raza" we mean those people who are descendants of or come from Mexico, Central America, South America, and the Antilles.

Program

I. Political Platform

DOMESTIC POLICY

A. La Raza will no longer tolerate that its people be used as instruments of repression against Third World people (armed forces and police). End the draft and exempt all Raza youth from military service.

B. Full equality of the Spanish language: This includes all federal, state, municipal, and private agencies which must provide and carry out all functions within our community in English and Spanish.

C. La Raza Unida Party feels it is of the utmost importance to struggle for the concept of Community Control. By this we mean Community Control over all institutions of the community — schools, hospitals, libraries, welfare agencies, police, etc., that affect La Raza.

    1. The community must control all money, government or private, "with no strings attached" that will be allocated for La Raza and its community.

    2. La Raza Unida Party calls for the establishment of councils of La Raza to administer all institutions within our community. All councils will be democratically elected by the community.

D. La Raza Unida Party calls upon the community to break with the two-party system (Democratic-Republican) which has been one of the key instruments in the oppression of La Raza.

E. The constitutional right of farmworkers to organize their union and formulate their own demands must be respected.

F. La Raza Unida Party supports the struggles of all Third World peoples in the U. S.

G. La Raza Unida Party supports all attempts by the American working class to organize and struggle independently for their well-being.

H. All Raza people 18 years of age or older must have the constitutional right to vote be they felons, immigrants, or nationals.

I. La Raza Unida Party demands that the pollution of our environment halt. La Raza Unida Party takes the position that the pollution of our environment is a crime against our people.

That the elimination of this pollution be completely financed by the corporations that produce it. That there be community control boards on a national level to ensure that these corporations eliminate the damage that they have created to our environment. La Raza Unida Party recognizes that the ecology of our environment has been used as an issue to obscure the fundamental political and economic problems of this society on all levels, local and national. To La Raza Unida Party ecology is just one aspect of the manifold problems that we face.

FOREIGN POLICY

La Raza Unida Party supports the right of self-determination of all nations. We are opposed to the intervention of the United States into the internal affairs of any nation. We demand an end to United States support to every oppressive regime from Mexico to Vietnam.

A. We demand the release of all political prisoners in Latin America, especially our brothers in Mexico.

B. Free Puerto Rico.

C. Immediate withdrawal from Southeast Asia.

D. Support of the Palestinian Liberation Struggle.

E. Free all colonies and territories of the United States.

II. Economic Platform

La Raza Unida Party feels that economic control of our lives and of our community is of the utmost importance.

A. Equality of the Spanish language in all the places of employment and business.

B. Rank-and-file democratic control of the unions; the elimination of all racist practices in the labor movement.

C. La Raza Unida Party calls for full employment of La Raza at all levels of the economy.

D. Escalator clauses in all union contracts to assure automatic wage increases with the rising cost of living.

E. A guaranteed annual income wage beginning at 18 years of age.

F. A shorter work-week with no reduction in pay.

G. One hundred percent taxation on all profits of corporations or businesses which engage in discrimination against La Raza.

H. Rent control agencies under the direct control of La Raza community, which would provide adequate housing for all persons of La Raza that would not cost more than 5 percent of his or her annual earnings.

I. Public ownership and control of all public utilities.

J. A minimum wage that meets a decent standard of living for all in La Raza.

K. The right of Raza *ancianitos* to secure an equitable old age must be provided by this society. Aged Raza citizens have helped to build this society and should, therefore, be provided with free medical care, free housing, free food, and all the essential things needed to continue to lead a dignified life.

L. La Raza Unida Party demands that the right of the ill to have adequate and free medical and hospital attention be met.

III. Education Platform

The community should have control of the entire educational system from the nursery schools through college.

A. Democratic elections of community control boards to supervise our schools within our communities.

B. Our educational system and curriculum will meet the needs of our children to obtain economic security, give them a knowledge of themselves and an understanding of our true history and culture.

C. Bilingual education.

D. Parent involvement in every phase of school life.

E. All Raza groups will be entitled to use school facilities to promote activities beneficial to the community and to further our liberation.

F. A full program of adult education.

G. Dismiss all school officials who victimize or insult Raza children on social or cultural grounds.

H. Free education from preschool through college with open enrollment and subsistence wages. Free lunches, breakfasts, and books.

I. The guarantee of high school rights that include freedom of expression, freedom to organize, to pass out literature, and all other rights which are safeguarded in the constitution must be provided.

IV. Self-Defense

A. We have the human right to defend our lives by any means necessary.

B. Community control of the police and all the judicial processes.

C. Free all political prisoners.

D. La Raza Unida Party supports and defends the full constitutional and human rights of La Raza — be they citizens, immigrants, or nationals.

E. All Raza men and women in the jails are political prisoners. The very nature of the judicial penal system in this country makes La Raza inmates political prisoners because that system does not afford them their basic constitutional rights.

1. La Raza has not had the benefit of trial by a jury of our peers.
2. La Raza does not have the money to pay for justice (that is, lawyers, court fees, adequate research assistance).
3. La Raza is railroaded by public defenders who misrepresent us and tell us to plead guilty.
4. The economic-social conditions that La Raza is forced to live in is the very reason for the offenses committed, which have in turn led to the imprisonment of all La Raza men and women now there.

F. Dismantling of the California Adult Authority Board — to be replaced by parole review boards in the community from which the prisoner comes.

G. Community control boards to administer the functioning of jails — these boards to be made up of 50 percent community elected officials and 50 percent inmates elected by inmates themselves.

H. Raza inmates have the right to form unions to implement collective bargaining.

I. Raza inmates must be paid federal minimum wages.

J. Full educational opportunities for all Raza inmates must be provided and include fully autonomous Raza departments.

K. On-the-job training for La Raza inmates in the field of their choosing.

L. Visitation rights which will include transportation for families and conjugal visitation.

V. Raza Women's Platform

PREAMBLE

We have arrived at a point in our struggle for self-determination where we have collectively, both men and women, decided to embark on a higher level of political activity in the form of our independent La Raza Unida Political Party.

We, the people of La Raza, want this party to fully encompass all the aspects of the needs of our people. We want this party to work for the eradication of all the inequalities and oppressive forces functioning to perpetuate our bondage.

We feel that the importance of the party will be determined by the measure to which it takes into account the needs of La Raza *as a whole,* and by the measure to which it actively works to meet those needs and to eradicate every form of exploitation which burdens us.

For our women who live under an economic structure which systematically uses and oppresses women to further its own ends, ends to making profits by any means necessary off the backs of whomever it is easily possible to physically identify, isolate, and create myths around, there exists a triple exploitation, a triple degradation; they are exploited as women, as people of La Raza, and they suffer from the poverty which straitjackets all of La Raza. Because of the particular nature of their oppression, within our women lies a tremendous potential for commitment to serious struggle. Their participation, if we eliminate all obstacles, will accelerate and strengthen our struggle to a fantastic degree.

We feel that without the recognition by all of La Raza of this special form of oppression which our women suffer, our movement will greatly suffer.

We want to eliminate the exploitation of man by man in every form — to eliminate the oppression of our women so that both men and women, in the process of our struggle and when our struggle bears fruit, will be equal human beings with all of the rights and responsibilities of a truly free people and without any kind of oppression in any form.

Bearing this in mind and recognizing that a people as a whole can never be liberated if an entire sector of that people remains in bondage, we of the Raza Unida Party state our position as follows:

A. We shall respect the right of self-determination for our women to state what their specific needs and problems are, and how they feel that these needs can be met and these problems can be eliminated, as a basic princple of our party.

B. The party encourages La Raza women to meet in Raza women's groups wherever the movement is functioning, in order to enable the women to discuss the direction that their participation is taking and the particular needs of Raza women they feel must be acted upon. We encourage that these groups be formed to enable the women to aid in the recruitment of more women to participate in a politically conscious way and in all levels of the struggle.

C. The party will include Raza women in all decision-making meetings, paying them due respect when they offer opinions and speak. Our women will always be fairly represented in planning committees, in public relations functions as spokeswomen, in workshops, and in discussion groups as leaders.

D. Raza men and women both will cooperate fully, in this party and at home, in the very difficult task we have before us of freeing our women and encouraging them in every way we can, at all times, to become involved in every level of the struggle and in working actively towards the elimination of all attitudes and practices that have relegated our women to the unquestionably bondaged positions they are now in.

CHILD CARE

A. Child-care centers controlled by Raza must be made available for Raza in schools, workplaces, and neighborhoods, totally free of charge, wherever our people are found.

B. These child-care centers will be open 24 hours a day and must accommodate children from the age of 45 days through the preschool ages.

C. Medical attention will be made available for the children and facilities will be available for children who may be sick — with the necessary medicine free of charge.

D. These centers will function as educational centers as well as care centers.

F. These centers will be controlled and run by both Raza men and women.

WORK

A. An end to inequality in pay because of sex or race. Statistics show that for the same job women now get paid half the wage earned by men. The poorest suffer from this the most. Raza women as a group are paid even less than their underpaid Raza male counterparts.

B. Fifty percent of Raza women who work, work as domestics. We want job openings in all areas of work for Raza women, specifically in full-time employment with salaries to meet the standard of living no matter what it may be and no matter how much it increases. All Raza women who apply for jobs, in no matter what area, must be accepted. If training is needed, it should be given with pay.

C. Maternity and paternity leaves with pay and with a guarantee of a job on return.

BIRTH CONTROL

A. Clinics and agencies within our communities that distribute any birth-control information and/or abortion counseling and information and clinics and agencies that pass out birth-control devices and perform abortions *must* be community-controlled, and a woman who is counseled must be thoroughly informed about all the dangers and possible side effects of any devices or operations.

B. No forced abortions or sterilizations of our women.

C. The ultimate decision whether to have a child or not should be left up to the woman.

EDUCATION

A. Intensive recruitment of Raza women into the schools —with Raza counselors and tutors to help the women stay in school and to encourage them to enter all areas of study.

B. Guaranteed jobs for all Raza women upon graduation in whatever field the women choose.

C. Part of the education of our women will be dedicated to the study of the history of the oppression of women within the framework of our background and to the study of the role which Raza women have played in the history of our people.

POLITICAL PARTICIPATION OF MEXICAN AMERICANS
IN CALIFORNIA

This Report, based on the 1971 Hearings in
Sacramento, California, closely examines political discrimination against Chicanos. Studying variables such as gerrymandering, reapportionment, English language tests, voting
requirements, etc., this Report documents
the failure of the Democratic and Republican
parties, as well as the State government and
othere levels of government, to mobilize against
the racism which has been a major factor in
denying Chicanos access to political power.
This document shows that these parties and
agencies have accepted this condition of political discrimination. This report serves as a
microcosm of the problems found in the other
Southwest States.

Source: U.S. Government Printing Office, 1971.

INTRODUCTION

On January 21 and 22, 1971, the California State Advisory Committee
to the United States Commission on Civil Rights conducted a public open
meeting on the subject: "Political Participation of Mexican Americans."

The meeting was held in the State Capitol Building in Sacramento two
weeks after the California Legislature began its 1971 session. Key members of the State Senate and Assembly were available for appearances before the Committee to discuss what was destined to be a major issue in the
Legislature this year: the redrawing of the state's Assembly, Senate and
United States Congressional district lines.

California has two United States Senators, 40 State Senators, 80 Assemblymen, and had, until the 1970 U.S. Census increased their number by five,
38 U.S. Congressmen.

One of the Committee's principal concerns was why only three elected
State and Federal level representatives out of 160 are Mexican American.*
. . .

---

* These are United States Congressman Edward R. Roybal, 30th District,
Los Angeles County; State Assemblyman Alex Garcia, 40th District, Los
Angeles County; and State Assemblyman Peter Chacon, newly-elected in
San Diego County's 79th District.

In addition to the issue of reapportionment and its effect on the Mexican American community, presentations were made on other matters pertinent to the participation of Mexican Americans in the political life of California. These included voter rights, Mexican American influence in major political parties, political use of police and the courts, political appointments and specific Mexican American political problems in both rural and urban areas.

POLITICAL RACISM IN CALIFORNIA

To begin to comprehend the acute problem which confronts the Mexican American in California's political life today, one must first realize that the racism which infests all of our other institutions is very much a part of the State's political system, as well.

While it is not a generally accepted public belief that the Mexican American community is victimized by racist attitudes to the degree that other minorities are, the Committee found that racism has been a major factor in denying the Mexican American access to our political and governmental institutions in California today.

The Committee found much evidence that the legislature, the State administration, and administrations at all levels of government in California have chosen to accept this condition rather than mobilize our society to combat it.

For many years, in spite of large and continually growing numbers in California, the Mexican Americans have been conspicuously absent from governmental positions in this State. This has been true at all levels of government: municipal, county, State and Federal (in those instances where federal officials work within the boundaries of California).

This has also been true of both elective and appointive offices.

Mexican Americans have not been successful in seeking election to public office; nor have the non-Mexican Americans who were winners at the polls appointed Mexican Americans to the many, important non-elective posts which they control, or otherwise involved them in the decision-making processes of government.

Before the State's second Mexican American Assemblyman was elected in November 1970, there were only two Mexican Americans among California's 160 elected representatives serving in the State Assembly, State Senate, U.S. Senate and U.S House of Representatives--a minuscule 1.25 percent in a state with between 12-15 percent Mexican American population.

These were some of the surface signs that the Mexican American was not being afforded an opportunity to share in the political experience and the political rewards of government in this State at any level.

Last year, the California State Advisory Committee to the United States Commission on Civil Rights began receiving an increasing number of complaints in support of this contention--complaints alleging that Mexican Americans are victims of deliberate discriminatory practices ranging from gerrymandering of districts to unconstitutional election procedures. . . .

The Committee study showed that many of the methods used in the past to exclude Mexican Americans from political participation in California were strikingly similar to those used to exclude blacks from political participation in the South.

Many, in fact, were the same: tests based on education and literacy, gerrymandering of voting districts to minimize minority representation, intimidation, and, on occasion, murder.

While the South had its poll taxes and grandfather clauses to discourage the black voter, California had its English-language voting requirements and threats of deportation to discourage the Mexican American voter.

Another, more insidious weapon which works to discourage Mexican Americans from running for political office, or more certainly from emerging victorious on election day, is the weapon of racist caricature.

In a recent paper on "Advertising and the Mexican American Consumer," Dr. Donald L. Carter, a Los Angeles advertising agency executive and professor at the University of Souther California, wrote:

"The image is a schizoid one. On one hand, the mass media, books, cinema, television and even the elementary school textbooks portray Mexicans as benign, shiftless, sweet, peasant-type people who are devout and trustworthy; but other portraylas in the organs of the mass media depict the Mexicans as villainous characters with shifty eyes and criminal proclivities."

One speaker, Ed Cano of the United States Department of Health, Education and Welfare, offered the Committee the following version of what happens when a nonMexican American voter is faced with the choice between a Spanish surnamed candidate and one with an Anglo-Saxon surname:

"Imagine the pictures that flash in the voter's mind:
'Jones, hmmm"--positive--' intelligent, witty,
respectable, competent. He will protect my interests.
Responsible, has credibility and connections, politically
astute, sophisticated.'

'Lopez'--no hesitation--'lazy, incompetent, is using ethnic
background to gain acceptance, not relying on personal
qualifications, irresponsible, militant, couldn't possibly
protect my interests, not too smart.'

Automatically, almost reflexively, Citizen X punches the
card next to the incumbent Mr. Jones. He walks out
thinking he has contributed to the 'best of all
possible worlds.' And once again, the door to political
participation for the Lopezes of California--indeed,
the nation--is summarily and irrevocably shut.

COMMITTE'S ANALYSIS AND RECOMMENDATIONS

I. Reapportionment

Mexican Americans, who number between 2 1/2 and 3 million persons in Calfironia, represent between 12-15 percent of the State's total population; yet, they hold less than two percent of the State's elective offices in the United States Congress and the State Legislature.

Out of 40 State Senators, none are Mexican American.

Out of 80 State Assemblymen, two--one of them newly elected--are Mexican American.

Out of 40 Congressional representatives--38 Congressmen and two U.S. Senators--one is Mexican "American.

More than half of the 42 speakers at the State Advisory Committee meeting offered comment on the subject of reapportionment. Whether they were legislators, attorneys, or representatives of Mexican American organizations, they agreed on one vital point:

The Mexican American in California has been gerrymandered out of any real chance to elect his own representatives to the State Legislature or the United States Congress in a proportion approaching his percentage of the state population.

Former Assembly Speaker Jess Unruh, who was prominent in the Assembly when the redistricting took place during the 1960's states:

"Reapportionments are designed by incumbents, for incumbents, as a service to incumbents."

With California's legislators, dividing and conquering Mexican Americans has become a reflexive act of self-preservation. To allow Mexican Americans to vote in community blocs would be to invite self-defeat at the polls. . . .

The State Advisory Committee sees the California State Legislature, with its power to reapportion, as a self-perpetuating body which will continue to exclude those who are not in it.

Most damning in the eyes of the Committee, was the legislators' apparent lack of serious concern about gerrymandering and their apparent unwillingness to take the necessary action to eliminate this insidious form of discrimination.

Their acceptance of gerrymandering based on racism is both immoral and illegal.

It leads the Committee to the inevitable conclusion that unless public opinion in California is marshalled to cause a complete reversal of the present attitude of legislators, or unless the courts order a fair and just reapportionment, there is no hope that Mexican Americans will be afforded fair representation for at least the next decade.

We should also note that in California, the Governor shares responsibility for reapportionment with the legislature. Governor Reagan was invited to appear before the Committee, but failed to do so. Nor, despite our invitation, did he send a representative.

The Committee is concerned at the degree of racism which is directed at the Mexican American in California, and it is doubly concerned that the actions taken by California's State legislators have continued to reflect the racism in their communities rather than the statesmanship and leadership which is essential if the overall problem of racism is to be resolved.

Instead of dealing with this racism, the legislators have accepted and benefitted from it.

As a result, California has by far the worst record in the Southwest with regard to Mexican American legislative representation.

"Texas, whose reputation for repression of and discrimination against Chicanos is well known, has ten times as many Assemblymen and twice as many Congressmen," Mario Obledo, executive director of the Mexican American Legal Defense and Educational Fund (MALDEF), told the Committee, adding: "New Mexico has a history of Mexican American senators and governors. Arizona's recent election saw a Mexican American as the Democratic Party's candidate for governor."

The Committee further concludes that the recent disruptions within the Mexican American community can be attributed in part to that community's lack of political representation. The community has no elected official who can speak out in complete candor on the problems and issues facing it. No major elected official in California--whether Mexican American or other-wise--has more than a 30 percent Mexican American constituency. For a present incumbent with a 20-30 percent Mexican American constituency to given voice to the true aspiration and concerns of the Mexican American community would be to invite defeat at the hands of his Anglo constituency, for it is the Anglo majority that is his real master.

There are no immediate or simple solutions for Mexican Americans seeking political office in California today. By placing its own selfish in-terests ahead of the political rights of California's Mexcian Americans, the State legislature has compounded the multiple hadnicaps of an identifi-able Spanish surname and other political disadvantages which face Mexican Americans here today.

Therefore, the Committee's first recommendation is that the power to reapportion be removed from the State Legislature and placed in the hands of a body which is representative of all of the people in California.

There is a precedence for such an action. A number of other States in the Union have already adopted other methods of reapportioning their State Houses and Congressional districts.*

---

*The National Municipal League's Model State Constitution (Section 4.04) provides that the reapportionment authority be removed from legislative control and entrusted to the administrative authority of the governor's office, subject to the review and modification by the state's highest court. For pur-poses of reapportionment, the governor would be advised by a non-partisan board of citizens. By 1967, eight states (Alaska, Arizona, Arkansas, Hawaii, Michigan, Missouri, New Jersey, and Ohio) had removed reapportionment from legislative control. New York National Municipal League, 1967.

The Committee's second recommendation is that, if the legislature does not apportion the Mexican American and other minority communities justly, the United States Department of Justice be asked to file a civil rights action enjoining the implementation of California's 1971 Reapportionment Act.

If the 1971 reapportionment, as presently being drafted by the State Legislature, once again makes a patchwork quilt of the Mexican American community and attempts to exclude its voice from our halls of government in Sacramento and Washington, D.C., we will view this as a denial of civil rights which the Federal government has the authority and responsibility to correct. We would urge the federal government to use all the weapons in its legal arsenal to cause the State Legislature and the Governor to apportion fairly and in a manner which conforms with the Constitution of the United States. . . .

And that is the choice to be made.

II. Voting Rights

The California State Election Code has kept many Mexican Americans from exercising their right to vote.

Robert Garcia, an Assembly staff member, described the Code as a collection of laws "written with the premise that it ought to be difficult for people to vote" and filled with "arbitrary barriers that have kept us from electing more Chicanos." . . .

Key recommendations included (1) that lengthy residency requirements --which tend to work against the poor and the migrant--be shortened, (2) that ex-felons should uniformly be permitted to vote; (3) that a system of permanent registration be adopted; (4) that a system of registration by m mail be developed; (5) that ballots be printed in Spanish when appropriate; (6) that all language and literacy requirements be abolished; (7) that the number of available deputy registrars be increased; (8) that the speaking of a language other than English be permitted at a polling place; and, (9) that the possibility of granting State citizenship to legal resident aliens be explored.

In his written statement, Senator Cranston said that he was drafting legislation to delete the English speaking requirement from the naturalization process, which he called a citizenship hindrance to "thousands of Mexican nationals lawfully residing in California."

Recently the California Supreme Court ruled that the State Constitution violated the United States Constitution in its requirement that all voters be literate in English. This decision opened the voting booths to more Mexican Americans.

There are other barriers presently preventing Mexican Americans from voting or otherwise fully enjoying their rights as citizens.

In view of this, the Committee submits a third recommendation that a commission be established by the legislature to examine all California laws to determine which statutes discriminate against Mexican Americans or other minorities because of their culture or language. The commission should be composed of representatives from all minority groups.

III. Appointment of Mexican Americans to Positions in Government

Out of 15,650 elected and appointed officials in municipal, county, State and Federal levels in California, only 310--just 1.98 percent--are Mexican American.

This information was provided to the Committee by a Civil Rights Commission staff study which further showed that:

- None of the tope 40 State officials are Mexican American.
- None of the tope 28 advisors on the Governor's staff are Mexican American.
- Of the 4,023 positions in the executive branch of State government, including the boards, commissions and advisories, only 60--1.5 percent-- are filled by Mexican Americans.
- Of 10,907 city and county government officials in California, only 241--2.2 percent--are Mexican American.
- None of the 132 top State court positions--including seven Supreme Court Justices, the Judicial Council, the Administrative Office of the Courts, the Commission on Judicial Qualifications and the State Court of Appeals-- are held by Mexican Americans.
- At the Federal level--legislators, judges, marshals, commissioners, United States Attorneys and their assistants--there were 525 offices specifically serving Californians. Of these seven--1.33 percent were held by Mexican Americans. None of the four U.S. attorneys or 87 assistant U.S. attorneys serving in California are Mexican American.
-In the U.S. Court of Appeals and the U.S. District Court in California (which include U.S. judges, referees, probation officers, commissioners and marshals) there are 262 positions, only 6 of which are filled by Mexican Americans. None of these 6 are judges or referees. . . .

Of the nearly 700 State Senate and Assembly staff members listed in the 1970 State Legislative handbook, only 7 had Spanish surnames. These positions are not covered by rules or guidelines of the legislature's own creation, the state Fair Employment Practices Commission, or by Title VII of the Federal Civil Rights Act of 1964. . . .

(1) It has denied them the opportunity to learn the "system!--the process of government which established the rules by which they must live.

(2) It has excluded them from participation in forming policies--policies which have stunted their growth educationally, denied them economic opportunities, limited their access to the State's system of justice, and generally worked to "keep them in their place" as second-class citizens.

(3) It has denied them the use of government facilities by closing off avenues through which they could voice their problems and grievances.

The lack of Mexican Americans in appointive and elective policy positions in government is dramatically reflected by the fact that in many departments of the State, Mexcian Americans comprise less than two percent

of the work force, and that the department with the best hiring record has
only seven percent Mexican Americans on its work force.

"For All The People...By All the People, " a 1969 U.S. Civil Rights
Commission report to the President and the Congress-a report based in
part on a study of California's municipal and State governments--found that:
"Not only do State and local governments consciously and overtly discriminate in hiring and promoting minority group members, but they do not foster
positive programs to deal with discriminatory treatment on the job.". . .

The only remedy for State and local government job applicants or employees who are victims of discrimination is a costly, time-consuming private court suit.

The State Advisory Committee makes a fourth recommendation that the
Governor, members of the legislature and key elected and appointed officials at all levels of government take immediate steps to correct the racist
patterns of political appointment which have created the imbalance which
exists in policy level positions today.

The State Advisory Committee makes its fifth recommendation that
Title VII of the 1964 Civil Rights Act be expanded to cover state and local
government agencies, and that the jurisdiction of the Equal Employment Opportunity Commission and the Fair Employment Practices Commission be
expanded to cover the personnel practices of these State and local agencies.

IV. Major Political Parties and the Mexican American

Political power and authority in California lies with the elected officials,
the wealthy contributors, and the influential pressure groups. Under California law, political parties are without any real authority. They are prohibited from making pre-primary endorsements and may not contribute financially to primary candidates.

For all practical purposes, the political parties in California are owned
and controlled by the State Legislature or the Governor. Elected officials
and nominees appoint all of the members of the State parties' Central Committees. These appointments are made from among their own supporters.

Inasmuch as the districts in California are now apportioned in a manner which excludes Mexican Americans from public office and makes their
nomination in the primary only a remote possibility, their opportunity to
participate fully in party positions is drastically limited. Only the legislature can provide a remedy for this inequity--a just reapportionment. Unless
such a reapportionment occurs, both parties can expect to lose much of the
support they now receive from Mexican American voters.

As many speakers emphasized to the Committee, the vast majority of
Mexican American voters are Democrats. Estimates ranged up to 90 percent. The Democratic Party, the speakers complained, has taken the Mexican American for granted. The Republican Party, with few Mexican Americans and few pressures from that community, has not been at all responsive
to its needs, they said. Several speakers stated that unless a fair reapportionment bill is enacted this year, a new party representing the interests of
Mexican Americans will be formed before the 1972 elections.

As the Committee's sixth recommendation, it urges the leaders of both political parties to use all of their influence with the legislature and the Governor to ensure the enactment of a fair and just reapportionment bill.

One important area in which the political parties can ensure an opportunity for fair and meaningful participation in the political process is in the selection of delegates to the national conventions which nominate presidential candidates. In the past, neither major party has afforded fair representation to Mexican Americans on its delegation. As a result of its 1968 Chicago convention, the Democratic Party, both nationally and in California, has adopted guidelines for proportionate representation of Mexican Americans at its 1972 convention. The Republican Party has taken no comparable action.

Mexican Americans view the committments made by the Democratic Party to reform its delegate selection process with justifiable skepticism. They have grown accustomed to broken promises by politicians.

It is the Committee's view that Mexican Americans are entitled as a matter of law to fair representation at Presidential conventions. Unless such representation is afforded at the 1972 conventions, the delegations may be subject to legal challenge.

As the Committee's seventh recommendation, it urges that the delegations selected and the proceudres followed by both parties be carefully reviewed and analyzed after the selection process is completed, and appropriate challenges be instituted in the event that Mexican Americans are once again denied fair representation.

As the Committee's eighth recommendation, it urges that the Republican Party adopt guidelines for the purpose of affording fair representation to Mexican Americans at the 1972 Presidential convention and that the Democratic Party fully implement the guidelines it has adopted.

V.   Representation in Los Angeles and Other Urban Areas

The Civil Rights Commission staff report shows that among the 90 top officials, mayors, councilmen, etc.--in California's three largest cities--Los Angeles, San Diego and San Francisco--there is one Mexican American.

The report shows that in cities with 50,000 to 500,000 population, there are 64 mayors, one percent of whom are Mexican American; 332 councilmen 20 percent of whom are Mexican American; and 926 other officials, 15 percent of whom are Mexican American.

Within these city governments, Mexican Americans represent 2.7 percent of the officials.

Although there are 1.1 million Mexican Americans residing in Los Angeles County, this ethnic group is unrepresented on the five-member County Board of Supervisors and the 15-member Los Angeles City Council.

Los Angeles City Councilman Thomas Bradley joined Mexican American speakers in charging that this lack of representation is due to gerrymandering and other schemes designed to limit Mexican American political influence.

One councilmanic District which Mexican Americans share with blacks has 260,000 residents, which white Anglo districts have populations as low as 162,000.

This discrepancy was successfully challenged in court by the Mexican American Legal Defense and Educational Fund (MALDEF). Six weeks after MALDEF's chief counsel in Los Angelese, Joe Ortega, described the condition to the Committee, the California Supreme Court ruled that the city of Los Angeles must reapportion its councilmanic districts on the basis of equal numbers of people rather than registered voters, the criteria it had used. . . .

The Committee makes its ninth recommendation that the power to reapportion at city and county levels of government be taken from the hands of incumbents and placed with a commission representative of the people of the area.

The Committee also heard complaints that those municipal, county and school board elections which require candidates to run "at-large"--citywide, countywide, or districtwide, instead of from specified smaller districts --minimize minority voting power. In some communities, political racism appears to be the motive for maintaining "at large" elections.

The Committee's tenth recommendation is that cities and counties with sizable defined ethnic communities that lack representation should consider conducting elections on a district, rather than at-large basis.

SUMMARY OF PROCEEDINGS

REAPPORTIONMENT

The principal concern of the State Advisory Committee's two-day meeting was the 1971 reapportionment of California's state legislative and Congressional districts, and it brought comments from many speakers of diverse backgrounds and experiences.

Yet not one of those speakers defended the past gerrymandering of Mexican American communities.

Typical of statements heard by the Committee were:

Jess Unruh a Democrat and former assembly speaker: "Quite obviously the Mexican American community has been reapportioned more with regard to how it would maximize the Democratic representation that it has as to how it would maximize the Mexican American representation."

Senator Dennis Carpenter, Chairman, Republican State Central Committee: "Those district lines which now exist have not produced what I would call an unfair number of Mexcian American legislators in California. They are districts which were established by the Democratic Party."

Mario Obledo, executive director, Mexican American Legal Defense Fund: "Gentlemen, any individual can look at the statistical information that is available to the public in the State of California with regard to Chicano representation in the Assembly and in the Senate of this State, and it will show a prima facie case of, if not de jure segregation, de facto segregation against the Mexican American."

U.S. Congressman Edward R. Roybal, in a written statement said:
"The Supreme Court decisions over the last decade relating to legislative reapportionment have lulled many citizens into the supposition that gerrymandering and other techniques used to minimize minority group political influence have become obsolete. Nothing could be further from the truth. In fact, the rigid 'one man one vote' reapportionment guidelines outlined by the Court in recent years have in some ways heightened, rather than reduced, the propensity for unjust redistricting of legislative districts. . . .

U.S. Senator Alan Cranston, also in a written statement: "Despite the rapid emergence of political activism in the Mexican American community, access to the state's political institutions remains virtually closed to this community. The reasons for this are complex, but they have a common root: the Mexican American has been systematically excluded from the opportunities available to the Anglo community that lead to political, economic and social success." . . .

Two professors from California State College at Los Angeles, Henry Pacheco and Dr. David Lopez Lee, brought the Committee a detailed map which they had prepared of Los Angeles County, showing the various degrees of density of the Mexican American population there.

They also brought along a fact sheet which stated that the East Los Angelese community, with a Mexican American population of 600,000 persons, was sliced up into nine State Assembly districts, seven State Senate districts, and six United States Congressional districts. The districts were cut up in such a way that none of them had more than 35 percent Mexican American voter registration, Pacheco said.

The Assembly offered a good example of gerrymandering practices. Using the legislature's own figures, five districts--the 40th, 45th, 48th, 50th and 51st--dip into East Los Angeles to take between 20-30 percent registered Mexican American voters each, with four other districts--the 52nd, 53rd, 56th and 66th--dipping in for smaller amounts. The amounts are large enough to insure the reelection of Democratic incumbents, Pacheco explained--but small enough to prevent a Mexican American candidate from winning the district.

Professor Pacheco suggested that the county which presently has one Mexican American Assemblyman, one Mexican American Congressman and no Mexican American State Senators--should provide the Mexican American community six Assembly seats, three State Senate seats and three U.S. Congressional seats. . . .

Jesse Ramirez, executive director of the Chicano Federation of San Diego County, reported:

"San Diego County has 15 to 20 percent Mexican Americans, and for the first time in our history we have a representative in Sacramento. Thirteen municipalities, one Mexican American City Councilman; no representation on the County Board of Supervisors; no city managers, no top department

heads anywhere in the county, so the representation we have speaks to what
one young man said earlier, 'Taxation without representation.' The ethnic
distribution runs one way, the boundaries run another way."

Richard Calderon, a research project supervisor who was narrowly defeated for the United States Congress by the then-incumbent State Senator
George Danielson in the June, 1970, Democratic Party primary, stated that
he felt a district with 35 percent Mexican American voter registration was
sufficient to elect a Mexican American candidate. . . .

Calderon, from Eastern Los Angeles County, said that in his campaign
against Danielson, which he lost, 25,518 votes to 23,506 votes, he handily
carried all of the towns with any number of close to 35 percent or greater
Mexican American voter registration.

"It was in the marginal areas of 20 to 25 percent that we had problems,"
he said. "Some we won. Some we didn't."

Calderon described the intent behind the gerrymandering of East Los
Angeles:

"Why were we cut up? Well, the primary consideration was a self-ser-
ving consideration, and it happened that in 1960, the Democratic Party was
also in power. It benefits the Democratic Party to cut up our community,
because what they are doing is slicing into a rich pie where the registration is 90 percent or better Democratic. By each district taking a chunk
from that rich pie, they come out with districts that are 60 percent or better
in Democratic registration, so it gives them the opportunity to get more
Democratic districts."

Jess Unruh, who was Speaker of the California Assembly throughout
most of the '60s, spoke at length about the "political realities" of reapportionment and what actually happened during his term as Speaker.

"In 1961, we did an Assembly and Congressional reapportionment," he
said. "We did not do a Senatorial reapportionment because that was before
the one-man one-vote court edict. In 1965, we again realigned the Assembly
and Seante lines, and in 1967, we realigned the Congressional districts.

"In no case have I seen anything out of this except the actions of the
legislature to protect the members of the legislature and to favor the party
in power.

"In 1961, pursuant to a direct request, I think the principal thing that
motivated the legislature in reapportionment after that all-important principle of protecting incumbents was to give to the then new Democratic President, John Kennedy, as big a working majority in the Congressional delegation of California as was possible. We did that.

"In 1965, it was totally and completely for the protection of incumbents.

"In 1967, it was to protect the incumbent Congressmen.

"I would suggest," Unruh continued, "that is what would govern this
reapportionment at both the Assembly, the Senate and Congressional level.
That is the way it is done. . . . They will first of all make a deal to protect
themselves. Secondly, they will attempt to give their party whatever advantage there is. Thirdly, they will look after other groups who manage to get
the most pressure on them after that."

Lawrence Glick, deputy director of the U.S. Civil Rights Commission's Office of General Counsel, quoted a comment to the Committee by Senator Moscone that "the Democratic Party wants to be a more effective instrument for the Mexican American people." Then he queried Unruh on whether it would be possible for the Democratic leadership in California to face the reapportionment dilemma head on, and if an incumbent had to be eliminated, would it be done?

"Certainly that would be better for the Mexican American population," Unruh responded, "but that just isn't going to happen. It just isn't going to happen." . . .

Senator Mervyn Dymally, a Democrat, and chairman of the Senate Elections and Reapportionment Committee, assessed the Mexican Americans' hopes for '71: "The fair and just thing regarding reapportionment of the State Senate is to see that the Mexcian American communities within California have an opportunity to be represented. Unfortunately, however, neither the committments which I make nor the Democratic Party nor the State Senate may make and intend to fulfill will guarantee Mexican American representation in the State Senate....There are now 20 million people within our State. So each of the 40 State Senate Districts will contain approximately half a million people. Los Angeles County, which is slightly under seven million people, will retain its 14 seats. No gain....A seat for the Mexican American community would have to displace a current incumbent....No current Senate incumbent can realistically be expected to offer up his seat willingly to the Mexican American community. This is part of our problem."....

A young professor from California State College at Los Angeles, Carlos Penichet, told the Committee:

"As we have wandered through the halls of the legislature here and met with a number of representatives, I think all of us have an increasing impression that very little is going to be done about racial gerrymandering to the Chicano communities in this legislature.

"We have gotten mostly elusive comments. Very subtly, but directly we are being told that the primary considerations in this whole issue of reapportionment is that the incumbents in the Democratic Party are going to have to be protected. . . .

A week later, at the same auditorium, Governor Reagan, whose office declined to send a representative to the State Advisory Committee meeting, told the membership of the Republican State Central Committee:

"Thousands of Californians are still being cheated out of their correct proportional share of legislative and Congressional representation as a result of a cynically and deliberately contrived imbalance....Large communities of particular ethnic groups like our fine citizens of Mexican descent have been gerrymandered and cut up so they have no change to choose either legislative or Congressional voices representative of their particular problems. This time reapportionment must correct that injustice...."

Several of the Mexican American speakers made the point that California's political system was on trial in the 1971 reapportionment, and that if the Mexican American community was gerrymandered out of an opportunity for political representation once again, the consequences could be serious.

Armando Morales, a psychiatric social worker, cited the Mexican American's lack of political opportunity as a major factor in the recent East Los Angeles riots, and told the Committee:

"A democracy functions best when all people have a voice in government. Urban disorder is a luxury that discriminatory political interests can no longer afford. Everyone loses."

Mario Obledo, executive director of the Mexican American Legal Defense Fund, told the Committee that MALDEF was already researching the Constitutional dimensions of the problem, and was prepared to take the case to court if the legislature did not present a reapprotionment plan which was just to California's three million Mexican Americans.

Another frequently mentioned alternative was a massive community organizing effort behind La Raza Unida Party.

Richard Calderon predicted that the Mexican American community would form a Freedom Delegation--with strong support from Southern delegations--to impede the seating of California's regular delegation at the 1972 Democratic National Convention.

Senator Cranston summed up his statement:

"I cannot overstate the gravity of the existing situation. It affects not only an excluded community but all Californians.

"I believe that the survival of democratic government hinges upon the opportunities which it provides to disenchanted groups to translate their aspirations into political terms. Without these opportunities, the fundamental right to petition the government for redress of grievances becomes meaningless.

"Thos excluded from participation in political institutions may conclude that they have no stake in a society whose political system is closed to them," he warned.

In his remarks to the Committee, Los Angeles City Councilman Thomas Bradley drew the blunt conclusion:

"There are far too many people in this country who do not see this as a problem and who do not understand it in any way."

He suggested: "Until we get that kind of public awareness, we will never be able to take the next step toward finding the solution."

VOTING RIGHTS

Several ways by which the Mexican American in California has been excluded--both legally and illegally--from the voting process were cited at the meeting.

The State Election Code came under fire from a number of Mexican American witnesses, from attorneys representing California Rural Legal Assistance (CRLA) and the Mexican American Legal Defense and Education

Fund (MALDEF), from the Co-Chairman of the California Commission on Democratic Party Reform and from the Secretary of State himself.

In a recent case before the California State Supreme Court (Castro v. California), the court ruled that the State violated the United States Constitution's guarantee of equal protection under the law when it limited its voter literacy test to English. The court reasoned that a Spanish speaking citizen had an abundance of Spanish language new media in this state to assist him in learning about the candidates and issues and becoming as knowledgeable on them as his English speaking neighbor.

This decision, many of those appearing before the Committee commented, opened a new series of questions on language and voting rights.

Senator Alan Cranston, in his written statement, recommended:

"Our election laws for registration and voting must be liberalized to make it easier for Mexican Americans to participate in the electoral process in the most important place of all-the voting booth.

"In partial response to this problem, " he said, "I am drafting legislation, to be introduced early in this session of Congress, that will enable thousands of Mexican Nationals, lawfully residing in California, to become American citizens by deleting the English-speaking requirement from the naturalization process.

"Spanish-speaking registrars must be provided, as well as ballots and voter pamphlets printed in Spanish, " he added.

Robert Garcia, staff assistant to Assembly Speaker Bob Moretti, stated that the State Election Code was filled with "arbitrary barriers that have kept us from electing more Chicanos" and that the Code "was written with the premise that it ought to be difficult for people to vote.". . .

He recommended that:

--A system of registration-by-mail be developed. "This would greatly help farm workers and the rural Chicano, " he said.

--A system of permanent registration be adopted. "This is the ideal solution, but that is not going to come about, " he admitted.

As an alternative plan, he recommended purging of voter lists only after general elections.

"In Riverside County, 10,000 people were purged because they did not vote in the primary election in June of last year. A lot of those people were farm workers who leave Imperial Valley and Coachella Valley at that time to work in San Joaquin Valley and the Sacramento Valley. They can't leave a forwarding address because they never stay in one place very long. They stay two or three weeks and move on. When the sample ballot of disbursement is returned to the county clerk, the clerk sends out a double postcard to the address of that person. Of course, the post card is not returned within the required 30 days, and the person is removed from the eligible voter list, "Garcia said. He added that:

--California should adjust its residency requirements to conform to the new national 30-day residency requirements.

--Ex-felons should uniformly be permitted to vote.

"Based on a precedent set in a case in 1966, many county clerks are now registering ex-felons. If people aren't aware of the precedent, county clerks aren't likely to do that."

--When appropriate, ballots should be printed in Spanish.

The 1970 Voting Rights Act abolished all language and literacy requirements, Garcia pointed out, so "it doesn't make much sense for a person literate only in Spanish to try and read an explanation of a proposition in English. I have a difficult enough time trying to understand those."

"I think the argument that if you do it for the Spanish speaking people, you have to do it for all ethnic minorities can be dispelled by imposing some kind of numerical formula such as whenever ten percent of the electorate speaks a certain language, ballots in that language are needed."

Sacramento Attorney John Moulds III spoke in support of Spanish language ballots, a 19-day residency requirement for voting, registration-by-mail, and a statewide solution to the problem of ex-felons voting.

On the latter issue, he pointed out:

> I think the felony voting exclusion in California is much more serious than many of us know, particularly because it not only has racial and ethnic overtones, but it also has substantial economic overtones. It is sometimes a narrow thing in the State of California whether a man is convicted of a felony or misdemeanor. It is also true that it is possible, later on, to correct the record to take care of a felony and reduce it to a misdemeanor. This is the kind of thing that happens to a man who has private counsel, and it may not happen to the man who is a transient as he does not come back into the area from which he has a conviction. This can make a substantial impact, plus there is the general public impression that a person once convicted of a felony may not vote until he has gone through the complicated process of a certificate of rehabilitation and a pardon by the Governor. This is being remedied in some counties and should be remedied in more.

"There are approximately 40,000 adult inmates and parolees in the California Adult Authority corrections system. Of these, 20 percent, or ,8,000 are of Spanish surname, mostly from the Southern California area," he explained.

"Most Mexican American convictions are for narcotics offenses."

"Because of the numerous, interrelated institutional discriminatory practices that result in more poor Mexican Americans being arrested, convicted and imprisoned for narcotic offenses than middle-class persons, their punishment is made even more severe because they also lose their right to vote."

"And because they lose their right to vote, they become politically helpless to participate in the American democratic process to change those social conditions that caused-their initial downfall, and which will also cause their future downfall."

CRLA Attorney Don Kates, of Gilroy, stated that a CRLA suit caused the California Supreme Court to rule that the California Constitution was in violation of the United States Constitution in its requirement that all voters be literate in English.

Kates pointed out that in Los Angeles County alone there were 17 Spanish language newspapers and several radio and television stations accessable to persons who could read or speak Spanish. He cited "the discriminatory history of the English literacy requirement," defining its purposes as "to make sure that people born in foreign countries couldn't vote."

The California Supreme Court decision outlawing English literacy requirements came during the middle of last year's primary elections. Kates stated that most counties, especially urban counties, implemented the decision immediately.

"However, in a number of rural counties, particularly those where the existence of some Spanish-speaking voters might make a great deal of difference, the reaction was somewhat less than immediate compliance. In Imperial County, the registrar denounced the decision in the press and attempted to implement a scheme whereby anybody who wishes to register to vote under the Castro decision would have to vote in the county seat. Since the county stretches from San Diego to Arizona and from Riverside County to the Mexican border, that would mean people would have to drive 50 or even 100 miles round trip in order to vote or to register to vote. After threat of litigation by our office down there, the county counsel was able to convince the registrar of voters that he better allow registration in each incorporated area of the county, and that eventually occurred. However, I think the delay was sufficient that a large number of people who should have been allowed to vote for the first time in their lives in a primary were not allowed to vote."

Kates commented that in rural communities there are few, if any, Mexican American deputy registrars, in spite of the fact that under law, any competent person can be appointed as a deputy registrar and that the election code specifically encourages registration of voters.

Before the Castro decision, Kates said, there were instances where Mexican American deputy registrar applicants were turned down with the explanation that they'd probably register non-English speaking people. Now, he predicted, "every type of technical objection will be placed in the way of appointing any further Mexican American registrars."

Another issue concerning voting rights was raised by Cododac Colchado, Martin De Leon and Daniel M. Ruiz, teachers taking graduate study at the University of California at Davis. In a prepared paper, they quoted a recent article by Sacramento Bee reporter Dennis Campbell:

An inconsistency in California law denies 250,000 residents
the opportunity to vote. These are California's Spanish-
speaking aliens. They are permanent residents here. They

own property, pay taxes and are subject to our laws, but as non-citizens, they have no voice in the institutions which govern them. They are victims of a chain of inconsistencies:

1. Congress requires that aliens understand English before they can become United States citizens.

2. Since California aliens who do not understand English cannot become U.S. citizens, neither can they acquire California citizenship.

3. Without California citizenship, these Spanish speaking residents cannot vote.

4. Spanish speaking Californians who acauired citizenship by virtue of birth in the U.S. can vote, even though they cannot understand English.

The courts could remedy the paradox by declaring California's requirements of U.S. citizenship unconstitutional. This could be done on the same ground that the English literacy test was struck down in the Castro decision. If this were to happen, a resident alien in California could acquire State citizenship without becoming a U.S. citizen. . . .

In response to the Committee's questioning, California Secretary of State Edmund G. Brown, Jr. stated that he felt that Section 14240 of the Election Code, which states that all of the proceeds at the polls must be in English, was probably unconstitutional in light of the Castro decision.

"How else could they participate intelligently?" he asked.

In his statement to the Committee, Brown made four major points:

1. That valid arguments and other pamphlet material, as well as voting machine instructions, should be printed in Spanish in those areas where a high concentration of Spanish speaking voters resided.

2. The California Election Code has many restrictive requirements which tend to penalize migrant workers, the young, minorities and the poor. These should be changed, he said. He singled out pre-registering requirements of 54 and 90 days, and the need for bilingual registrars. "These registrars should be given adequate financial inducement so that they are really motivated to register people," he said.

3. Californians, with emphasis on those of Mexican descent, ought to be able to register on a given date and be declared permanent resident immigrants, "however they got here." Brown added: "In many places there is a fear that if they register to vote, their status may not be as secure as they think it is, and they may be deported, or some other governmental intrusion of a similar or unfavorable reaction might occur. So I think we have to give assurance to those people who have lived in our state for a reasonable period of time that they are welcome here, and have every right of every other person in the state. If such a situation were to be declared, then I think that --although those people who weren't citizens couldn't vote-- it would clear the air in such a way that many citizens who are now hesitant to come forward would be able to register."

4. The State of California must take some affirmative steps to hire Mexican Americans and other minorities. "I think that the matter of affirmative recruitment is shockingly inadequate, and that the State has demonstrated very clearly that it is indifferent to the needs, not only of Mexican American citizens, but of poor people in general."

Senator George Moscone, Co-Chairman of the California Commission on Democratic Party Reform, enumerated five recommendations dealing with voter registration which that Commission had prepared for adoption by the party. (All of the recommendations were adopted by the Democratic Party at its State Central Committee Conference in Sacramento the following weekend.)

The recommendations were:

(a) Abolition of residency requirements;

(b) Allow voter registration up to 19 days before an election;

(c) Allow voter registration or re-registration by mail;

(d) Abolish all language and literacy requirements:

(e) Adopt procedures to increase the number of available deputy registrars and simplify registration procedures.

"In the area of voting, we seek to protect the highly mobile and low income voter by abolishing consolidated precincts and printing ballots in Spanish," Moscone said. . . .

APPOINTMENT OF MEXICAN AMERICANS TO POSITIONS IN GOVERNMENT

The fact that only 1.98 percent of California's appointed and elected officials are Mexican American was criticized by State officials as well as by members of the Mexican American community at the meeting.

One speaker on this issue was Dr. Francisco Bravo of Los Angeles, a man who has received more key political appointments than perhaps any other Mexican American in the history of California. Dr. Bravo has received appointments at the municipal, State and Federal levels including Los Angeles City Police Commissioner and State Agricultural Commission; he has been given major appointments by both Democratic and Republican governors of the State. . . .

"We have had practically no appointments out of our 122 Commissioners in the city of Los Angeles. Since we constitute somewhere around 20 to 30 percent of the population, we should have 30 or 40 Commissioners. We usually have six to eight. In the time I served as Commissioner--the first Mexican American Commissioner in the city's history--there was one. Mayor Yorty came through with about 19, but this has been reduced to about six or eight now.

"In the State, we constitute about 15 percent of the population and we should have at least one Mexican American on each one of the boards and commissions. In the critical boards, like the Board of Education, Welfare, Custodial Institutions, Athletic Commission, we should have two or more."

Dr. Bravo stated that Governor Reagan had appointed 54 Mexican Americans to non-civil service jobs in his first four years in office. "We should have between 500 and 1,000 involved in appointed positions, " he said. During the administration of former Governor Edmund G. (Pat) Brown, 30 Mexican Americans were appointed, he said.

The question of finding qualified Mexican Americans is no irrelevant, Dr. Bravo stated. "We have a plethora of well-trained, didactically trained individuals in the various professions and skills, at the tope universities. "

He was particularly critical of the failure of California governors to appoint Mexican American judges.

"How many has Governor Reagan appointed during his regime? The answer to that is five. But only three are Mexican Americans. The others only carry the Latin or Spanish surnames. "

Dr. Bravo said that his experience as a board member and as president of the Los Angeles Police Commission made him realize the tremendous importance of appointing Mexican Americans to judgeships.

"Judges indeed are the last resort, " he said, "the last resort for Mexican Americans who are caught in the jungle of laws and of law enforcement people, prosecutors who are dedicated only to their particular job, and not to individuals or to the background of individuals, culturally speaking. . . .

The U.S. Civil Rights Commission staff report showed that there are 1, 179 superior, municipal and justice court judges and county constables in California, 21 of whom are Mexican American. Broken down, there are 407 Superior Judges in the state, three of whom are Mexican American (all in Los Angeles County). There are 315 municipal judges and 240 justice court judges. Nine of these are Mexican American. There are 217 constables, nine of whom are Mexican Americans. Thus, Mexican Americans represent about 1.7 percent of the city and county judiciary process.

Lorenzo Patino, a board member of the National Urban Coalition and a law student at the University of California at Davis, brought the Committee the official 1970 California Legislative Handbook, which lists State Assembly and Senate staff members, including consultants, administrative assistants, administrative secretaries, secretaries, typists and clerks.

Of 445 people listed as working for the Assembly, only five had Spanish surnames. Four of these were typists and the fifth was an intern, he said.

Of the 223 employees listed for the Senate, only two had Spanish surnames; both were administrative assistants.

"The only agency in the State of California which is not covered by the Fair Employment Practices' rules or guidelines is the State Legislature, which created F.E.P.C. I think it is tragic that the legislature is the greatest violator of the intent of its own legislation, " Patino remarked.

Secretary of State Edmund Brown stated that in the three weeks since he took office, he found affirmative recruitment--including that of the 120 persons working in his own office--"shocklingly inadequate. "

"The imbalance that has been pointed out before this Committee demonstrates an indifference and lack of recruitment, he said. . . .

MAJOR POLITICAL PARTIES AND THE MEXICAN AMERICAN

Few witnesses made direct reference to the failure of the Democratic and Republican Parties to involve the Mexican American in the party structures themselves. They seemed, instead, to accept it as common knowledge, and move directly into attacks on the policies and practices of both parties.

Abe Tapia, president of the Mexcian American Political Association, (MAPA), stated that "the two-party system has failed the Mexican. We don't need it. We don't want it."

Bert Corona, national MAPA organizer, said: "Both parties have been guilty of using the Spanish speaking and Chicano vote for their imperative of control of the legislature....They are cynical in their dealings with our needs and aspirations....Both parties ultimately have shown that they represent the big money interest."

Most repeated complaints against the parties included:

1. The parties, particularly the Democratic Party, have deliberately gerrymandered Mexican American districts, preventing Mexican Americans from electing their own representatives.

2. The parties, particularly the Democratic Party, have not given Mexican Americans any voice in selecting candidates to run in those districts with high Mexican American population.

3. The parties, particularly the Democratic Party, have not supported Mexican American candidates financially.

4. The Democratic Party has given only lip service to the needs of the Mexican American community, while the Republican Party still fails to understand those needs.

5. The parties have slighted the Mexican American community in providing resources for voter registration drives.

6. The parties court the Mexican American community only briefly during election time, and then jult it on the day after election.

7. The parties structure their conferences and conventions in such a way as to make them "rich men's pastimes", out of the reach of poor minorities. (Tapia referred to Democratic Party conference registration fees as a "poll tax" which excludes Mexican Americans.)

Senator H. L. Richardson, chairman of the Republican Senate Caucas, commented that "Mexican Americans have literally put all of their eggs in one basket. They have for years joined one party, and have for years been systematically taken advantage of, much in the same fashion as other minorities. They have lost their leverage. The Mexican American is a hip-pocket vote. The question is, how can you turn them out on any given election? Once they have committed themselves to this posture, then the only question is, how does the lily-white liberal divvy up the Mexican American community to serve as a consistent voting bloc for his district? ...As long as the Mexican American put all his eggs in one basket, he shouldn't be surprised when they get crushed."

Several of the Mexican Americans who addressed the Committee pledged their support to La Raza Unida, the Mexican American party which has won election victories in other Southwestern areas, including Crystal City, Texas.

Tapia said: "We need a candidate who comes from the community, is selected by the community, and we don't give a damn if the Democratic Party likes him or the Republican Party likes him.

"We are going to select him, not the parties. The Chicano community is going to select its own candidates. That is why I have been trying to resolve some of the problems in our community and unify our community so that we can, once and for all, determine what we are going to do with the two-party system that affects us every day.

"We are saying to them that the La Raza Unida Party is going to be one that is going to fight them, no matter what. We are going to make it a reality in the State of California, such as it is in Texas, New Mexico, Arizona, and Colorado."

Richard Calderon, who was narrowly defeated in the Democratic Primary for the United States Congress in 1970, foresaw "a strong possibility of La Raza Unida developing and qualifying for the 1972 general elections if no districts are drawn in our behalf".

Peter Chacon, freshman Mexican American Assemblyman from San Diego County, told the Committee that the major political parties "must realize they have a serious responsibility in seeing that Chicanos do have part of the political feast", and must appoint them to important positions within their parties.

Chairmen of the State central committees of both major political parties were invited to appear or send their representatives.

State Senator Dennis Carpenter, retiring chairman of the Republican State Central Committee, accepted the Committee's invitation.

Senator Carpenter stated that while he had a major interest in involving Mexican Americans in the Republican Party, "I want to state honestly that I am not satisfied with the progress I have made in this area."

Senator Carpenter referred direct questions on numerical participation of Mexican Americans to John Lopez, chairman of the Republican State Central Committee's Ethnic and Nationalities Committee.

Lopez estimated that of the central committees 1,250 regular voting members, 30 were Mexican Americans.

Lopez stated that he knew of no Mexican Americans who were officers of the Republican State Central Committee, and Senator Carpenter recalled one Mexican American who was a member of the California delegation to the 1968 Republican National Convention.

Senator Carpenter stated that there were two Mexican American Republican congressional candidates, "both of whom I helped financially," in 1970. Neither was successful, he said. . . .

Roger Boas, chairman of the State Democratic Central Committee, declined an invitation to appear, and did not send a representative.

State Senator George Moscone, Senate Majority Leader and co-chairman of the California Commission on Democratic Party Reform did speak.

He stated that, "For too long the way has been substantially blocked for members of minority races to enter the mainstream of political power and public office....California's traditional stance of non-partisanship and a tacitly-approved weak political party structure has only tended to maintain the status quo and the evils of political segregation.". . .

REPRESENTATION IN LOS ANGELES AND OTHER URBAN AREAS

Eighty percent of California's Mexican Americans--more than two million--live in urban areas. According to a study released in February, 1971, by the Economic & Youth Opportunities Agency (EYOA), Los Angeles County alone has more than 1.1 million Mexican Americans, with half of these clustered in the Greater East Los Angeles area.

Yet, speaker after speaker reminded the Committee, no Mexican Americans are serving on the two key elective bodies in that area: the 15-member Los Angeles City Council or the 5-member Lost Angeles County Board of Supervisors.

How the exclusion of Mexican Americans from the Los Angeles City Council came about was described by Councilman Tom Bradley.

"It did not come about by accident, " he said. "Over the years we have seen deliberate efforts through gerrymandering which precluded minorities from being elected. I know it from a firsthand point of view because I saw it happening with the black community for years. When that community would grow to a point where it was a threat to the City Council, they would suddenly redraw the lines and instead of running them north and south, they would run them east and west, anything that would cut up that ever-expanding population in that section.

"The same thing has been true with respect to Mexican Americans."

Councilman Bradley stated that an incumbent had an authomatic 12-20 percent advantage in an election and admitted that no incumbent councilman would willingly sacrifice his seat. He and some other councilmen attempted to solve the problem in 1968 by developing a plan to enlarge the City Council to 17 members. (It had been a 15-member body since 1925, when the city's population was 500,000, compared to its present 3,000,000.)

"We failed by one vote in getting the necessary support to put it on the ballot as part of our charter. Instead, we had to put it on the ballot as a separate issue and to tie it to the main charter reform. If the main ballot issue failed (which it did), no matter how many votes the expansion got, it couldn't win. The cares were stacked against us from the very beginning."

Armando Morales pointed out that the Chicano Law Students Association and the Congress of Mexcian American Unity both tried to persuade the Council to expand its membership. After an initial denial of the request, the Council agreed to the plan Bradley mentioned.

"Mexican Americans viewed this feeble, impractical attempt as a political maneuver designed to make Mexican Americans believe that the City Council was truly attempting to help them develop political power, " Morales commented.

He said that the County Board of Supervisors rejected a similar request to expand their membership.

In his presentation, Bert Corona of MAPA made the recommendations that the city reconstitute a councilmanic district that is 50 percent Mexican American and that the county put all of East Los Angeles into one supervisorial district.

Joe Ortega, chief Los Angeles counsel for the Mexican American Legal Defense & Education Fund, pointed out that the apportionment of the Los Angeles councilmanic districts was done on the basis of registered voters, a concept which MALDEF challenged in the suit, Calderon v. the City of Los Angeles.

"Registered voters and populations are not the same thing, " Ortega told the Committee. "In the Mexican American areas, because of, among other thins, lack of education, lack of sufficient command of the English language and lack of a familiarity and a competence in the political system, the people do not register to vote in the same percentages as they do in other areas.

"In the Ninth Councilmanic District, which is primarily in the East Los Angeles area and which has vast numbers of Mexican Americans, there are 260,000 persons. On the other hand, the Fifth Councilmanic District, which includes West Los Angelese, Westwood and Bel Air--almost entirely all white--has 162,000 people.

"It seems to me that that not only violates the principles of the one-man, one-vote rule, which the Supreme Court has enunciated, but it makes the Mexican American nothing less than a second class citizen. If he is underrepresented in City Hall, he does in fact receive poor governmental services, which, in turn, keep him from getting the proper skills and the proper economic well-being to be able to register to vote. The thing becomes a perpetuating system.

"If you deny him these services, he will not register to vote in the same frequency that other people do. Consequently, his vote continues to get debased more and more. "

On March 2, 1971, six weeks after Ortega spoke, the California Supreme Court held that the districts drawn by the city of Los Angeles do not reflect the one-man, one-vote rule and must be based on equal numbers of people rather than registered voters.

Ortega also mentioned the problem of gerrymandering councilmanic districts.

"The U.S. Census graphs show that there is a large concentration of Mexican Americans in a relatively small area of Los Angeles, the East and Northeast area. There is a very, very great concentration of Mexican Americans.

"This area, however, under the councilmanic scheme, is split up into three councilmanic districts. The Mexican Americans are spread in the ninth, thirteenth and fourteenth districts. "

"I think that it is clear why, even though the Mexican American comprises about 15 percent of the population of Los Angeles, there are not Mexican Americans on the City Council, " Ortega said.

Ortega was asked how he viewed a current move to dissolve all of the councilmanic districts in Los Angeles and to conduct all future elections on an at-large basis, where all of the voters in the city make their selections from all of the candidates.

"The election of representatives at-large has been held to be legally proper in some cases, " he responded, "but when it acts to delete a definite class vote, then it is illegal. I think it would be, in a case like Los Angeles. "

Two speakers from the Mexican American community offered the Committee detailed reports on the continuing conflict between the police and Mexican Americans in East Los Angeles, and its political implications.

The first was Armando Morales, a doctoral candidate at the University of Southern California School of Social Work and author of articles and books on police-community relations as they pertain to Mexican Americans. Morales is a member of the Boards of several civic and community organizations working to improve police-community relations.

Morales stated that East Los Angeles had been the scene of four urban riots within a 12-month period, and that the underlying reason for the police-community confrontations there was political power.

"East Los Angeles has had more civil turmoil than any area in the United States for the years 1970 and 1971, and in its plea for help from politicians, it has been totally ignored by Los Angeles Mayor Sam Yorty, the Los Angeles City Council, the County Board of Supervisors, Governor Reagan and even President Nixon, " Morales stated.

"This inattention merely reflects a symptom of political powerlessness, as only political power elicits political interest. Related to this and intensifying the problem is that Anglo-Saxon politicians are even less interested in the Mexican American poor. "

"The current overt conflict between Mexican Americans and law enforcement agencies in Los Angeles is plainly a political confrontation where the police are using their legal authority and power to suppress and oppress Mexican American efforts toward political organization and social change.

"No longer is the police assault being directed to murderers, rapists and thieves, but rather the police are out to stifle dissent, harass nonconformists and contain the politically militant minorities. The police target is not criminality, but social and political deviance from the status quo. "

"The silence of politicians only serves to give license to police to do what they wish. "

Morales complained of a "double standard" of government rule of "selective democracy, " in Los Angeles.

"Some people and some communities in Los Angeles enjoy the real advantages of a democracy, but others, such as Mexican Americans in East Los Angeles, do not. This is the primary reason why conflict exists between the police and Mexican Americans and the reason why these problems cannot be solved on the local Mexican American community level.

Political self-determination has to become a reality if one wishes to see a final end to the conflict between the Mexican American community and the police, " Morales emphasized.

The "double standards" of law enforcement range from drunk arrests to use of State conspiracy statutes to discourage political dissent, Morales claimed.

He stated that in East Los Angeles there are approximately 10,000 Spanish surnamed persons arrested annually for drunkeness or drunk driving; yet, in a middle-class Anglo-Saxon community across town, with the same rate of alcoholism, there are only 1,500 people being arrested per year for the same offenses.

"Americans have a right to political dissension and to demonstrate publicly, " he continued. "However, the District Attorney used the state conspiracy statutes against Mexican Americans on at least three occasions-- the East Los Angelese high school blowouts in May 1968, the 1969 Biltmore Hotel 'Nuevas Vistas Ten' education demonstration, and the December 1969, Catolicos de la Raza demonstrations at St. Basil's Catholic Church. Rather than dealing with alleged law violations, distrubing the peace, etc., as individual acts and therefore misdemeanor offenses, the district attorney chose to use the conspiracy laws, felony offenses, as a political tool to discourage political dissent."

Morales also mentioned the "harassment and unwarranted arrests" of activists by police, as well as raids on activists' headquarters and private homes.

Rosalio Munoz, former student body president of UCLA and chairman of the Chicano Moratorium Committee, explained the original role of his organization: to place the issue of the Vietnam War, where a disproportionate number of Mexican Americans were serving and dying, before the Mexican American community.

"The role of the committee is one of politics, " he said. "We engage in speech-plus activities, something very, very necessary to our community, because we have no real effective political representation. Because of this lack of representation and lack of effectiveness of the representation which we do have, political issues as defined by the standard institutions in this country do not relate to our people and their everyday lives."

The U.S. Commission on Civil Rights released the report on Mexican American and the Administration of Justice in the Southwest, which covered many of the problems which Mexican Americans encounter with law enforcement agencies and with the courts, in March 1970. The California State Advisory Committee to the Commission issued a report on the August 29, 1970 East Los Angeles riots and related police-community conflicts in September 1970. In that report it made several recommendations.

Dr. Julian Nava, a member of the Los Angeles Board of Education, told the Committee that there were 300 Mexican Americans serving on school boards nationally, and that in California, there are slightly more than 100.

"We have concluded that there is little prospect where school boards

are appointed that local powers are willing to appoint Mexican Americans,"
Nava continued. "We have also concluded that the election of Mexican Americans to school board membership is frequently the result of peculiar local
circumstances and that most of the Mexican American school board members are elected by coalitions and when elected have a numb er of strings at-
tached to it or restraints placed upon them for fear that if they speak up too
clearly regarding Mexican American needs their political support will be
withdrawn."

"It isn't a rosy picture, as I see it, for the future. The figure 100 may
sound impressive, but it is infinitesimally small in relation to the proportion of Mexican American school children in our state."

Dr. Nava identified gerrymandering and appointive school boards as
the two biggest obstacles to adequate Mexican American representation on
school boards.

"The appointive boards I have become acquainted with have always reflected the two or three major vested interests in that community: commerce,
banking, certain forms of industry or the agribusiness," he said.

The Civil Rights Commission staff report showed one Mexican American, Tony Sierra, of Calexico, on the State Board of Education. He was appointed by Governor Ronald Reagan, replacing Dr. Miguel Montes of Los
Angeles, an appointee of Governor Edmund G. Brown and the first Mexican
American to serve on the board in this century.

MEXICAN AMERICAN POLITICAL REPRESENTATION
IN SMALL COMMUNITIES AND RURAL AREAS

Mexican Americans are represented on the governing bodies of California's small communities and rural areas in very low proportion compared
to their population statewide.

The Civil Rights Commission staff study, conducted in January 1971,
shows that Mexican Americans comprise only two percent of the governmental leaders in cities under 10,000 population, and only three percent of the
governmental leaders in cities between 10,000 to 50,000 population.

In cities with under 10,000 population, there are 181 mayors, six, (three
percent) of whom are Mexican American; 724 council men, 44 (6 percent)
of whom are Mexican American; and 3,098 other officials, 39 (1 percent)
of whom are Mexican American.

In cities with 10,000 to 50,000 population, there are 155 mayors four (3
percent) of whom are Mexican American; 633 councilmen, 33 (5 percent) of
whom are Mexican American, and 1,815 other officials, 42 (2 percent) of
whom are Mexican American.

Rural counties, generally, appear to offer inadequate opportunities for
Mexican Americans to participate in governmental functions. . . .

Individuals from several rural areas appeared before the Committee,
including San Benito County, which has a school population greater than 50
percent Mexican American, yet--according to the California State Roster

for 1970--has only one Spanish surnamed official in city or county government, out of a total of 51 officeholders.

Speakers from these areas stated that pressures facing rural Mexican
Americans who attempt to become politically active are quite different from
those confonting urban Mexican Americans.

Frank Valenzuela, former mayor and city councilman in Hollister, San
Benito County, described how he was forced to leave his community due to
economic pressures when he spoke out against the use of braceros--con-
tract Mexican farm laborers--who were depriving local residents of work.

Don Kates, a California Rural Legal Assistance (CRLA) attorney with
offices in Gilroy, Santa Clara County, stated that Mexican Americans are
generally excluded from grand jury service and that this works against the
farm laborer in the rural communities.

"In this state, the grand jury investigates every type of local public ac-
tivity--how the hospital runs, how the jail runs, how the welfare program
runs, " Kates explained. "One of the things we have found in rural communities is the fact that there are laws governing how growers operate, the conditions in the field, minimum wage, and so on. All of these laws are criminal laws, and they are all violated with complete impunity. I have never
heard of a grower being prosecuted. In fact, I have just received answers
to a request in San Bernardino County in which the District Attorney admitted he had never heard of a grower being prosecuted for a crime against
the Mexican Americans in the history of that county, and I think I could con-
fidnetly say that there has never been, in rural California, the prosecution
of a grower for any crime, a violation of health and sanitation laws, minimum
wage laws, or anything of that type. "

Kates called grand jury service "the sole source of participation in
government for the common ordinary citizen. "

He stated that he made a study of the grand jury service in California's
20 counties with the greatest percentage of Spanish surnamed population.
In all of them, he said, Mexican Americans were consistently underrepresented. In 15 of them, the underrepresentation was so serious that it raised the
question of unconstitutional jury discrimination. Grand jury candidates are
selected in California by judges.

"The courts have held that if the minority group percent of the population is three times as great as minority group percent of grand jurors over
a period of some years, a presumption of unconstitutional selection will be
held to have been raised. We found that in 15 counties (out of the 20 studied)
there was more than a three-to-one discrepancy. In one county, no Mexican
American had been a grand juror for 30 years. "

Kates concluded:

"If the grand jury were composed, in part, of people who care about the
farm workers in the field, it would be possible we would have some indict-
ments and have some inquiries into why the District Attorney's offices find
it important to prosecute people for some crimes but not important to prosecute them for others. ". . .

The trio, Cododac Colchado, Martin De Leon and Daniel M. Ruiz, prepared a paper for the Committee in which they stated that more than a third of the nation's migrant farm workers work at least part of the year in California.

"An estimated 190,000 agricultural migrant workers and their families were on the move in 43 counties in California during 1968," their report stated. "About 81 percent of them were of Mexican origin."

These workers' right to vote has been compromised "by means ranging from outright intimidation to restrictive laws which make registration difficult," the report said.

Andy Tobar described his efforts to encourage Mexican Americans in Mendota, a small town with 80 percent Mexican American population but less than 50 percent Mexican American voter registration, to become candidates for municipal office. He had talked to more than ten potential candidates, he said, none of whom would run. He added:

"Some were just beginning their businesses and they were fearful that their vote might jeopardize their business and their family's livelihoods. Some did not feel they were qualified. Because they were so fearful that they would do an inadequate job, they preferred not to get involved. Yet, in my experience with City Council meetings and Board of Trustee meetings, I think that Chicanos are more than qualified. But the thing is, we have never really been shown why we should get involved."

Tobar pointed out that in his experience, the media would not pay the same attention to Mexican American candidates that it would to other candidates, and, by stereotyping Mexican Americans, it reinforced Mexican Americans' feelings of inferiority."

"I think the responsibility also has to be on the media," he said. "They have got to take positive steps so that La Raza can look at themselves in a very positive sense, and once we start building our own self-image and the people around us start looking at the Chicano as a person who is capable of having intelligence, then we can start winning the elections." . . .

PARTICIPATION OF MEXICAN AMERICANS
IN CALIFORNIA GOVERNMENT

Background

In 1960 the U.S. Census reported that of California's total population of 15,717,204, the Spanish surnamed population was 1,426,583 or 9 percent. In July 1967 the California State Department of Finance estimated that of a total 1967 population of 19,478,000, the Spanish surnamed population was 2,162,100 or 10.9%. Since the Spanish surnamed population increased 1.9 percent in the seven years 1960-1967, projected growth for the years 1968-1970 would be 8 percent. In other words, we can estimate that for 1970, Spanish surnamed people comprise 11 percent of the State's population. [1]

Also in 1967 the State Department of Education issued by counties the percent of Spanish surnamed enrollment in the public schools. [2] By correlating this data with the State's estimates of each county's population in 1970, it can be estimated that over 80 percent of the Spanish surnamed population is concentrated in 12 of the 58 counties. These counties, each of which has total populations of over 100,000 persons, are Fresno, Kern, Los Angeles, Merced, Monterey, Riverside, San Bernardino, San Juoaquin, Santa Barbara, Santa Clara, Tulare, and Ventura.

Six additional counties (Colusa, Imperial, Kings, Madera, San Benito and Yolo) although relatively low in population, have high percentages of Spanish surnamed public school populations. By estimating the 1970 Spanish surnamed population of these counties and adding them to the above 12 counties, we cann account for over 90 percent of the Spanish surnamed population.

Three additional counties should be noted. In 1967, San Francisco, Santa Cruz, and San Diego Counties' Spanish surnamed school populations were 14 percent, 13 percent, and 11 percent respectively; the 1960 U.S. Census Report suggests that nay of the remaining Spanish surnamed population, as estimated by the state, can be accounted for in these counties.

Mexican Americans in Federal, State and Local
    Elected and Appointed Offices[4]

Each year the Secretary of State of California issues a book entitled
California Roster of Federal, State, County and City Officials.[5] This book
includes the names and locations of every major elected and appointed official of the state at all levels of government; it is compiled with the "cooperation of Federal, State, County, and City and other agencies."[6] State
civil service employees are included only when their positions rely directly
or indirectly on appointment by the Governor's office, other executive office officials and/or the State Legislature; city and county officials are included only when their positions rely directly or indirectly on appointments
by elected officials.[7]

The 1970 Roster lists 15,650 positions at all government levels; only
310 or 1.98 percent were held by Mexican Americans.[8] The majority of
these (241) were officials in city and county offices; 1.2 percent of California's Federal and State offices were held by Mexican Americans, although
they comprise nearly 12 percent of the State population.

1970 California Roster of Federal, State, County and City Officials

Category of Office	Total # in Office	Total # Mexican Ameri-cans
Federal Elected and Appointed	525	7 (1.3%)
State Legislators and Advisors	195	2 (1%)
Executive Offices of State	2,291	13 (Less than 1%)
State Boards, Commissions and Advisories	1,732	47 (2.7%)
City and County Government Officials	10,907	241 (2.2%)
TOTALS - Gov't all levels	15,650	310 (1.98%)

In the Roster, there is a listing of the top officials for each State in the
Union. California's list includes 40 top State offices. . . .

Mexican Americans in Offices of the Federal Government
Few Mexican Americans are found in elected and appointed positions
of the Federal Government specifically serving Californians. In the national

legislature (Senate and House of Representatives) there is only one Mexican American.[10] In the U.S. Court of Appeals and the U.S. District Courts (which include U.S. judges, referees, probation officers, commissioners and marshals) there are 262 positions; only six are Mexican American (2 percent). None of these six are judges or referees. In California there are four U.S. Attorneys and 87 Assistant U.S. Attorneys; none of these are Mexican American.[11]

Mexican Americans in Office of the State Government

Legislature. In the California State Legislature there are 120 seats, and one of these is held by a Mexican American.[12] When combined legislative staff is examined (including the Senate and Assembly Attaches, the Office of the Auditor General, the Joint Legislative Budget Committee technical staff and the Legislative Counsel) out of nearly 75 staff advisors, only one is Mexican American (1.3 percent)

Judiciary. At the State level in the courts there are 132 positions including the seven Supreme Court Justices, the Judicial Council, the Administrative Office of the Courts, the Commission on Judicial Qualifications and the State Court of Appeals.[13] No Mexican Americans hold any of these high offices.

Executive. In California there are seven elected officials responsible for the administration and enforcement of State laws and regulations: the Governor, the Lt. Governor, the Secretary of State, the State Controller, the State Treasurer, the Attorney General, and the State Superintendent of Instruction. These seven officials, none of whom are Mexican American, and the State Legislature, select and appoint all State Boards, Advisories, and Commissions.

The Roster lists 28 advisors in the Governor's office none of whom are Mexican American. One hundred officials are listed in the Lt. Governor's office; two are Mexican American. In the Secretary of State's, Treasurer's, and Superintendent of Instruction's offices there are 31 staff advisors; none of whom are Mexican American.[14] There are no Mexican Americans among the State Controller's 12 assistants although there are three Mexican Americans who are among the 144 Tax Appraisers, a position appointed by the Controller. In the Attorney General's office there are 283 deputies, representatives and assistant attorney generals; one assistant attorney general is Mexican American.

The 135 boards, commissions and advisories at the State level in California provide a continuous feedback to the State officials on the needs and concerns of the population. Some of these boards set policy and make budget decisions which broadly affect the entire state. These include the State Board of Education, State Board of Equalization, Public Employment Retirement System, Regents of the University of California, Commission on Housing and Community Development, and the Governor's Cabinet. Of the 69 persons on these boards, only two (2.8 percent) are Mexican American.

Finally, the Roster itemizes high level civil service staff which provide advisory assistance to the elected officials and to the appointed boards and commissions. Many of these positions are personally selected by elected officials and are responsible for day to day policy and planning. There are 1,686 offices in the Roster, seven of which are occupied by Mexican Americans, or less than one percent.

Mexican Americans in Offices of County and City Government

Statewide Participation. The Roster lists a total of 10,907 officials in the county and city governments; 241 (2.2 percent) of these are Mexican Americans.

Governing the 58 counties in California are 296 county supervisors and 1,402 other elected and appointed officials. There are nine Mexican American supervisors (3.4 percent) and 13 Mexican Americans who occupy other official offices (less than one percent). Not included in the above tabulation are the superior court judges, municipal court judges, justce court judges, and county constables. There are 1,179 such offices in the State 21 of which are Mexican American. Specifically, there are 407 Superior Judges in California, three of whom are Mexican American, and all of whom work in Los Angeles County. There are 315 Municipal judges and 240 justice court judges; nine of these are Mexican Americans. Finally, there are 217 constables; nine of these are Mexican Americans. In other words, Mexican Americans represent about 1.7 percent of the county and city judiciary process.

In 1970 there were 403 incorporated cities in the state. There were 181 cities with populations under 10,000; 155 cities with populations from 10,000 to 50,000; 64 cities with populations from 50,000 to 500,000; and three cities with populations over 500,000 (Los Angeles, San Diego, and San Francisco). [15]

Participation of Mexican Americans in Local Government - By Size of City

Population	Mayors Non MA/MA	Councilmen Non MA/MA	Others* Non MA/MA
0-10,000	175/6	680/44	3059/39
10,000 to 50,000	151/4	600/33	1772/42
50,000 to 500,000	63/1	312/20	911/15
Over 500,000	3/0	32/1	66/0

*First number is total nonMexican American; 2nd number is Mexican American.

In cities with under 10,000 population, there are 181 mayors, six (3 percent) of whom are Mexican American; 724 councilmen, 44 (6 percent) of whom are Mexican American; and 3,098 other officials, 39 (1 percent) of whom are Mexican American. In summary, Mexican Americans are in 2 percent of the county and city governments' decision making positions in cities of this size.

In cities with 10,000 to 50,000 population, there are 155 mayors, four (3 percent) of whom are Mexican American; 633 councilmen, 33 (5 percent) of whom are Mexican American; and 1,815 other officials, 42 (2 percent) of whom are Mexican American. Mexican Americans occupy 3 percent of the decision making positions in these cities.

In cities with 50,000 to 500,000 population, there are 64 mayors, one (1 percent) of whom are Mexican American. Within these city governments, Mexican Americans represent 2.7 percent of the officials.

Finally, in California's three largest cities, there are 99 mayors, councilmen and other officials, only one of whom is Mexican American.

Participation of Mexican Americans in 18 selected counties. As mentioned above, most of the Mexican American population reside in 18 of California's 58 counties. A review of the participation of Mexican Americans in local government, specifically in these counties and cities, will perhaps give a more realistic assessment of the Mexican American representation at the local level.[16]

Participation of Mexican Americans in 18 Selected Counties
(City and County Government Officials)

County	Total # Officials	Total # MA	%MA
Fresno	256	17	7
Kern	181	1	-
Los Angeles	1247	41	3
Merced	140	6	4
Monterey	205	3	1
Riverside	295	13	4
San Bernardino	254	7	3
San Joaquin	75	-	-
Santa Barbara	124	3	2
Santa Clara	271	11	4
Tulare	144	3	2
Ventura	192	6	3
Colusa	32	-	-
Imperial	118	9	7
Kings	79	3	4
Madera	60	-	-
San Benito	51	1	2
Yolo	80	1	1
TOTAL	3,806	125	3.2%

In 16 of the 18 counties, less than 5 percent of the city and county officials are Mexican American; four of the counties have less than 1 percent
or zero percent participation of Mexican Americans (Kern, San Joaquin,
Colusa, and Madera Counties). Five additional counties have less than 3
percent participation of Mexican Americans in local government. (Monterey,
Santa Barbara, Tulare, San Benito, and Yolo Counties). The largest number
of Mexican Americans in the State reside in Los Angeles County; yet there
are no Mexican Americans in county government decision making positions.
In the 78 cities within L.A. County, there are only 41 (3 percent) Mexican
American officials out of 1,247 offices.

In two of the 18 counties, Fresno and Imperial, 7 percent of the city
and county officials are Mexican American. Although these counties have
very high percentages of Mexican Americans in their populations. Fresno's
Spanish surnamed school population is 29 percent and Imperial's is 45 percent.

'In conclusion, the majority of Mexican Americans reside in 18 counties;
yet, out of 3,804 offices in these county and city governments, Mexican
Americans occupy only 125 or 3 percent.

FOOTNOTES

1. U.S. Census figures for 1970 on the Spanish surnamed are not yet available. Therefore, we have used State 1967 figures, to estimate 1970 Spanish
surnamed percent of total population.

2. See State Department of Education Report, Racial and Ethnic Survey
of California Public Schools, Part One, Sacramento, 1967 Appendix E.

3. Every effort was made to obtain the number of Mexican American and/
or Spanish surname registered voters. However, figures were not available
for either the State as a whole or for individual counties. A standard formula for estimating registered voters (the average of total number registered for both primary and general elections multiplied by the percent of
Spanish surname in the population) suggests that there were over 900,000
Spanish surnamed registered voters in 1970. However, there is no information available on exact location and density of these potential voters. Those
contacted for possible number of Spanish surname registered included both
the Democrat and Republican Central Committees, the Secretary of State,
Los Angeles County Registrar of Voters and the Los Angeles County Planning Commission.

4. In tabulating the number of Mexican American officials in the California
Roster, an effort was made to eliminate those Spanish surnamed individuals
whose ethnic heritage is other than Mexican. Commission staff attempted
to verify as many names as possible by letter or telephone, but staff and
time limitations prevented verification of all 15,000 plus names. In some

cases names of individuals of Mexican American heritage with non-Spanish surnames were added to the totals. Therefore, the remainder of the paper refers to Mexican American specifically rather than the larger Spanish surnamed group.

5. All the data is derived from the California Roster unless specifically noted otherwise. 1970 California Roster of Federal, State, County and City Officials compiled by the Secretary of State, Office of Procurement, Documents, Sacramento, California.

6. California Roster, Inside Front Cover.

7. Not all city and county officials are included, but in general most major elected and appointed officials with decision-making powers are recorded. A typical entry for a city would include mayor, councilmen, city clerk, district attorney, police chief, fire chief, treasurer, city manager, parks and recreation director, public service department manager, superintendent of buildings, planning director and school superintendent.

8. Some individuals occupy more than one office. In that case they are counted twice, or as many different times as their names appear in a new capacity.

9. California Roster, pp 186-187.

10. In addition to the one Mexican American from California, there are two Congressmen from Texas, one Congressman and one Senator from New Mexico.

11. The Roster does not include all Federal appointments in 1970 such as Manuel Ruiz, U.S. Commission on Civil Rights or Martin Castillo, former Chairman, Cabinet Committee for the Spanish Speaking.

12. In November 1970 one additional Mexican American was elected to the State Assembly.

13. Some of the judges are in several capacities within this category and are counted twice in those cases.

14. See below for civil service employees with policy and decision making powers.

15. San Francisco is both a city and a county and is tabulated in both categories.

16. None of California's unincorporated areas are included in these tabulations.

17. Judiciary is not included here. Mexican American representation in local judiciary is discussed elsewhere in the paper.

THE CHICANO RENAISSANCE

by Philip D. Ortego y Gasca

This article by Dr. Ortego y Gasca is a classic.
He examines the Chicano literary renaissance in
relationship to the rise of the Chicano Movement
of the sixties and then places it within the context
of American literature and American society. He
postulates that the significance of this renaissance
lies in the identification of Chicanos with their
Mexican-Indian past, from which they have drawn
their literary symbols and metaphors and this, in
turn, has changed the Chicanos' own psychological
and literary image and consequently, society's
view of them.

Source: Reprinted by permission of Dr. Philip
D. Ortego y Casca

In *Understanding Media,* Marshall Mc-Luhan explains that "the medium is the message . . . that the personal and social consequences of any medium—that is, of any extension of ourselves—result from the new scale that is introduced into our affairs by each extension of ourselves."[1] Applying McLuhan's proposition to the Chicano movement, for example, we can see that the Chicano movement is the medium for extending ourselves (Chicanos) in American society, and, as such, the Chicano movement becomes the message. Such slogans as *Ya Basta, Venceremos,* and *Chicano Power* are only elements of the total message; they are simply part of the new scale introduced into Chicano affairs by each of our individual thrusts toward greater participation in American society. Indeed, the personal and social consequences of our extensions into American society have been the result of a new scale of values and aspirations that we have created with each extension of ourselves.

In particular, these extensions appeared first in the form of beneficial societies, then social clubs, and, after World War II, as political organizations. Our extension into the arts—generically including painting, sculpture, architecture, music, dance, literature, drama, and film—is a more recent phenomenon, although there were, of course, Mexican-American artists at various times since 1848.

These artists, however, did not reflect any significant thrust by Mexican Americans into artistic endeavors. They represented only individual successes in penetrating the artistic iron curtain because the animosities engendered by the Mexican-American War created Anglo-American resistance to Mexican-American participation in most spheres of American life except at the lower rungs of the societal ladder. Consequently, Mexican Americans became the backbone of such American enterprises as the cattle industry, the railroad, the cotton industry of the Southwest, mining, and, of course, the fruit and produce industry. The Mexican-American way of life paralleled the black-American way of life, although for the former there was no Emancipation Proclamation.

Nevertheless, the Mexican American was nurtured and sustained in spirit and soul by his music, dance, *cuentos* (folktales), and remembrance of things past—all contributing to the maintenance and development of Mexican-American folk music, folk art, and folklore. Unlike other peoples of the United States—except groups with English-speaking backgrounds, such as the Irish, Scotch, and

[1]Marshall McLuhan, *Understanding Media: The Extensions of Man,* 2d ed. (New York: New American Library, 1964), p. 23.

English—Mexican Americans were reinforced continuously in their language, culture, and heritage by their very proximity to Mexico and the almost uninterrupted flow of immigration (legal and otherwise) from Mexico.

There are no accurate or reliable population figures from 1848 to 1900, but the census reports for those years indicate a steady and consistent growth of Americans of Mexican descent. Recorded Mexican immigration from 1900 to the present indicates that, because there was no quota on Mexican immigration until 1965, well over one million Mexicans have come to the United States. The actual figure may be closer to one and one-half million if other means of entry into the United States employed by Mexican nationals are considered. It is clear from these statistics and from the fact that now more than ten million Mexican Americans are living in this country that Mexican Americans are essentially a native group, most of whom were born in the United States.

Mexican Americans have always been "Americans" in the true sense of the word because they were very much a part of the landscape when the Anglo Americans arrived in the Southwest. Despite their early settlement and their large numbers, Mexican Americans have been the most shamefully neglected minority in the United States. In the Southwest, where approximately seven of the ten million live, they subsist on levels of survival far below the national norms. The reason for this low subsistence level, many Mexican Americans argue, is that they are victims of the Treaty of Guadalupe Hidalgo—a treaty that identified those who came with the conquered lands of the Southwest as defeated people. Those who came afterwards in the great migrations of the first three decades of the twentieth century have been equally victimized by stereotypes engendered by the Mexican-American War.

In recent years there has been an increasing social and political consciousness, leading to demands for reformation of the socioeconomic structure that has kept Mexican Americans subordinated these many years. With this increasing social and political consciousness has come the awareness of their artistic and literary heritage. Throughout the Southwest the sleeping Mexican-American giant has begun to flex his dormant muscles.

Redefining American literature

The decade of the 1970s promises to be one in which this awakening, this renaissance, will be manifested by a growing desire of Mexican Americans not only to attain status in sociopolitical and economic areas but to seek a more substantial literary identity in the ever-widening mainstream of American literature. In the 1970s Mexican-American writers, scholars, and teachers will attempt to redefine American literature as a fabric woven not exclusively on the Atlantic frontier by the descendents of New England Puritans and southern Cavaliers, but as one woven also in the American Southwest with marvelous Hispanic threads that extend not only to the literary heritage of the European continent but also to the very heart of the Mediterranean world.

Like the British roots in the new American soil, the Hispanic roots have yielded a vigorous and dynamic body of literature that, unfortunately for us, has been studied historically as part of a foreign contribution rather than as part and parcel of our American heritage. Moreover, we seldom learn about the extent to which the Hispanic literacy tradition has influenced American literature. The works dealing with the southern and southwestern parts of the United States, therefore, have become the neglected aspect of the American experience; the implication is that such works are not properly within the traditional definition of American literature because they were not written in English.

Language, however, is hardly a logical reason for not recognizing non-English material as American literature, although it was written in the United States—as in the case of Isaac Bashevis Singer—or what has become the United States—as in the case of the chronicles of the South and Southwest by the Spanish and their progeny. In the pluralistic cultural and linguistic context of contemporary America, we can no longer consent to the suggestions of American literary historians that

American literature properly begins with the arrival of British colonials in America.

American literature actually begins with the formation of the United States as a political entity. Thus, the literary period from the founding of the first permanent British settlement at Jamestown, Virginia, in 1607, to the formation of the American union represents only the British period of American literature. So, too, the literary period from the first permanent Spanish settlement at Saint Augustine, Florida, in 1565, to the dates of acquisition of these Spanish and Mexican lands by the United States should, in fact, represent the Hispanic period of American literature. More appropriately, the British and Spanish periods should both be listed under the rubric "Colonial American Literature." The Mexican period of the Southwest should simply be labeled "The Mexican Period."

Loss of a literary birthright

The neglect of the Spanish and Mexican literature of the Southwest has produced unfortunate literary consequences for Mexican Americans because they have come to see themselves and their Mexican kinsmen portrayed in our national literature by means of racial clichés and distorted caricatures. Like other minority groups, Mexican Americans were and continue to be inaccurately and superficially represented in literature, movies, television, and other mass media. This situation sometimes has been caused by prejudice, but it has also been caused by those well-meaning romanticists who have seriously distorted the image of the Mexican American for the sake of their art.

Mexican Americans have been characterized at both ends of the spectrum of human behavior (seldom in the middle) as untrustworthy, villainous, ruthless, tequila-drinking, and philandering *machos* or else as courteous, devout, and fatalistic peasants who are to be treated more as pets than as people. More often than not Mexican Americans have been cast either as bandits or as lovable rogues; as hot-blooded, sexually animated creatures or as passive, humble servants. The pejorations and generalizations are to be deplored, and Mexican Americans today are beginning to rise up against the perpetuation of such racial clichés.

Whatever the reasons for deliberately or inadvertently neglecting the Hispanic aspect of American literature, the fact remains that not only have Mexican Americans been deprived of their literary birthright but all other Americans have been deprived of an important part of a literary heritage that is also rightfully theirs. Mexican Americans actually have a rich literacy heritage. That they have been kept from it bespeaks a shameful and tragic oppression of a people whose origins antedate the establishment of Jamestown by well over a century (and even more, considering their Indian ancestry). Moreover, the shame and tragedy are compounded when Mexican-American youngsters learn about their Puritan forebears but not about their Hispanic forebears about whom they have as much right—if not more—to be proud.

Heretofore, Mexican Americans have been a marginal people in a sort of no man's land, caught between the polarizing forces of their cultural-linguistic Indo-Hispanic heritage and their political-linguistic American context. They have become frustrated and alienated by the struggle between the system that seeks to refashion them in its own image and the knowledge of who and what they really are. As a result, this cultural conflict has debilitated many Mexican Americans.

Mexican-American youngsters are taught about the cruelty of their Spanish forebears and the savagery of their Mexican-Indian forebears; they have been taught about the Spanish greed for gold, of the infamous Spanish inquisition, of Aztec human sacrifices, of Mexican bandits, and of the massacre at the Alamo. They seldom, if ever, learn of the other men at the Alamo, their Mexican forebears—unknown and unsung in American history—who were killed fighting on the Texas side. American children probably have never heard of such men as Juan Abamillo, Juan Badillo, Carlos Espalier, Gegorio Esparza, Antonio Fuentes, José Maria Guerrero, Toribio Losoya, Andres Nava, and other Texas Mexicans at the Alamo.

In order to be fully comprehended, the ethnic phenomenon of Mexican Americans since World War II must be viewed in the more personal context of their literature. What we have seen instead has been the myriad educational, sociopolitical, and socioeconomic accounts by Anglo investigators and researchers who have pursued the phenomenological chimeras of the queer, the curious, and the quaint. To understand the significance of human movements, we must assess the evidence from the arts. There is little doubt that the contributions to the American experience by Mexican Americans and their forebears have yet to be understood and measured.

In the Southwest the relationship between Mexican Americans and Anglo Americans is similar to that of a legally adopted child and adoptive parents. The analogy describes the circumstances of Spanish-speaking peoples in all the Hispanic territories acquired by the United States. To pursue the analogy to its proper conclusion, we must ask whether, in trying to educate the child about his proper past, we talk about the heritage of the adoptive parents or the *actual* heritage of the adopted child? To indoctrinate the child with the heritage of his new parents as if it were his own is to perpetrate the grossest kind of fraud at the expense of the child.

Information about the literary accomplishments of Mexican Americans during the period from the end of the Mexican-American War to the turn of the century, for example, has been negligible. As Américo Paredes has pointed out, "With few exceptions, documents available for study of the region are in English, being for the most part reports made by officials who were, to put it mildly, prejudiced against the people they were trying to pacify."[2]

American writers have tended to minimize the literary achievements of Mexican Americans in the Southwest for reasons ranging from jingoism to ignorance. It should be noted, however, that no sooner had the Spanish established their hold on Mexico than they started a printing press in Mexico City

in 1529, more than a century earlier than any established in the British colonies of North America. Indeed, there was a substantial Spanish-reading public in New Spain and Mexico, including the North Mexican states, until the lands were ceded to the United States in 1848. Spanish literature was read and written in both the Spanish peninsula and in the New World. Such Spanish playwrights as Pedro Calderón de la Barca and Lope de Vega extended their literary influence to Spanish America just as the Mexican-born playwright Juan Ruiz de Alarcón extended his literary influence to Spain.

Oral transmission of heritage

In the Southwest the people who had come with the land continued to tell and retell the tales that their forebears had brought from the Old World and from Mexico. These folktales had been passed on from generation to generation until they became a decidedly strong oral tradition. Mexican Americans were therefore not "absorbed" into the American "culture" without a literary past and heritage of their own, as so many Americans believe.

To be sure, much of what they knew about that literary heritage had been acquired orally. Folk drama, for example, was immensely popular among the Mexican Americans, who continued to stage the old plays in much the same fashion as the early English folk dramatists had staged their plays in town squares, churches, or courtyards. In the Mexican Southwest, liturgical pastorals depicting the creation and fall of man and of Christ's resurrection evolved into "cycle plays" similar to those of Spain and England. Like the developing culture on the Atlantic frontier, the Southwest brought forth a new literature by New World men.

By the time of the Mexican-American War, the Mexican Southwest had been thoroughly nurtured on drama, poetry, and folktales of a literary tradition of several hundred years. Mexicans who became Americans continued the Indo-Hispanic literary tradition not only by preserving the old literary materials but also by creating new ones in the superimposed American political ambiance. To cite only

[2]Américo Paredes, Folklore and History, in *Singers and Storytellers*, ed. Mody C. Boatright, Wilson M. Hudson, and Allen Maxwell (Dallas: Southern Methodist University Press, 1961), pp. 162–63.

one sphere of literary activity, by 1860 there were a number of Mexican Americans engaged in newspaper work. In New Mexico alone, ten out of eighty journalists of the period were Mexican Americans because most Anglo-American papers published bilingual editions for the vast numbers of Spanish readers in the Southwest. Moreover, Mexican Americans were employed to translate the English-language news into Spanish.

Disparaging images of Mexican Americans

Nevertheless, Mexican Americans were poorly regarded by the vast majority of Anglo Americans who came in contact with them, and many of the literary portraits of Mexican Americans by Anglo-American writers exerted undue influence on generations of Americans down to our own time. The disparaging images of Mexican Americans were drawn by such American writers as Richard Henry Dana, who, in *Two Years Before the Mast,* described Mexican Americans as "an idle, thriftless people" who could "make nothing for themselves."[3] In 1852 Colonel John Monroe reported to Washington:

The New Mexicans are thoroughly debased and totally incapable of self-government, and there is no latent quality about them that can ever make them respectable. They have more Indian blood than Spanish, and in some respects are below the Pueblo Indians, for they are not as honest or as industrious.[4]

Four years later W. W. H. Davis, United States Attorney for the Territory of New Mexico, writing of his experiences with Mexican Americans, said that "they possess the cunning and deceit of the Indian, the politeness and the spirit of revenge of the Spaniard, and the imaginative temperament and fiery impulses of the Moor." He described them as smart and quick but lacking the "stability and character and soundness of intellect that

give such vast superiority to the Anglo-Saxon race over every other people." He ascribed to them the "cruelty, bigotry, and superstition" of the Spaniard, "a marked characteristic from earliest times." Moreover, he saw these traits as "constitutional and innate in the race." In a moment of kindness. however, Davis suggested that the fault probably lay with their "spiritual teachers," the Spaniards, who never taught them "that beautiful doctrine which teaches us to love our neighbors as ourselves."[5]

In 1868 the *Overland Monthly* published an article by William V. Wells, "The French in Mexico," in which he wrote that "in the open field, a charge of disciplined troops usually sufficed to put to flight the collection of frowzy-headed mestizos, leperos, mulattoes, Indians, Samboes, and other mongrels now, as in the time of our own war with them, composing a Mexican Army."[6] In our time Walter Prescott Webb characterizes the Mexicans as possessing "a cruel streak" that he believes was inherited partly from the Spanish of the Inquisition and partly from their Indian forebears. Webb asserts:

On the whole, the Mexican warrior . . . was inferior to the Comanche and wholly unequal to Texans. The whine of the leaden slugs stirred in him an irresistible impulse to travel with, rather than against, the music. He won more victories over the Texans partly by parley than by force of arms. For making promises and for breaking them he had no peer.[7]

Even John Steinbeck in *Tortilla Flat* portrayed Mexican Americans as lovable carousers claiming Spanish blood in the face of their color, "like that of a well-browned meerschaum pipe."[8]

---

[3]Richard Henry Dana, *Two Years Before the Mast* (New York: Bantam Books, 1959), p. 59.

[4]U.S., Congress, *Congressional Globe,* 32d Cong., 2d sess., January 10, 1853, Appendix, p. 104.

[5]W. W. H. Davis, *El Gringo: Or, New Mexico and Her People* (New York: Harper & Brothers, 1857), pp. 85–86.

[6]William V. Wells, The French in Mexico, *The Overland Monthly,* 1:232 (September 1868).

[7]Walter Prescott Webb, *The Texas Rangers: A Century of Frontier Defense* (Austin: University of Texas Press, 1965), p. 14.

[8]John Steinbeck, *Tortilla Flat* (New York: Bantam Books, 1965), p. 2.

That the defenders of the besieged Alamo were flying the Mexican flag of 1824, not the Texas flag, had been forgotten by the time of the Civil War. Forgotten too is the great heroic effort of Mexican Americans in the Union Army during the Civil War. In Texas, the fact that José Antonio Navarro's "Memoirs" are part of Mexican-American literature has been obscured by time and ethnic myopia.[9] Most Americans probably are unaware that Navarro, a Mexican American, was a member of the first Texas State Senate or that his son Angel III was graduated from Harvard in 1849. In the commemoration of the Texas heroes we hear little about Lorenzo de Zavala, another Mexican American, who served as the first vice-president (ad interim) of the Texas Republic. Instead we hear about the "outrages" of Juan Cortina and his revolt of 1859, despite the fact that Cortina was actually a Union-inspired guerrilla fighting both the Texas Confederates and the French Mexicans.

Neglected writers

There were many Mexican American writers in the last half of the nineteenth century, but they have remained as neglected as the people they represent. In New Mexico, for example, Donaciano Vigil, editor of the newspaper *Verdad,* compiled a *History of New Mexico to 1851;*[10] and in 1859 Miguel Antonio Otero wrote *The Indian Depredations in the Territory of New Mexico.*[11] In California, Juan Bautista Alvarado completed a "History of California."[12] In northern California, Mariano Guadalupe Vallejo wrote prolifically on a number of topics, composing sonnets for his children and for special oc-

casions. He culminated his literary activities with a five-volume "History of California" that Herbert E. Bancroft hailed as standing without rival among its predecessors in thoroughness and interest.[13] Many Mexican Americans kept diaries (a major type of Hispanic literature) and wrote letters to each other about their day-to-day activities. These letters—most of them unpublished—reveal as much about the Mexican-American experience as the letters of John Winthrop and Roger Williams reveal about the Puritan experience in America.

Historical background

Quest for statehood

What most characterized the post-Civil War period in the Southwest was the quest for statehood by the territories of Colorado, Utah, Oklahoma, Nevada, Arizona, and New Mexico. The admission of Texas into the Union had of course precipitated the Mexican-American War, but the *fact* of statehood allowed Texas a measure of "progress" that was not realized in the other territories until later in the nineteenth and twentieth centuries. California became a state in 1850; Colorado, in 1876; Utah, in 1896; and Oklahoma, in 1907. Arizona and New Mexico, however, did not become states until 1912. The delay has been attributed to the fact that the preponderance of Mexican Americans made statehood unpalatable to the rest of the nation.

Although Mexican Americans had proved their loyalty to the United States in both the Civil War and the Spanish-American War (more than half of the Rough Riders in Cuba were Mexican Americans), ethnic hostilities toward Mexican Americans did not lessen. For example, Senator Albert J. Beveridge of Indiana, an outright anti-Hispano, led the resistance against statehood for Arizona and New Mexico on the grounds that Mexican Americans were unaspiring, easily influenced, and totally ignorant of American

---

[9]Jose Antonio Navarro, Memoirs, Archives Division of the Texas State Library.

[10]Donaciano Vigil, *History of New Mexico to 1851,* New Mexico State Archives, Santa Fe, New Mex.

[11]Miguel Antonio Otero, *The Indian Depredations in the Territory of New Mexico,* Library of Congress, Washington, D.C.

[12]Juan Bautista Alverado, Historia de California, 1876, Bancroft Library, Berkeley, Calif.

[13]Mariano Guadalupe Vallejo, Recuerdos historicos y personales tocante a la Alta California: historia politica del pais, 1769–1849, 1875. Translated as History of California, by Earl R. Hewitt, Bancroft Library, Berkeley, Calif.

ways and mores and that, although fifty years had passed since the Mexican-American War, Mexican Americans were still aliens in the United States, most of them having made no effort to learn English.[14] According to Beveridge, such linguistic resistance was treasonous, to say the least, despite the fact that for part of the first decade of the twentieth century Miguel Antonio Otero, a Mexican American, was governor of the Territory of New Mexico (1897–1906), having been appointed by President McKinley and then reconfirmed by President Roosevelt after the assassination of McKinley in 1901.

Mexican Americans strove to become part of the United States in their own way, but they were regarded with disdain by a sizable segment of the Anglo-American population of the Southwest. Ironically, although Mexican Americans were being rejected by American society, the turn of the century saw the creation of "Spanish heritage and landmark" societies that vigorously espoused the restoration of "Spanish" missions in the Southwest. Mexican Americans were the butt of injustice after injustice while their lands, goods, properties, and persons were craftily secured by squatters, unscrupulous lawyers, and con artists who shamelessly bilked them because of their language handicap. Despite the fact that Mexican Americans constituted the majority of the population in the Southwest at first, they were quickly eased down the social rung with the increase of Anglo Americans in the area. By 1870 Mexican Americans ceased to be the majority in California. They had become a minority very early in Texas, although in New Mexico they held on until after the turn of the century. Nonetheless, Mexican Americans were slowly but surely reduced to conditions of peonage approximating the level of servitude into which the blacks had been forced.

Rags-to-riches mystique

Against this background emerged the rags-to-riches mystique that was to influence

American life well into the twentieth century. Horatio Alger's characters, Tattered Tom, Ragged Dick, and Phil the Fiddler, became the American standard for success through hard work. A Mexican American's "wealth," however, was judged as the product of connivance rather than of fortitude and application. For instance, when the Mexican-American Lugo family of southern California lost its wealth in 1865, Benjamin Hayes quickly suggested that the finger of Providence was responsible for the decay of the Mexican Americans.[15]

Not even Mariano Vallejo's "true history of California," which was meant to show Anglo Americans that Mexican Americans were not as they were caricatured in conversation and literature, could counteract the firmly lodged prejudices of Anglo Americans toward Mexican Americans.[16] Perhaps Leonard Pitt best summarizes the situation of Mexican Americans at the end of the nineteenth century when he writes, "By emphasizing injustice, violence, and broken promises in their memoirs, the Californians [Mexican Americans] came closer to a meaningful truth than the Yankees who spoke of Providence."[17]

Indeed, the providence of the Yankee was fraught with peril for the Mexican Americans, despite the fact that the Yankees had guaranteed them full citizenship and had agreed to regard them as equals rather than as conquered people. The Yankee rationalization for broken promises that Vallejo bemoaned was simply that "progress has its price" or that the Mexican Americans were "culturally unsuited to the new order" or else that the Mexican Americans had "brought it on them-

---

[14]In 1902 Beveridge filed a majority report for his committee investigating statehood for New Mexico and Arizona. The report objected to statehood.

[15]Benjamin D. Hayes, *Pioneer Notes ... 1849–1875*, ed. Marjorie Tisdale Walcott (Los Angeles: Marjorie Tisdale Walcott, 1929), p. 280.

[16]In 1875 Vallejo wrote to his son, Platon, that he was completing his "true history of California" to serve as a guide for posterity. See Nadie Brown Emparan, *The Vallejos of California* (San Francisco: Gleeson Library Associates, University of San Francisco, 1968), p. 129.

[17]Leonard Pitt, *The Decline of the Californios: A Social History of the Spanish-Speaking Californians, 1846–1890* (Berkeley and Los Angeles: University of California Press, 1970), p. 283.

selves." The American pretense at ethical behavior appears all the more reprehensible because of blatant bigotry.

By 1900 Anglo Americans in the Southwest had so taken over the Mexican Southwest that what had once been Mexican and Spanish had been neatly appropriated and transformed into an American "tradition." Mexican water and mining laws were retained in toto by Anglo-American settlers and governments. Spanish words were transformed into English equivalents. *La riata* became *lariat; juzgado* became *hoosegow; calabozo* became *calaboose; chiapas* became *chaps,* and so forth. The American *cowboy* became simply an altered reflection of the Mexican *vaquero,* saddle, ten-gallon hat, and all. The language of America had absorbed a considerable number of expressions, but Mexican Americans themselves were kept at arms-length as "outsiders," to be forgotten for another fifty years.

Resistance to Anglo aggression

It would, however, be an egregious error to conclude that Mexican Americans were passive in defending themselves against Anglo-American "aggressions." In 1883, for example, Mexican-American agricultural workers went on strike for better wages and working conditions in the Panhandle; in 1903, Mexican-American sugar beet workers went on strike for similar reasons in Ventura, California.

To counter their exclusion from Anglo-American schools, many Mexican Americans formed private and parochial schools, such as El Colegio Altamiro, founded in Texas in 1897. To overcome rural depredations, Mexican Americans in New Mexico formed the Knights of Labor in 1890, a mutual assistance and protective organization. Some Mexican-American organizations, such as Los Gorras Blancos (the White Caps) of New Mexico, were called marauders by Anglo Americans, but their purpose was primarily to protect themselves from such violent repressions as that which in 1904 took the life of Colonel Francisco J. Chaves, a surgeon and Civil War veteran who had become a Mexican-American spokesman, leader, and territorial superintendent of public instruction.

Migration from Mexico

As has already been noted, La Raza in the United States was to be culturally and linguistically renourished as no other group—save English-speaking—had been. In the decades between 1880 and 1940, almost three-quarters of one million Mexicans officially migrated to the United States. Mexican migration to the United States was one of the truly major mass movements of people in the Western Hemisphere. The phenomenon reflects "the failure of roots," as Ernesto Galarza explains.[18]

At the same time, however, Mexican migration to the United States reflects the growth of technology in North America. From 1880 to 1910, for instance, President Porfirio Díaz sped the construction of 15,000 miles of railroad lines linking the mineral wealth of Mexico to American smelters just north of the border. Mexicans not only worked the rails but were caught by the mystique of something better at the end of the tracks. Unquestionably the railroad provided the best escape for Mexicans in their exodus from war-torn Mexico. "Al norte!" was frequently the best alternative for Mexican refugees. Although the "depopulation" of Mexico was of great concern to the Liberal Party of Mexico, which had effectively brought Porfirismo's administration to an end and had promised to repatriate Mexicans in *el destierro,* the political and socioeconomic situation worsened in Mexico, thereby swelling instead of diminishing the ranks of fleeing Mexicans.

Travel either way across the Mexican-American border was relatively easy until the 1920s. It was not until 1924 that the Border Patrol was established to curb the illegal entry of Mexicans into the United States. Devoid of really natural barriers, the Mexican-American border is no more than a line staked out by markers from the Pacific to El Paso, or a barbed wire fence in places, or, during certain seasons, an almost dry river bed from El Paso to the Gulf of Mexico supporting the ubiqui-

[18]Ernesto Galarza, *Merchants of Labor: The Mexican Bracero Story* (Santa Barbara, Calif.: McNally & Lofton, 1964), p. 17.

tous undergrowth of chapparal and mesquite. Mexicans settled easily in the Southwest, for, unlike European immigrants, Mexicans were really migrating to an area similar to that from which they came and that was peopled by their kinsmen. Indeed, there was *mucha raza en el norte.*

Significance of the renaissance

Perhaps the significance of the Chicano Renaissance lies in the identification of Chicanos with their Indian past. It matters not what etymologies are ascribed to the word "Chicano"; the distinction is not in whether the word is a denigration but in that it has been consciously and deliberately chosen over all other words to identify Mexican Americans who regard themselves as Montezuma's children. They have thus cast off the sometimes meretricious identification with the Spanish templar tradition foisted on them by Anglo-American society because of its preference for things European. To reinforce their identification with their Indian past, Chicano writers have appropriated for their literary symbols Aztec and Mayan figures, including the great Aztec calendar stone.

Significantly, a literature draws from the history and myths of its people's past. Those of Mexican-Indian ancestry are well aware of the extent to which the myths and history of their Indian past are operating in the Mexican-American ethos. Understandably, it is to the Mexican-Indian past that the Chicano Renaissance has turned for its most meaningful literary symbols and metaphors. The selection of Quinto Sol as the name of a publishing group is itself a manifestation of the Chicano writers' deliberate identification with their Indian past, for the Aztecs were the people of the Fifth Sun (*Quinto Sol*). According to their mythology, there had been four previous epochs, each governed by a sun. The first epoch ended with the inhabitants of earth devoured by ocelots; the second world and sun were destroyed by wind; the third, by a rain of fire; and the fourth, by water. According to the Aztecs, the sun and world in which they lived—the fifth sun—was destined to perish as a result of earthquakes and famine and terror.

Chicano publications

Mexican Americans have been struggling within the predominantly Anglo-American culture of the United States for over 122 years. Although Mexican Americans have been writing all that time, the realization of Mexican-American literature as the *élan vital* in the life-styles of the people themselves has happened only within recent years. In the fall of 1967, a cohort of Mexican-American writers at Berkeley, California, formed Quinto Sol Publications in a tiny office over a candy store. Their purpose was "to provide a forum for Mexican American self definition and expression on . . . issues of relevance to Mexican Americans in American society today."[19]

Alternatives is the key word in what has since blossomed into the Chicano Renaissance. Mexican Americans had been completely disenchanted with the plethora of writings about them, writings that depicted them in a variety of literary contexts resorting to the most blatant stereotypes and racial clichés, all of them by "intellectual mercenaries" as the Quinto Sol group called them in the first issue of their literary quarterly magazine, El Grito: A Journal of Contemporary Mexican American Thought.[20] The promise of El Grito was that it would be the forum for Mexican Americans to articulate their own sense of identity. Even more important, the printed word was seen as a very important medium in the Chicano struggle for equality.

To compound the problem, Mexican Americans have not only been deprived of their literary birthright but they have effectively been kept from articulating their experiences in American literary outlets. In the last twenty years, for example, few Mexican Americans have published in the "leading" American literary quarterlies. In 1947 Mario Suarez published two sketches entitled "El Hoyo" and "El Señor" in the *Arizona Quarterly,* a literary journal that published the fiction of such other Mexican-American

---

[19]Editorial, *El Grito* 1:4 (Fall 1967).

[20]Ibid.

writers as Arnulfo D. Trejo and Amado Jesús Muro and the prose works of such Mexican-American scholars as Rafael Jesús Gonzalez.

Some Mexican-American writers had managed to find literary outlets, but at the expense of their art as Mexican Americans. Understandably, the greatest outpouring of Mexican-American writing since 1900 has been in prose, all of it essential in laying the foundation for what was to erupt as the Chicano Renaissance in the last years of the 1960s. The prose (much of it cast as polemics and rhetoric) helped to refashion first their psychological image and then their literary image. Mexican-American writers who sought to break the long-standing and readily accepted stereotypes about Mexican Americans in print found little or no favor with magazine editors because the images of the "Mexican" in American literature were hard to put aside.

As recently as 1968 an editor of a high school multiethnic text who was looking for material on Mexican Americans rejected a "nonfolk story" by this writer and suggested that the ninth-year reader in which J. Frank Dobie's popular "Squaw Man" appeared would provide an idea of the kind of material he was seeking for the reader. Of course, what he really wanted was the "queer," the "curious," and the "quaint" kind of "folksy" stories most editors have come to expect about Mexican Americans.

At another time, this writer suggested to the editor of a prestigious midwest literary quarterly the idea of publishing an issue on Mexican-American literature because he had just devoted an issue to American-Indian literature. The response betrayed the editor's lack of knowledge about Mexican Americans and their literary achievements, for he indicated he had heard that Quinto Sol Publications had published an anthology of Mexican-American writing but that he had not seen it. Because this writer had indicated he was working on an anthology also, the editor wondered if there would be anything of special significance left over for a special issue with two anthologies available.

Until the 1960s, fiction, such as Floyd Salas's *Tattoo the Wicked Cross* and John

Rechy's *City of Night,* was rare.[21] Both authors are Mexican-American writers who have penetrated the literary iron curtain not as ethnic writers but just as writers. This success simply attests to the fact that, as black writers who have written nonblack works, Mexican-American writers are capable of writing non-Mexican-American works. Like the market for black works, the market for Mexican-American works was limited to those who wrote what most editors expected; and what most editors had come to expect was the image of the Mexican American as an indolent, passive, humble servant who lived for *fiestas* and *mañana.* Chicano writers, however, are no longer struggling to penetrate the literary iron curtain; they have come to realize that the only viable outlets for their works are those that they create for themselves. In this way was born the Chicano Renaissance and hundreds of literary outlets, from mimeographed magazines to such slick publications as *El Grito* and the Los Angeles-based *Con Safos.*[22]

El Grito has become to the Chicano Renaissance what *Partisan Review,* for example, became to the New Criticism. It has published a variety of fiction, poetry, and prose appealing to the wider Mexican-American community. Principally, however, it has sought to show the patent falsity of Anglo-American works that purport to "explain" the Mexican American in terms of debilitating profiles and criteria. From the beginning, Octavio Romano and Nick Vaca, founders and editors of *El Grito,* have attempted to rearticulate the identity of Mexican Americans from the perspective of Mexican Americans. They have taken American social scientists, in particular, to task for perpetrating false images of Mexican-American culture. In addition, *El Grito* has provided an outlet for emerging Mexican-American writers.

Perhaps *Con Safos* best articulates Chicano life in the barrio. (Most Mexican Americans

---

[21]Floyd Salas, *Tattoo the Wicked Cross* (New York: Grove Press, 1967); and John Rechy, *City of Night* (New York: Grove Press, 1963).

[22]*Con Safos,* P.O. Box 31085, Los Angeles, Calif. (Published irregularly as sufficient material becomes available for an issue.)

are still in the barrios or have come from them.) *Con Safos* has a slick news magazine format, and, like *El Grito,* runs first-rate exposé pieces. Although *Con Safos* is more pictorial, *El Grito* regularly has provided space for portfolios of Mexican-American artists. Both magazines are essentially experimental in approach; they publish what reflects the Chicano community however it may be written—in Spanish or English or both —and rely heavily on striking covers employing Mexican-Indian motifs. There is no question of which magazine better articulates the Chicano experience, for both magazines articulate the essential problems of Chicanos everywhere.

Other Chicano magazines are springing up as Chicanos become increasingly aware of the power of the pen and the persuasiveness of print. For several years Francisca Flores, a fiery and undaunted Chicana from Los Angeles, published *Carta Editorial* by herself and at her own expense, commenting on the ills besieging Mexican Americans. What the Anglo-dominated mass media failed to cover in the Chicano community, Francisca Flores reported fearlessly in her small four-page newsletter. To be properly informed on what was happening in Mexican-American affairs, one had to read *Carta Editorial.* In 1970, *Carta Editorial* was absorbed into *Regeneración,* still edited by Francisca Flores but with a news magazine appearance and an expanded core of commentators and contributors.[23] What makes the venture of *Regeneración* significant is that the "new" magazine is really a revival of the journal that Ricardo Flores Magon, the Mexican exile, published in the United States while keeping clear of Porfirio Díaz's secret police. Magon started out by publishing *Liberación* in Mexico until he was forced to flee Díaz's wrath.

In the United States, Magon found refuge first in the Mexican-American community of San Antonio, Texas, and then in St. Louis, Missouri, where he founded *Regeneración.* Later, forced to leave St. Louis, he made his way to Los Angeles, where he continued his

attack on Porfirismo. He was finally taken into custody by American federal agents on the charge of having violated American neutrality laws. He was imprisoned at San Quentin, where his health failed and where he died. There is no doubt that *Regeneración* was instrumental in the downfall of Díaz.

There has been a special literary relationship between Mexicans and Mexican Americans, for when Mexican intellectuals and writers have fled from Mexico, they invariably have come to the United States and to Mexican-American communities. Many successful and abortive plans involving Mexico have been hatched in Mexican-American homes and communities. Benito Juarez's successful recapture of Mexico from the French was made possible by Mexican-American assistance in the form of money and material —and sometimes men. Porfirio Díaz himself launched his political career from Texas. During the Mexican Revolution of the twentieth century the Mexican-American Southwest provided asylum for many revolutionaries. It is little wonder that the heroes of the Chicano movement are Pancho Villa and Emiliano Zapata and that the Mexican revolutionary writers, Mariano Azuela, José Vasconcellos, and Martin Guzman, are read voraciously by Mexican Americans seeking their own liberation. No contemporary Mexican writers have influenced the Chicano movement so much as has Octavio Paz and his *Labyrinth of Solitude,* a work that goes far in exploring the Mexican mind and thought, not in its Hispanic origins so much but in relation to the Indian origins of Mexico.[24]

The Chicano theater

El Teatro Campesino, the Chicano migrant theater that grew out of the *Huelga* at Delano in 1965, has transformed the ancient Aztec myths for the *campesino* stage to Chicano relevancy. In one magnificent *acto* entitled "Bernabe," the Chicano link to the ancient Indian heritage is strengthened and

[23]*Regeneración,* P.O. Box 54624, T.A., Los Angeles, Calif. (Published monthly.)

[24]Octavio Paz, *Labyrinth of Solitude* (New York: Grove Press, 1961).

articulated masterfully. This message is being carried everywhere in the United States (and abroad) by El Teatro Campesino in its various annual tours. Luis Valdez, director of the company, describes Chicano theater as "beautiful, *rasquachi*, human, cosmic, broad, deep, tragic, comic, as the life of *La Raza* itself."[25] The consequence of El Teatro Campesino has been the creation of similar theatrical companies elsewhere, including universities with as few as a dozen Chicano students.

The distinctive character of Chicano theater lies in its seeming "artlessness." There is no attempt to create setting or atmosphere or character. Valdez, for example, employs *calavera* (skull) masks to create the illusion of temporality. All the skull masks are identical. Only the actions, dress, and voices of the actors differentiate them as characters. The end result is a kind of stylized theater resembling the Japanese Kabuki theater or the Greek mask plays.

In 1969, El Teatro Campesino filmed Rodolfo "Corky" González's stirring epic poem, "I Am Joaquín." Although the poem created considerable impact on the Chicano community, the film version has elevated it to a new dimension. Few, if any, Chicanos who view it are left unstirred because González has skillfully woven myth and memory and desire into a masterwork of poetry. Joaquín becomes the enduring spirit of the Chicano soul and spirit buffeted by alien winds in the country of his forebears where he walks as if he were a stranger. Joaquín's final words are not an empty incantation but a promise that he will endure.[26]

Chicano poetry

The heart of Chicano poetry lies in the imperative cry of Joaquín. The works of such other Mexican-American poets as Luis Omar Salinas, Abelardo Delgado, Miguel Ponce, and José Montoya reflect the existential problems of survival that Chicanos face day in and day out. There is anguish and frustration in the vision of Chicano poets, but there is also determination bred from the knowledge of who they are. In "Aztec Angel," for example, Salinas glorifies the beauty of the Aztec mother and child, thus encouraging pride in the heritage of the Chicano.[27] In the poem "The Chicano Manifesto," Delgado writes of the impatient *raza*, but tempers that impatience with an appeal for brotherhood.[28]

The message from Chicano poets for change is loud and clear. There is no mistaking the insistent plea for reformation. Although the spirit of Chicano poetry may be considered revolutionary, its intellectual emphasis, however, is on reason as it attempts to move the hearts and minds of men by appealing to their better natures.

The Chicano novel

The Chicano novel is a post-World War II phenomenon. José Antonio Villarreal's novel, *Pocho*, was published in 1959.[29] At that time it received scant attention and quickly went out of print. Although it appeared a decade too early, it stands in the vanguard of the Chicano novel for depicting the Chicano experience in the United States. Villarreal's style was influenced by the American "pop" novel of the 1950s, and his portrayal of the linguistic characteristics of Chicanos was clearly influenced by the work of Ernest Hemingway and Steinbeck. The novel's strength, however, is in the author's skillful presentation of the Mexican background of the Chicano migration to the United States.

[25]Luis Valdez, Notes on Chicano Theater, *El Teatro* (Official newspaper of El Teatro Campesino, published by El Centro Campesino Cultural, P.O. Box 2302, Fresno, Calif.), p. 4.

[26]Rodolfo González, I Am Joaquín, *El Gallo* Newspaper, 1967.

[27]Luis Omar Salinas, *Crazy Gypsy* (Fresno, Calif.: Origenes Publication, La Raza Studies, Fresno State College, 1970), p. 51.

[28]Abelordo Delgado, *Chicago: 25 Pieces of a Chicano Mind* (Denver: Migrant Workers' Press, 1970), pp. 35-36.

[29]José Antonio Villarreal, *Pocho* (Garden City, N.Y.: Doubleday and Co., 1959).

Two recent novels by Chicanos represent the nexus between the Chicano and Anglo worlds at this time and indicate the direction the Chicano novel will probably take. Richard Vasquez's novel, *Chicano,* will be of special interest to Chicano readers because, in a manner similar to that of *Pocho,* it deals with the substance of their lives and experiences.[30] *Chicano* details the odyssey of Hector Sandoval from Mexico to the United States during the Mexican Revolution and the travails of his children, Neftali, Jilda, and Hortencia, and their heirs in California. *Chicano* is an important novel for its portrayal of the Chicano migration, although some critics contend that the values of the novel have been misplaced in a rendition of the traditional fictions about Chicanos.

On the other hand, Raymond Barrio's *The Plum Plum Pickers* is a more exciting work, not because it is experimentally in the same mold as *Cane*—a novel that figured prominently in the Negro Renaissance of the 1920s—but because Barrio has been concerned less with presenting a panorama of Chicano life than with dealing entirely with the contemporary situation of the migrant couple, Manuel and Lupe, caught in the grip of agricultural exploitation.[31]

Essentially, *The Plum Plum Pickers* focuses on the proletarian view of life. Lupe is drawn as a significant figure in the novel, not as a female trifle caught at the edges of that fictive *machismo* so dominant in *Pocho* and *Chicano.* In *The Plum Plum Pickers,* Barrio has gone beyond the form of the "pop" novel to create a significant work of American literature.

The linguistic aspect

Another important aspect of the Chicano literary renaissance to consider is the linguistic aspect. Chicano writers are expressing themselves on the printed page in their Chicano language, evolved from Spanish and English, and their particular experiences in American barrios, *colonias,* and ghettos. Like black English, the Chicano language is at the heart of the Chicano experience; but unlike black English, the Chicano language deals not only with dialects of American English but with dialects of American and Mexican Spanish. Moreover, it has produced a mixture of the two languages resulting in a unique kind of *binary phenomena,* in which the linguistic symbols of two languages are mixed in utterances using either language's syntactic structure.

For the bilingual (Spanish-English, for instance) writer, this structure involves using either his English or Spanish idiolect at will to produce a "stereolect." For example, Alberto Alurista's poetry in *El Espejo-The Mirror: Selected Mexican American Literature* (published by Quinto Sol) reads as follows:

> Mis ojos hinchados
>> flooded with lagrimas
> de bronce
> melting on the cheek bones
> of my concern
>> razgos indigenes
> the scars of history on my face
>> and the veins of my body
> that aches
>> vomito sangre
> y lloro libertad
>> I do not ask for freedom
> I am freedom.[32]

In order to understand contemporary Mexican-American literature, it is important to understand the function of binary phenomena in Chicano communication and expression. It is equally important, however, to understand that these phenomena are not of Mexican-American origin, for binary phenomena occur wherever there is linguistic contact and coexistence. In New York, for example,

---

[30]Richard Vasquez, *Chicano* (Garden City, N.Y.: Doubleday and Co., 1970).

[31]Raymond Barrio, *The Plum Plum Pickers* (Sunnyvale, Calif.: Ventura Press, 1969).

[32]Octavio I. Romano-V, ed., *El Espejo-The Mirror: Selected Mexican American Literature* (Berkeley Calif.: Quinto Sol Publications, 1969), p. 172. Reprinted by permission of the poet.

binary phenomena ("stereolecticism") occur among American speakers of Yiddish. In literature, such contemporary American writers as Philip Roth and Saul Bellow use many Yiddish expressions in their works.

Linguistically, it is important to keep in mind the primacy of language in the life of an individual or of a society or culture because the language we speak shapes our particular view of the world. Thus, to comprehend the Chicano experience, one must critically examine the language of Chicanos, not with preconceived notions of what is correct or standard in language usage in Spanish or English but with knowledge of the role language plays in human intercourse. We can no longer tag the Chicano language as "poor Spanish" or "poor English" or as "Mex-Tex," "Spanglish," "Pachuco," or other such denigrations. We must guard against stupidities that suggest that Mexican Americans are nonlingual because they speak neither English nor Spanish. We must bear in mind that we do not depreciate the language of Chaucer's time by calling it "Frenglish," though more French than English was spoken by the upper classes.

Ironically, California proved to be the birthplace of the renaissance that Aurora Lucero had hoped New Mexico would produce. In 1953 she wrote optimistically:

There now remains but one renaissance to be effected—the literary. With the happy accident that New Mexico possesses more traditional literary materials than any other Hispanic region it should be possible to bring about such a rebirth in the reenactment of the lovely old plays, in the keeping alive the lovely old folk dances and in the singing of the old traditional songs.[33]

The Chicano Renaissance came into being not in relation to the traditional past but rather in the wake of growing awareness by Mexican Americans of their Indian, not Hispanic, identity. The Chicano Renaissance is but the manifestation of a people's coming of age. It has been long over overdue, and in another country, like Milton's unsightly root, it bore a bright and golden flower.

---

[33] Aurora Lucero, *Literary Folklore of the Hispanic Southwest* (San Antonio, Tex.: The Naylor Company, 1953), p. 210.

CHICANO HISTORIOGRAPHY

Dr. Garcia, in a well reasoned and scholarly article, examines three concepts of Chicano history: Chicano history as a tool of the Chicano Movement; Chicano history as a unique ethnic experience and Chicano history as comparative history. He selects the latter as the most feasible and views it in light of the "Bolton Thesis" and calls for the "creation" of a Chicano history which should be interwoven into the history of the Americas.

One of the major intellectual tasks for Chicanos is to answer the question--"What is Chicano history?" This, of course, is an extension of the old controversy: "What is history?" Numerous intellectuals have grappled with this question, and given a variety of answers. It is not my intention to review what these are; what I intend, however, is to deal with the problem of Chicano history, and how it is being met, or should be met, by Chicanos.

There are at least three conceptions of Chicano history which can be defined. One is the view of Chicano history as a tool to support various goals (self-determination, liberation, cultural pride, political power, etc.) of the Chicano Movement. This type of history emphasizes only the "good" aspects of the Chicano experience, and resembles the "great men" historical school of thought. Heroes like Montezuma, Hidalgo, Morelos, Juarez, Murieta, Cortina, etc. are stressed and held up as standards for Chicanos to emulate. Unfortunately, in so doing, the truth about many of these individuals is distorted. The idea, for example, that many Chicanos have of Juarez as the embodiment of Indian Mexico is inaccurate, for he was the representative of the European-oriented Mexican bourgeois.

This view of history, however, is understandable, for every group, every nation has used its past for nationalistic purposes. And, undoubtedly, there is something to say for this method, for it does instill in Chicanos a sense of identity and pride (although one can question whether it simply substitutes mistaken identity for non-identity). Yet, there are limitations to this perspective, the most serious being that it constitutes a shallow history, one that does not take into account the varied and complex forces that are found in any given historical period.[1]

Besides this conception of Chicano history--which is intellectually unacceptable--there are two other views of Chicano history. One is that the history of the Mexican in the United States should be studied in isolation, apart from the intellectual, social, economic, and political currents that affect other peoples. The major premise for this point of view is that the Chicano is unique--that he represents a unique historical type. Thus, one would examine Chicano migration, labor, family, politics, etc., quite independent from that of any other group. A reflection of this attitude is seen in United States history courses taught under Chicano Studies where the chief objective is to teach the history of the Chicano apart from that of the rest of the United States.[2]

The third conception of Chicano history is quite the opposite. Chicano history, according to this argument, should be comparative history. The emphasis is to study the Chicano in relation not only to the Anglo-American, but, also, to other minority groups in this country; also, to study the Chicano in relation to Mexican history, to Latin American history, to European history, and, indeed, to world history.

It is my belief that this last conception is the correct one. I cannot support the idea that the Chicano is unique, with the implication, therefore, that he has little in common with other peoples. This is wrong, and Chicano historians should strongly oppose this misconception. The Chicano is different, but he is not unique. He has the same human desires, aspirations, fears, etc., etc., as other peoples. Moreover, beyond the human factor, the Chicano is not divorced from historical currents (colonialism, industrialization, urbanization, etc.) that have affected others. The same problems, issues, situations the Chicano has faced, and continues to face, have, likewise, been encountered by other groups. By no means should we study our people in a vacuum, for to do so means to continuously contemplate our "brown navels", and that, to me, is a limited activity. What I am arguing, then, is that we study the experience of the Mexican in the United States in its widest perspective. In so doing, Chicano historians can have no better guide than the theory advanced by one of the notable historians of this century, Herbert Eugene Bolton.

In a presidential address delivered at the Forty-seventh Annual Meeting of the American Historical Association in Toronto in 1932, Bolton argued that a broader treatment of American history was needed. It was needed in order to remove American history from a strictly nationalistic basis. "European history cannot be learned," Bolton contended,

> from books dealing alone with England, or France, or Germany, or Italy, or Russia; nor can American history be adequately presented if confined to Brazil, or Chile, or Mexico, or Canada, or the United States. In my own country the study of thirteen English colonies and the United States in isolation has obscured many of the larger factors in their development, and helped to raise up a nation of chauvinists. Similar distortion has resulted from the teaching and writing of national history in other American countries.[3]

What Bolton was calling for was a study of American history beyond the confines of the United States or of any individual American nation. American history should be hemispheric history--a study of the common factors in the development of the Western Hemisphere. Bolton, further understood the practical necessity of such a wide-ranging history, for he was making his appeal at the dawn of Franklin Roosevelt's "Good Neighbor Policy." "The increasing importance of inter-American relations makes imperative," Bolton insisted, "a better understanding by each of the history and the culture of all."[4] Yet, it was from an intellectual, rather than a political perspective that Bolton was presenting his theory. As he put it, a larger view of American history was essential not only for its political and commercial implications, but "it is quite desirable from the standpoint of correct historiography."[5]

It was Bolton's purpose, therefore, to suggest that there were common threads in the histories of the American nation-states; indeed, in the histories of all American people. And that each national history could best be understood in relation to that of the other American nations.[6]

What did these nations, these people, have in common? Bolton believed there were many similarities in the background of the American nations. Similarities in colonial systems; for example, each experienced the effects of mercantilism, feudalism, black slavery, of the subjugation of the Indians, and of the influence of the frontier. Each was faced with the issue of independence, of consolidating that independence, and of structuring a nation-state.[7] This is not to imply that Bolton did not believe there existed differences in America, but as Lewis Hanke suggests, Bolton simply judged it wiser to stress similarities because of the previous emphasis on the gulf between the United States and the rest of the Americas.[8] Similarities, a common history, the "Epic of Greater America," this is what Bolton deemed important.

Since its enunciation, the Bolton Theory has aroused a considerable controversy among American scholars. Perhaps the most critical of these is the Mexican historian, Edmundo O'Gorman, who believes Bolton's major fault was he did not demonstrate the essential unity of the Americas. What is lacking, O'Gorman insists, is the proof that there exists a common American culture. Until this is proven, historians cannot talk of a common history. What unities Bolton ascribed to Americans are unities which O'Gorman believes are to be found in any group of men, "simply because they have all been born and raised, they all eat and work."[9] Thus, these are "unities of Nature and not of human nature, which is the essence of history."[10] And Bolton's Theory will not be history until the existence of an American culture is proven; as long as this is not done, "it will remain just a beautiful, fallacious illusion."[11]

In similar fashion, Roy F. Nichols argues that there exists conflicting cultures in America between the United States and the Latin American nations. "The various aspects of this dual experience (the United States and Latin America) are most apparent," Nichols writes,

> in the cumulative cultural achievement. Here the basic cleavage is most vividly revealed, for two widely divergent cultures have appeared. They are so different, that in my opinion, we cannot speak of an American culture or of any social phenomenon that approaches hemispheric cultural solidarity.

Such conditioning factors as attitudes on race, religion, economic enterprise, politics, and general standards of artistic and literary value are culturally divisive rather than unifying.[12]

From an economic viewpoint, Sanford Mosk argues that the differences between the Americas, especially the United States and Latin America, are greater than the similarities. The basis of this difference is found in the divergent economic development of both areas. The inability of Latin America to break from its colonial heritage, Mosk contends, is the culprit in preventing it from achieving the modernization and industrialization of its economy as the United States has done.[13] This has produced "in effect, two Americas in this hemisphere."[14]

In contrast to these criticisms--and these, of course, are only a sample--of the Bolton Theory, several other scholars have spoken in support of it. The Argentine historian, Enrique De Gandia, for example, rejects O'Gorman's idea that there must be a unity of culture before one can refer to a common American history. "The unity of a country," he writes, "does not depend on the unity of its culture."[15] And he singles out the unity Spain achieved despite divergent cultures such as the Latin, Visigothic, and Arabic cultures.[16] On the question of whether there exists an American culture, De Gandia argues that what culture exists is not a peculiar American one; instead, it is an extension of European culture, although each American nation possesses distinct traditions, which, in turn, represent national cultures, but, again, within a European framework.[17]

What De Gandia argues, therefore, is that though there may not exist a particular American culture, there does exist a unifying cultural core throughout the Americas, which is European in origin. Yet, even beyond the question of cultural unity, he insists that the very fact America was founded from similar motives, which created similar problems, and which, in turn, led to similar reactions, is enough to allow discussion of a common American history. "The unity of America," De Gandia writes, "is independent of the unity of its culture."[18]

The reference to a common European tradition is the chief argument that most scholars have used to substantiate Bolton. Philip C. Brooks argues that throughout the era of the conquest of the environment and of the mixture of races in America, the common factor was the European heritage. "Dr. Bolton is on his strongest point," he notes,

when he talks of the expansion and rivalries of Spanish, French, and other colonizers in North America. This is partly because of the weight of evidence presented in his own writings. But it is also partly because that story has been the dominant one in the history of the Americas.[19]

Arthur P. Whitaker cautions, however, that in looking at American history through a broad panorama one should not be mis-directed by the expression of ideals like democracy, liberty, etc., the so-called "Pan-American ideals." To do so would be to produce historical writing which Whitaker labels "Hemispheric neo-romanticism."[20] This view, he explains, is based on the idea that all men everywhere are essentially the same, and this, in Whitaker's opinion, would reduce American history to a dull grey. What is needed, he insists, is a different unifying idea, one wide enough to allow "free play for the rich variety of human behavior which has always been American. It must bring together," Whitaker further points out,

> in a relationship that respects this individuality, societies as different as those which produced Cotton Mather and St. Rose of Lima, Benjamin Franklin and Lucas Alamon, Abraham Lincoln and Juan Manuel de Rosas, Franklin Roosevelt and Juan Vicente Gomez.[21]

The unifying idea that Whitaker suggests is that of looking at American history as the record of the common experience shared by what he calls the "Atlantic Triangle" consisting of Latin America, Anglo-America, and Europe.[22] It is through this perspective that Whitaker agrees with Bolton that the Americas possess a common history.

What does all this mean to Chicano history? What it means, in my opinion, is that though there may be some justification to the criticisms of people such as O'Gorman and Mosk, it is my belief that the Bolton Theory and its supporting arguments are more valid, and ones which are applicable to the study of Chicano history. I have already stated that Chicano history can best be understood using the comparative method. In so doing, the obvious theory to apply is Bolton's. If there exists common historical strands in American history, what we must do is discover where the Chicano experience fits in.

What historians must do is compare the Chicano experience with that of other peoples in the Americas. What common elements, for example, are to be found in Chicano culture with that of the Anglo-American? With the Mexican? With the Brazilian? The Cuban?, etc., etc. What common political, economic, and social issues have Chicanos shared with other groups in this hemisphere, as well as with others in Europe, Africa, and Asia?

Studies could be done on such topics as: the comparison of Mexican immigration to the United States with that of other groups not only to this country, but to the rest of the Americas; the comparison of Chicano migration from rural areas to urban ones with similar American movements; a comparison of the impact of industrialization on the Chicano with that of other American people; the comparison of the growth of the Chicano labor movement with other labor movements in America; a comparison of the rise of a Chicano middle class with that of other middle class movements, in Mexico, for example; the comparison of anti-colonial sentiments among Chicanos with similar sentiments in other American areas, etc., etc. There is no question--at least in my mind--that by using Bolton's Theory of a common American history the study of the Chicano experience in the United States will be enhanced, and the result will be a rich source of historical writing.

Let me, at this point, comment on the argument used by many of Bolton's supporters that the unifying link in the American experience is the European heritage, and on what the implication of this argument is for Chicano history. Many Chicanos, for understandable reasons, have gone to the point of outright rejection of anything that can be considered white, Anglo, or European. Instead, the constant reference point is the Indian heritage, whether it be Mayan, Aztec, Pueblo, etc. Obviously, because the Chicano is a mestizo, he possesses an Indian background; I do not quarrel with this; what I do object to is the rejection of our European past. I cannot believe we can understand the history of the Chicano without understanding the European heritage. The fact is the Indian was defeated, unfortunately, but defeated. We cannot deny this. As a consequence, the history of America since the European conquest has been shaped by European factors adjusted to the American environment. Chicanos are a product of this European adjustment, and we cannot understand our culture nor our history without recognizing this. Studying Aztec history and culture may be of some use, but it will not be productive of comprehending the entire historical reality of the Chicano.

This is not to imply we go to the false extreme, as many have done, of calling ourselves Spanish, Spanish-Americans, or Hispanos. The fact is we are Mexicans. This is a distinction Bolton, for example, was unable to make. In an article published in 1930 entitled, "Defensive Spanish Expansion and the Significance of the Borderlands," Bolton made the point that the Southwest was the "meeting place and fusing place of two streams of European civilization, one coming from the south (the Spanish), the other from the north (the English)." [23] And in describing the Spanish influence in the Southwest, Bolton mentioned the continued use of the Spanish language, the fact that names of states, rivers, mountains, etc. possessed Spanish names. [24] "Many towns have Spanish quarters," he wrote, "where the life of the old days goes on, and where one can always hear the soft Castillion tongue." [25]

Now, Chicanos know there are very few, if any, places in the Southwest where the "soft Castillion tongue" can be heard! The point, of course, is Bolton did not recognize that the civilization, the culture, that existed in the Southwest at the time of the United States conquest in 1848 was not Spanish, but Mexican. It was, therefore, a mestizo society, one which had fused the Indian elements with the Spanish ones to create a distinct national culture. De Gandia, for example, recognizes the existence of national cultures, such as the Mexican, but at the same time acknowledges that not only the culture of Mexico, but the political, economic, and social currents of the Mexican experience were ones that for the most part, were generated from a European source. [26] And this is what Chicanos have to understand: We can be proud of being Mexicans, Chicanos, and, at the same time, recognize the European influence, and attempt to understand it, and in so doing, know ourselves better. I am not saying we should be proud of our European heritage--that is up to each individual--what I am saying is that to neglect it is to neglect reality.

Leopoldo Zea, the Mexican philosopher, writes that "Mexicanism in itself cannot be a legitimate goal, but only a point of departure, a means toward a broader and more responsible task." [27] What Zea says about "Mexicanism" is, also true for "Chicanismo"; it is not a goal, but a means. And, I submit, it is a means toward a universal understanding of men. We look at ourselves and at others for the purpose of comprehending the human condition. Franz Fannon writes, "It is a question of the Third World starting a new History of Man . . . we must invent and we must make discoveries . . . For (America), for ourselves and for humanity, comrades, we must turn over a new leaf, we must work out new concepts, and try to set afoot a new man."[28]

A "new man"--this should be the purpose of Chicano history-- not a "new Chicano", but a "new man"! One who will rise above nationality, culture, race, etc., and recognize himself in his fellow- man. It seems to me that if we do not make this our goal, Chicanos run the risk of not only isolating ourselves, but, also, putting ourselves in a position contrary to that of others, who are, likewise, fighting for their liberation.[29]   Let me quote again from Leopoldo Zea, who is appealing to the people of Latin America, but his words are quite relevant for Chicanos:

> We are no longer a collection of ill-defined countries suspended somewhere between reality and fantasy. We now discover that our goals are also those of many other nations of the world in a situation similar to ours. Consequently, statesmen and Latin American men of culture can now affirm that Latin America is creating universal history--it is sharing an endeavor with others whose conditions are similar to ours.[30]

And again,

> Thus an experience which has seemed unique to us and, because of our absurd inferiority complex, worthless, turns out to be one shared by many other men and nations. Other people who had seemed to us exotic and foreign now show us that, in spite of many social and cultural differences, their problems are ours and our solutions can be theirs, or vice-versa. By digging deep into ourselves, by rooting out a host of our own prejudices--masks that prevent us from recognizing ourselves in others and being recognized in turn--we will find the source of the genuine universality sought by all philosophers and presupposed by the most prestigious cultures: Mankind.[31]

If we make our destination universal history, as Zea puts it, then I suggest that our logical point of departure is the Bolton Theory. By looking at ourselves in relationship to the other peoples of America, we will be better able to understand men in general. As Chicanos, we have been marginal men for a long time, but now the margin--throughout the world--is becoming the center, and, therefore, as Chicanos we are in an advantageous position (due to our Latin American and Anglo- American backgrounds) to offer new insights to the history not only of the Southwest, or of the United States, but of America, and hopefully, relate these to the rest of the world.

The United States historian, John W. Coughey, a student of Bolton's, writes that he cannot picture Bolton "beating a drum for integration, yet a cardinal belief of his was that people of all races and nationalities are very much alike."[32]   A common history, a universal history, this, in essence, is what Bolton called for, and there is no reason why Chicanos cannot be the leaders in the creation of such a history.

FOOTNOTES

1. The idea, for example, held by many Chicanos that Aztec society was "ideal" is a fallacious one, for the Aztecs held to many reprehensible traits, not the least being a war-like attitude, slavery and imperialism.

2. "Historical Nationalism" is, probably, an appropriate term for this conception.

3. Herbert Eugene Bolton, "The Epic of Greater America," in Herbert Eugene Bolton, Wider Horizons of American History (New York, 1939), z.

4. Ibid.

5. Ibid.

6. Ibid., 3.

7. Ibid., 9-10.

8. Lewis Hanke, (ed.), Do the Americas Have a Common History (New York, 1964), 46-47.

9. Edmundo O'Gorman, "Do the Americas Have a Common History," Ibid., 105-106.

10. Ibid.

11. Ibid., 107.

12. Roy F. Nichols, "A United States Historian's Appraisal," Ibid., 219-220.

13. Sanford A. Mosk, "Latin America versus the United States," Ibid., 165-187.

14. Ibid., 165.

15. Enrique De Gandia, "Pan Americanism in History," Ibid., 128.

16. Ibid.

17. Ibid., 131.

18. Ibid., 130.

19. Philip C. Brooks, "Do the Americas Share a Common History," Ibid., 136-137.

20. Arthur P. Whitaker, "The Americas in the Atlantic Triangle," Ibid., 143.

21. Ibid., 143-144.

22. Ibid., 144.

23. Bolton, Wider Horizons, 98.

24. Ibid., 98-99.

25. Ibid.

26. De Gandia, "Pan Americanism," 131.

27. Leopoldo Zea, Latin America and the World (Norman, Oklahoma, 1969), XI.

28. As quoted in Vincent Harding, "Beyond Chaos: Black History and the Search for the New Land," in John A. Williams and Charles F. Harris, Amistad 1 (New York, 1970), 289.

29. See the opinions expressed by Vincent Harding in Ibid., 267-292.

30. Zea, Latin America, 8-9.

31. Ibid., 9. A good example for Chicanos and others to emulate is the idea of "La Raza Cosmica" expressed by the Mexican philosopher, Jose Vasconcelos, who saw the "ultimate man" as a synthesis of all the different races of the world. See my article "Jose Vasconcelos and La Raza," El Grito, Vol. II (Summer, 1969), 49-51.

32. John W. Coughey, "Herbert Eugene Bolton," in Wilbur R. Jacobs, John W. Coughey, and Joe B. Frantz, Turner, Bolton, and Webb: Three Historians of the American Frontier (Seattle, 1965), 46.

BIBLIOGRAPHY

I   General Bibliographies

Barrio, Ernie, et. al. Bibliografia de Aztlan: An Annotated Chicano
Bibliography. San Diego: Centro de Estudio Chicanos, San Diego
State College, 1971.

Cabinet Committee on Opportunities for Spanish Speaking People. The
Spanish Speaking in the United States: A Guide to Materials.
Washington, D. C.: Government Printing Office, 1971.

Center for Latin-American Studies, Stanford University. The Mexican-
American: A Selected and Annotated Bibliography. Stanford, California: The Center, 1969.

Charno, Stephen M. (Comp). Latin American Newspapers in United
States Libraries. Austin: University of Texas Press, 1969.

Ching, D. C. (Comp). "Reading, Language Development and Bilingual
Child: Annotated Bibliography," Elementary English. Vol. 46.
(May, 1969), pp. 622-28.

Cortes, Carlos (Ed). The Mexican American: Mexican American Bibliographies. New York: Arno Press, 1974.

Heathman, James E. and Cecila J. Martinez. Mexican-American Education - A Selected Bibliography. University Park, New Mexico:
New Mexico State University, 1969.

Jordan, Lois B. Mexican Americans: Resources to Build Cultural
Understanding. Littleton, Colorado: Libraries Unlimited, Inc.,
1973.

Latin American Library. Children's Books About Mexican-Americans
and Children in Mexico. Oakland, California: Oakland Public
Library, 1968.

Messinger, Milton A. The Forgotten Child: A Bibliography, With Special
Emphasis on Materials Relating to the Education of Spanish-
Speaking People in the United States. Austin: University of Texas,
1967.

Navarro, Eliseo A. (Comp). The Chicano Community: A Selected Bibliography for Use in Social Work Education. New York: Council on
Social Work Education, 1971.

Nogales, Luis (Comp). The Mexican American: A Select and Annotated Bibliography. Stanford, California: Stanford University, 1969.

Ohannessian, Sirarpi. Interim Bibliography in the Teaching of English to Speakers of Other Languages. Washington: Center for Applied Linguistics of the Modern Language Association of America, 1960.

Padilla, Amado M., and Rene A. Ruiz. Latino Mental Health: Bibliography and Abstracts. Washington, D. C.: Government Printing Office, 1974.

Rios, Hermino and Lupe Costello. "Toward a True Chicano Bibliography: Mexican-American Newspapers: 1848-1942." El Grito, Vol. III, No. 4 (Summer 1970), pp. 17-24.

Talbot, Jane Mitchell and Gilbert R. Cruz. A Comprehensive Chicano Bibliography 1960-1972. Austin, Texas: Jenkins Publishing Co. - The Pemberton Press, 1973.

Wagner, Henry R. and D. Litt. The Spanish Southwest 1542-1794: An Annotated Bibliography. New York: Arno Press, 1967.

II   General Readings

Burma, John H. (Ed). Mexican-Americans in the United States: A Reader. Cambridge, Mass.: Schenkman Publishing Co., Inc., 1970.

Cabrera, Y. Arturo. Emerging Faces: The Mexican-Americans. New York: Wm. C. Brown Co., 1971.

Clark, Margaret. Health in the Mexican-American Community, A Study. Berkeley, California: University of California Press, 1959.

Gomez, Rudolph (Ed). The Changing Mexican-American: A Reader. El Paso, Texas: Pruett Publishing Co., 1972.

Grebler, Leo, et al. The Mexican-American People: The Second Largest Minority. New York: The Free Press, 1970.

Kiev, Ari. Curanderismo: Mexican-American Folk Psychiatry. New York: The Free Press, 1968.

McWilliams, Carey. Brothers Under the Skin. Boston: Little, Brown and Company, 1964.

Meier, Matt, and Rivera, Feliciano. Readings on La Raza: The Twentieth Century. New York: Hill and Wang, 1974.

Padilla, Amado M., and Ruiz, Rene A. Latino Mental Health: A Review
   of Literature. Washington, D. C.: (DHEW Publication No. HSM
   73-9143), Government Printing Office, 1973.

Rivera, Feliciano. Guideline for the Study of Mexican-American People
   in the United States. San Jose, California: Spartan Bookstore,
   1969.

III   Mexican and Southwest Heritage

Alba, Victor. The Mexicans: The Making of a Nation. New York: Pega-
   sus, 1970.

Gergusson, Harvey. Rio Grande. New York: Wm. Morrow and Co.,
   1967.

Haring, C. H. The Spanish Empire in America. New York: Oxford
   University Press, 1947.

Hollon, W. Eugene. The Southwest: Old and New. Lincoln: University
   of Nebraska Press, 1970.

Meinig, D. W. Southwest: Three Peoples in Geographical Change 1600-
   1970. New York: Oxford University Press, 1971.

Paz, Octavio. The Labyrinth of Solitude: Life and Thought in Mexico.
   New York: Grove Press, Inc., 1961.

Prescott, William H. The Conquest of Mexico. 2 vols. New York: E. P.
   Dutton and Co., Inc.

Ramos, Samuel. Profile of Man and Culture in Mexico. Austin: University of Texas Press, 1962.

Ruiz, Ramon Eduardo. The Mexican War: Was it Manifest Destiny?
   New York: Holt, Rinehart and Winston, 1963.

Spicer, Edward H. Cycles of Conquest: The Impact of Spain, Mexico
   and the United States on the Indians of the Southwest 1533-1960.
   Tucson: The University of Arizona Press, 1967.

Von Hagen, Victor W. The Aztec Man and Tribe. New York: Mentor
   Books, 1961.

Wolf, Eric. The Sons of the Shaking Earth: The People of Mexico and
   Guatemala - Their Land, History and Culture. Chicago: The University of Chicago Press, 1959.

Womack, John. Zapata and the Mexican Revolution. New York: Vintage Books, 1968.

Zea, Leopoldo. The Latin-American Mind. Norman: University of Oklahoma Press, 1963.

IV History

Acuna, Rodolfo. Occupied America: The Chicanos Struggle Toward Liberation. San Francisco: Canfield Press, 1972.

Alford, Harold J. The Proud Peoples: The Heritage and Culture of Spanish-Speaking Peoples in the United States. New York: David McKay Company, Inc., 1972.

Forbes, Jack. Aztecas del Norte: The Chicanos of Aztlan. Greenwich, Connecticut: Fawcett Publications, 1973.

Galarza, Ernesto, et. al. Mexican Americans in the Southwest. Santa Barbara, California: McNally and Loftin, 1960.

Gonzalez, Nancie L. The Spanish Americans of New Mexico: A Heritage of Pride. Albuquerque: University of New Mexico Press, 1967.

McWilliams, Carey. North From Mexico: The Spanish-Speaking People of the United States. New York: Greenwood Press, 1968.

Mier, Matt S. and Rivera, Feliciano. The Chicanos: A History of Mexican Americans. New York: Hill and Wang, 1972.

Moquin, Wayne and VanDoren, Charles. (Eds). A Documentary History of the Mexican Americans. New York: Bantam Books, 1971.

Pitt, Leonard. The Decline of the Californios: A Social History of the Spanish-Speaking Californians, 1846-1890. Berkeley, California: University of California Press, 1971.

Romano-V., Octavio Ignacio. The Anthropology and Sociology of the Mexican Americans: The Distortion of Mexican American History, a Review Essay. Berkeley, California: Quinto Sol Publications, 1969.

Ruiz, Ramon Eduardo and Tebbell, J. South by Southwest: The Mexican American and His Heritage. Garden City, N. Y.: Doubleday, 1969.

Sanchez, George G. Forgotten People: A Study of New Mexicans. Albuquerque: University of New Mexico Press, 1940.

Servin, Manuel P. The Mexican-Americans: An Awakening Minority. Beverly Hills, California: Glencoe Press, 1970.

Weber, David J. Foreigners in Their Native Land: Historical Roots of the Mexican American. Albuquerque: University of New Mexico Press, 1973.

V   Education

Acuna, Rudolph. Story of the Mexican Americans: The Men and the Land - A Junior High School Text. New York: American Book Co., 1970.

Beals, Ralph Leon. No Frontier to Learning: The Mexican in the United States. Minneapolis: University of Minnesota Press, 1957.

Brussell, Charles B. Disadvantaged Mexican American Children and Early Educational Experiences. Austin, Texas: Southwest Educational Development Corp., 1968.

Bustamonte, Charles J. and Patricia L. The Mexican-American and the United States: An Intermediate School Level Text. Mountain View, California: Patty-Lar Publications Ltd., 1970.

Carter, Thomas P. Mexican Americans in School: A History of Educational Neglect. New York: College Entrance Examination Board, 1970.

Chicano Coordinating Council on Higher Education (CHE). El Plan de Santa Barbara: A Chicano Plan for Higher Education. Santa Barbara, California: La Causa Publications, 1970.

Duran, Livie Isauro and Bernard, H. Russell. Introduction to Chicano Studies: A Reader. New York: The Macmillan Company, 1973.

Hernandez, Luis F. A Forgotten American: A Resource Unit for Teachers on the Mexican American. New York: Anti-Defamation League of B'nai B'rith, 1967.

Litsinger, Dolores Escobar. The Challenge of Teaching Mexican-American Students. New York: American Book Co., 1973.

Manuel, Herschel T. Spanish-Speaking Children of the Southwest. Austin, University of Texas Press, 1965.

Nava, Julian. Mexican Americans Past Present and Future: Junior High Text. New York: American Book Co., 1968.

Stone, James C. and DeNevi, Donald P. Teaching Multi-Cultural Populations: Five Heritages. New York: Van Nostrand Reinhold Co., 1971.

U. S. Civil Rights Commission. Mexican American Educational Study Report 1: Ethnic Isolation of Mexican Americans in Public Schools of the Southwest. Washington, D. C.: Government Printing Office, 1971.

_____. Mexican American Educational Study Report 2: Unfinished Education, Outcomes for Minorities in Five Southwestern States. Washington, D. C.: Government Printing Office, 1971.

_____. Mexican American Educational Study Report 3: The Excluded Student, Educational Practice Affecting Mexican Americans in the Southwest. Washington, D. C.: Government Printing Office, 1972.

_____. Mexican American Education Study Report 4: Mexican American Education in Texas, a Function of Wealth. Washington, D. C.: Government Printing Office, 1972.

_____. Mexican American Education Study Report 5: Teachers and Students, Differences in Teacher Interaction with Mexican American and Anglo Students. Washington, D. C.: Government Printing Office, 1973.

VI   Literature

Alurista. Floricanto en Aztlan. Los Angeles: Chicano Cultural Center, University of California, 1971.

_____. Nationchild and Pluma Roja. San Diego: Toltecas en Aztlan - Centro Cultural de La Raza, 1972.

Anaya, Rudolfo A. Bless Me, Ultima. Berkeley, California: Quinto Sol Publications, Inc., 1972.

Barrio, Raymond. The Plum Plum Pickers. New York: Canfield Colophon Books, 1971.

Boatright, Mady Boggin, (Ed). Mexican Border Ballads and Other Lore. Austin, Texas: Folklore Society, 1962.

Campa, Arthur L. Spanish Folk-Poetry in New Mexico. Albuquerque: University of New Mexico Press, 1946.

Delgado, Abelardo. Chicano: 25 Pieces of a Chicano Mind. Denver, Colorado: Barrio Publications, 1970.

Gonzalez, Rudolfo. I Am Joaquin: An Epic Poem. New York: Bantam Books, 1973.

Kirack, Alex. Space Flutes and Barrio Paths. San Diego, California: Centro de Estudios Publications, San Diego State College, 1972.

Ludwig, Ed and Santibonez, James. The Chicano: Mexican American Voices. Baltimore: Penguin Books, 1971.

Paredes, Americo. With His Pistol in His Hand. Austin: University of Texas Press, 1971.

Robinson, Cecil. With the Ears of Strangers: the Mexican in American Literature. Tucson, Arizona: The University of Arizona Press, 1969.

Romano-V, Octavio Ignacio (Ed). El Espejo - The Mirror: Selected Mexican-American Literature. Berkeley, California: Quinto Sol Publications, Inc., 1969.

Salinas, Luis Omar and Foderman, Lillian. From the Barrio: A Chicano Anthology. San Francisco: Canfield Press, 1973.

Sanchez, Ricardo. Canto y Grito mi Liberacion: The Liberation of a Chicano Mind. New York: Anchor Books, 1973.

Simmen, Edward (Ed). Pain and Promise: The Chicano Today. New York: Mentor Book, 1972.

_____. The Chicano: From Caricature to Self-Portrait. New York: Mentor Books, 1971.

Shular, Antonia Castaneda, et al. Literatura Chicana: Texto y Contexto. Englewood Cliffs, New Jersey: Prentice-Hall, Inc., 1972.

Valdez, Luis and Steiner, Stan. Aztlan: An Anthology of Mexican American Literature. New York: Vintage Books, 1972.

Vasquez, Richard. Chicano. New York: Doubleday and Co., Inc., 1970.

Villasenor, Edmund. Macho! New York: Bantam Books, 1973.

Villarreal, Jose Antonio. Pocho. New York: Anchor Books, 1970.

Zeta Acosta, Oscar. The Autobiography of a Brown Buffalo. San Francisco: Straight Arrow Books, 1972.

VII   Politics and Sociology

Barker, George C. Pachuco, an American-Spanish Argot and Its Social Functions in Tucson, Arizona. Tucson, Arizona: University of Arizona Press, 1958.

Blowis, Patricia Bell. Tijerina and the Land Grants: Mexican-Americans Struggle for Their Heritage. New York: International Press, 1971.

Camejo, Antonio (Ed). La Raza Unida Party in Texas: Speeches by Mario Compean and Jose Angel Gutierrez. New York: Pathfinder Press, 1970.

_____. Documents of the Chicano Struggle. New York: Pathfinder Press, 1971.

Carranza, Elui. Pensamientos on Los Chicanos: A Cultural Revolution. Berkeley, California: California Book Co., Ltd., 1969.

De La Garza, Rudolph O., et al. Chicanos and Native Americans: The Territorial Minorities. Englewood Cliffs, New Jersey: Prentice-Hall, Inc., 1973.

De Shepro, Theresa Aragon. Chicanismo and Mexican American Politics. Seattle: Centro de Estudios Chicanos, University of Washington, 1971.

Delgado, Abelardo. The Chicano Movement. Denver, Colorado: Barrio Publications, 1971.

El Tratado de Guadalupe Hidalgo 1848: Treaty of Guadalupe Hidalgo, 1848. Sacramento: Telefact Foundation in Cooperation with California State Department of Education, 1968.

Galarza, Ernesto. Merchants of Labor: The Mexican Bracero Story. San Jose, California: Rosicrucian Press, 1964.

_____. Spiders in the House and Workers in the Field. Notre Dame: Notre Dame Press, 1970.

Gamio, Manuel. Mexican Immigration to the United States: A Study of Human Migration and Adjustment. New York: Dover Publications, Inc., 1971.

_____. The Mexican Immigrant: His Life Story. New York: Arno Press, 1969.

Garcia, F. Chris (Ed). Chicano Politics: Readings. New York: MSS Information Corp., 1973.

Gardner, Richard. Grito! Reies Tijerina and the New Mexico Land
Grant War of 1967. New York: Harper Colophon Books, 1970.

Gutierrez, Jose Angel. El Politico: The Mexican American Elected
Official. El Paso, Texas: Mictha Publications, 1972.

"La Causa Chicana: Una Familia," Journal of Social Casework. (special
edition), Vol. 52, No. 5 (May, 1971).

Lopez & Rivas, Gilberto. Los Chicanos: Una Minoria Nacional Ex-
plotada. Mexico 12 D.F.: Editorial Nuestros Tiempo, S.A., 1971.

Lozada, Froben, et al. La Raza! Why a Chicano Party? Why Chicano
Studies? New York: Pathfinder Press, 1970.

McWilliams, Carey. Factories in the Fields: The Story of Migratory
Farm Labor in California. Hamden, Connecticut: Shoe String,
1969.

Martinez, J. Mexican Emigration to the U.S. San Francisco: R. & E.
Research Associates, 1971.

Matthiessen, Peter. Sal Si Puedes: Cesar Chavez and the New American
Revolution. New York: Delta Books, 1969.

Morin, Raul. Among the Valiant: Mexican Americans in W. W. II and
Korea. Los Angeles: Border Publishing Co., 1963.

Nabokov, Peter. Tijerina and the Courthouse Raid. Berkeley, California:
Ramparts Press, Inc., 1970.

Nelson, Eugene. Huelga: The First Hundred Days of the Great Delano
Grape Strike. Delano, California: Farm Worker Press, 1966.

Pendas, Miguel and Ring, Harry. Toward Chicano Power: Building La
Raza Unida Party. New York: Pathfinder Press, 1974.

Perez, Jose G. Viva La Huelga: The Struggle of the Farm Workers.
New York: Pathfinder Press, Inc., 1973.

Rendon, Armando B. Chicano Manifesto. New York: Collier Books,
1971.

Roman-V, Octavio. Voices: Readings from El Grito, A Journal of
Contemporary Mexican American Thought. Berkeley, California:
Quinto Sol Publications, Inc., 1971.

Samora, Julian. Los Mojados: The Wetback Story. Notre Dame: University of Notre Dame Press, 1971.

_____, (Ed). La Raza! Forgotten Americans. Notre Dame: University of Notre Dame Press, 1967.

Santillan, Richard. La Raza Unida: Chicano Politics. Los Angeles: Tlaquilo Publications, 1973.

Schockley, John Staples. Chicano Revolt in a Texas Town. Notre Dame: University of Notre Dame Press, 1974.

Steiner, Stan. La Raza: The Mexican Americans. New York: Harper and Row, 1968.

Taylor, Paul S. Mexican Labor in the United States 1928-30. (2 vols). New York: Arno, 1970.

United States Commission on Civil Rights. Mexican Americans and the Administration of Justice in the Southwest. Washington, D. C.: U. S. Government Printing Office, March, 1970.

Vidal, Mirta. Chicano Liberation and Revolutionary Youth. New York: Pathfinder Press, 1971.

_____. Chicanos Speak Out: Women - New Voice of La Raza. New York: Pathfinder Press, 1971.

Tapes on the Chicano

Acculturation of the Hispanic American. Audio tape. Southern Colorado State College, Pueblo, Colorado.

Californians of Mexican Descent. Audio tape. Pacifica Tape Library, Berkeley, California. KPFA Division of Documentaries. Programs prepared by Colin Edwards.

Distortion of Mexican American History. Audio tape. Pacifica Tape Library. Berkeley, California. Narrated by Dr. Octavio Romano.

Educational Needs of Chicanos. Audio tape. Pacifica Tape Library, Berkeley, California. Narrated by Y. Arturo Cabrero.

Interview with Reies Tijerina. Audio tape. Pacifica Tape Library. Berkeley, California.

Mexican-American: An Examination of Stereotypes. Tape, 8 cassettes with teacher's guide. Produced by Henry Olguin and distributed by BFA Educational Media. Division of Columbia Broadcasting System, Santa Monica, California.

Mexican-American Series. Audio tape. Center for Study of Democratic Institutions, Santa Barbara, California.

Mexican Folk Songs. Tape. Open 7 in. reel or cassette. 30 min., 1965. Produced by Pennsylvania Department of Public Instruction. Distributed by the National Center for Audio Tapes, Bureau of Audiovisual Instruction, University of Colorado, Boulder, Colorado.

Films

Californians of Mexican Descent. 16mm film, 5 tapes (two track) 30 min., each. Pacifica Foundation (KPDA), Berkeley, California.

Change: Education and the Mexican American. 16mm film, 57 min., sound, black and white. Produced and distributed by Extension Media Center, Film Distribution, University of California, Berkeley.

Chicano. 16mm film, 22 3/4 min., sound, color. Distributed by BFA Educational Media, Santa Monica, California, 1971.

Chicano. 16mm, 27 min., sound, color. Distributed by McGraw-Hill Contemporary Films, New York, 1971.

Chicano from the Southwest. 16mm film, 15 min., sound, black and white/color. Produced and distributed by Encyclopaedia Britannica Educational Corporation, Chicago, 1970.

Decision at Delano. 16mm film, 26 min., sound, color. Produced and distributed by Cathedral Films, Burbank, California, 1967.

Education and the Mexican-American. 16mm film, 57 min., sound, black and white. Two parts. Produced by the University of California, University Extension Department of Urban Affairs. Distributed by University of California Extension Media Center, Berkeley, 1969.

Felipa: North of the Border. 16mm film, 17 min., sound, color. Produced by Bert Salzman and distributed by Learning Corporation of America, New York, 1971.

Harvest of Shame. 16mm film, 17 min., sound, color. Produced by CBS News, New York. Distributed by McGraw-Hill/Contemporary Films, New York.

Henry . . . Boy of the Barrio. 16mm film, 30 min., sound, black and white, Atlantis Productions, Inc., Thousand Oaks, California, 1969.

Huelga. 16mm film, 52 min., sound, color. Produced by Kin Film Productions, Seattle, Washington. Distributed by McGraw-Hill/ Contemporary Films, New York, 1967.

I Am Joaquin. 16mm film, 22 min., sound, color. Produced by El Teatro Campesino. Distributed by the Centro Campesino Cultural, Fresno, California, 1969.

A Mexican American Family. 16mm film, 16 min., sound, color. Produced and distributed by Atlantis Productions, Inc., Thousand Oaks, California, 1970.

Mexican-American: Heritage and Destiny. 16mm film, 29 min., color, sound. Narrated by Ricardo Montalban. Produced and distributed by Handel Film Corporation, Los Angeles, California, 1971.

Mexican-Americans: An Historic Profile. 16mm film, 29 min., black and white. By Maclovic Barraza, Chairman of the Board of the Southwest Council of La Raza. Anti-Defamation League of B'nai B'rith, New York.

Mexican-Americans: Invisible Minority. 16mm film, 38 min., color. Produced by National Educational Television and Radio Center and distributed by Indiana University Audio-Visual Center, 1969.

Mexican-Americans: Quest for Equality. 16mm film, 28 min., black and white, sound. Produced and distributed by the Anti-Defamation League of B'nai B'rith, New York.

Mexican Rebellion. 16mm film, optical sound, 29 min., black and white. Distributed by San Francisco Newsreel, San Francisco, California, 1968.

North From Mexico. 16mm film, 20 min., color, sound. Produced by Center for Mass Communication of Columbia University Press. Distributed by Greenwood Press, Westport, Connecticut, 1971.

Pancho. 16mm film, 25 min., sound, color. Produced by Robert K. Sharpe. Produced and distributed by the U. S. Office of Economic Opportunity, Washington, D. C., 1967.

Pilgrimage (Delano to Sacramento). 16mm film, 1 record, 10 min., color. Distributed by Multi-Media Productions, Palo Alto, California.

Salazar Family: A Look at Poverty. 16mm film, optical sound, 14 min., black and white. Produced and distributed by the University of California, Media Extension Center, Berkeley, California, 1970.

Tijerina. 16mm film, 30 min., black and white, bilingual. Distributed
    by University of California, Extension Media Center, Berkeley,
    California.

Unfinished Revolution. 16mm film, 54 min., sound, black and white.
    Produced and distributed by National Educational Television and
    Radio Center, and Westinghouse Broadcasting Company, New
    York, 1962.

Viva La Causa--The Migrant Labor Movement. 16mm film, 40 min.,
    sound, color. Produced and distributed by Denoyer Geppert Com-
    pany, Chicago, 1971.

Voice of La Raza. 16mm film, 60 min., sound, color. Distributed by
    William Graves Productions, New York.

The Westward Movement: Texas and the Mexican War. 16mm film,
    18 min., sound, color. Distributed by Encyclopaedia Britannica
    Educational Corp. Chicago, 1966.

Why? La Basta: Chicano Moratorium at Laguna Park. 16mm film,
    12 min., color, sound. Produced and distributed by Cintech Pro-
    ductions, Long Beach, California.

                          Periodicals

Aztlan: Chicano Journal of the Social Sciences and the Arts, Mexican
    American Culture Center, University of California, 405 Hilgarde
    Avenue, Los Angeles, California 90024. Quarterly. Spanish-En-
    glish. 1970 -.

Civil Rights Digest, 1405 Eye Street, N. W., Washington, D. C. 20425.
    Quarterly. English. 1967 -.

El Grito, Quinto Sol Publications, Inc., P. O. Box 9275, Berkeley,
    California 94719. Quarterly. Spanish-English. 1967 -.

La Luz, 360 S. Monroe, Suite 320, Denver, Colorado 80209. Monthly.
    Spanish-English. 1972 -.

La Raza, P. O. Box 31004, Los Angeles, California 90031. Monthly.
    Spanish-English. 1967 -.

NAME INDEX